Nicolas Roeg Film by Film

NICOLAS ROEG FILM BY FILM

by
Scott Salwolke

McFarland & Company, Inc., Publishers
Jefferson, North Carolina, and London

To Monica—for her patience

British Library Cataloguing-in-Publication data are available

Library of Congress Cataloguing-in-Publication Data

Salwolke, Scott.
 Nicolas Roeg film by film / by Scott Salwolke.
  p. cm.
 Includes bibliographical references, filmography, and index. ∞
 ISBN 0-89950-881-2 (lib. bdg. : 50# alk. paper)
  1. Roeg, Nicolas, 1928–   — Criticism and interpretation. I. Title.
 PN1998.3.R635S26 1993
 791.43′0233′092 – dc20   92-56690
                                                            CIP

Manufactured in the United States of America

McFarland & Company, Inc., Publishers
 Box 611, Jefferson, North Carolina 28640

TABLE OF CONTENTS

INTRODUCTION

Nicolas Roeg has taken risks with his films that few other directors have taken, and he has paid a price for this decision. Although he has directed some of the most innovative films of the past quarter century, he remains an anonymous figure, seldom mentioned in most histories of film. He has yet to have a major commercial success, and critics have always been divided about his work. The mainstream critics have often labeled him pretentious or inaccessible, and even his staunchest supporters seem to have been silenced. Not only have his last few films received limited commercial releases, they have garnered almost no critical attention.

On the basis of a dozen films Roeg's place in history should be assured. He combines the British film industry's past with the innovations brought forth by the French New Wave. His work often echoes the films of Britain's most famous directors; scenes from his films borrow directly from the works of Alfred Hitchcock, Carol Reed, and Richard Lester. In their color scheme and in their presentation of themes, his films most recall the works of Michael Powell and like Powell's films, Roeg's films were often neglected on release only to be reexamined more favorably at a later date. Roeg's editing and battles with censorship are the direct result of his fascination with French films, particularly those of Alain Resnais.

What lies behind the neglect Roeg has suffered? In fact, there have been a variety of factors, some of which Roeg has had little control over. The first is that his films demand attention. They cannot be viewed in the same manner as can a film by Steven Spielberg or Brian DePalma, in which the images hurtle at the viewer. Roeg's films seem subliminal by comparison. They are filled with references to other mediums which help to expand on the film's central theme, but these references are often so brief that most viewers can easily miss them or if they do notice them, they may not make the necessary association. The editing also frustrates viewers, with its nonlinear approach; past, present, and future are often juxtaposed in the same sequence. More problematical is Roeg's tendency to create lead characters who are unemotional and detached. He concedes that his films are not typical fare, but makes no apologies: "I suppose I am outside the mainstream of British cinema. But then I have to watch the films I make. I can't make films to please the organizers of a film year or whatever. I'm not actually complaining, but it seems that the result of refusing to compromise is that one simply has to survive as best one can."[1]

Survive Roeg has, making films in his own way. Through it all he has held to the belief that film is not just a commercial medium, but also an art form. He says: "I believe film is an art. I believe it, I truly believe that. Thought can be transferred by the juxtaposition of images, and you mustn't be afraid of an audience not understanding. You can say things visually, immediately, and that's where film, I believe, is going. It's not a pictorial example of a published work. It's a transference of thought."[2]

But if Roeg's films are inaccessible, as it has been argued, then what accounts for their lasting popularity? *Performance* and *Bad Timing* are cult films, with audiences examining them over and over. *Walkabout* has become a mainstay with college and church organizations (who seem willing to overlook its nudity). *Don't Look Now* remains a popular video release, considered by many to be one of the best horror films ever. Even Roeg's most recent release, *The Witches*, seems destined to become the children's classic many predicted it would be when it was first released.

In fact, many of the difficulties the films have encountered can be attributed to their distributors, who seem unsure how to market them. *Performance, Eureka,* and *The Witches* were all shelved for a time before they were unceremoniously dumped on the market. *The Man Who Fell to Earth* was reduced by twenty minutes for its American release, and many of Roeg's other films have been similarly altered, although none quite so dramatically. *Castaway* was released by Cannon as a sexual-fantasy retreat, something it most definitely was not.

A further difficulty may lie with Roeg himself, who often remains as inaccessible as many find his films. He does not make the traditional rounds of the media when a film is released, because he believes the work should stand on its own. An intensely private man, he has given few details of his personal life and with the exception of a handful of interviews, has told little of his early life. One can often see Roeg, however, in the characters in his films, and he has described this relationship between his own life and his directing:

> With film, certainly the way I approach it, one has to delve into one's life to put "truth" onto the screen. One delves into one's emotions and tries to translate that to the story one wants to tell. All our imagination

is bound by experience. And when all that is ultimately portrayed in the characters of the film, it becomes a melancholic affair.[3]

What most often comes through in Roeg's interviews is his surprise that his films are called inaccessible:

> I don't believe my films are inaccessible. If they were, I would be inaccessible myself. What I am trying to do, like anyone who works in any form of art, is to express an emotion. The film audience is so curiously demanding in conservatism. People never say of dance or theater, "I don't understand what is happening." Yet film is the newest and should be the freest of all.[4]

In another interview he stated,

> I am concerned with breaking barriers, challenging assumptions, and moving the possibilities of film on a bit. Part of my job is to show that the cinema is the art of our time and can break through previous terms of reference. That doesn't mean ignoring them so much as expanding them as far as possible. Usually producers read scripts, and they want something rooted in the reality they know. I'm more anxious to look for what we don't know.[5]

Roeg remains disappointed that his films have not received the acceptance that they deserve or that he desires. "As I've said before, all I hope from my work is that someone out there will say, 'Hey, I've got a sort of curious, twisted mind like yours, so I know what you're talking about.' That's all we're doing with our work anyhow is saying, 'Hey, is anybody out there?' That's all we're doing with our lives, really. 'Is there anybody out there who understands me?'"[6]

This book examines each of Roeg's films in a linear fashion, considering each detail in an attempt to understand its meaning in terms of the film and his career. It is a format that Roeg would probably disparage, but one that seems necessary because of the inaccessibility of his films. Those that are available are often in a form which differs from Roeg's original cut. Even today there is no definitive version of his first film, *Performance*. I hope that this book will not only introduce Roeg's work to some readers, but also help clarify it for others.

Notes

1. *Films and Filming*, August 1985, p. 16.
2. *American Film*, April 1983, p. 22.
3. Jonathan Hacker and David Price, *Take 10*, p. 368.
4. *Vogue*, August 1985, p. 380.
5. Ibid., p. 333.
6. *Lighting Dimensions*, October 1987, pp. 76–77.

ONE

Performance

Nicolas Roeg was forty when he directed his first film, but he had already been working in the film industry for nearly half his life. He had first found work in a London studio, translating French films into English. If the job seemed hardly rewarding, it did give Roeg his first lesson in film. "What first really hooked me into thinking that this was a job that I would like to become deeply involved in was as a young man sitting at 'Lingua Synchrome,' where they dubbed French films into English. Running the films backwards and forwards to get the words right, I realized that film was a time machine."[1]

Roeg soon found other work in film, first serving as a clapper boy, then working behind the camera. He admits he had no burning ambitions at this time, but as the years progressed, so too did his expectations. By the start of the sixties he had become a director of photography, receiving critical acclaim for his work on such diverse films as *The Masque of the Red Death, Fahrenheit 451, Far from the Madding Crowd,* and *A Funny Thing Happened on the Way to the Forum.* His distinctive style often influenced the look of the film, regardless of the director or the genre. This was not enough for Roeg, however. Part of the impetus driving him was the work coming out of the French New Wave, in particular the films of Alain Resnais. If Roeg was impressed with *Hiroshima Mon Amour, Last Year at Marienbad* was a revelation, with its manipulation of time and inclusion of fantasy and memory.

Believing that film offered more than had previously been realized, Roeg began to take on other responsibilities, as if in preparation for something greater. He wrote *A Prize of Arms,* and *Sanders,* two films that had little to recommend them, but proved educational for him in terms of plotting. It was his collaboration with Richard Lester which gave his career further impetus. He helped to adapt *A Funny Thing Happened on the Way*

1

to the Forum, but it was Lester's next work, *Petulia,* which anticipated Roeg's style. Here too, he was not credited as co-writer, but one can already see the juxtaposition of seemingly unrelated events, the subliminal flashbacks, and a modern approach to a pessimistic love story that Roeg would make his own.

It was with the completion of *Petulia* that Roeg decided to pursue his own directing career. His initial choice was *Walkabout,* based on James Vance Marshall's children's story, and for the script he turned to playwright Edward Bond. When Bond presented him with the final script, it was only 65 pages, but Roeg felt it was perfect for what he intended. The film companies were not impressed, however, and Roeg's directorial career was on hold before it had begun. It was at this point that Roeg was contacted by an old friend about another project. Sometime artist, sometime screenwriter Donald Cammell was beginning a new project, and Roeg came on as his collaborator. The result would be *Performance.*

The genesis of *Performance* has been well documented (particularly in Alexander Walker's *British UK,* in which most of the participants are interviewed): how Mick Jagger's popularity in the musical field was the original impetus for the film, how the directors faced difficulties as it progressed, and how the production company was so shocked by the film's rushes that it finally shelved the film and then later dumped it on the market. Despite all the material about the film, however, no one has been able to determine adequately who contributed what in the direction. Donald Cammell served as both writer and co-director, while Roeg assumed double duty as writer and director of photography. The central image of the picture is that of two men coming together; it is also the central image for the making of the film. To discount one man's contribution may be to give undue praise to the other, but because this book is devoted to Roeg, his name will often be mentioned alone. This is not to detract from Cammell or any of the collaborators on Roeg's films; it is simply a matter of convenience.

In fact, it was Cammell who was first brought onto the project; he was commissioned to write a script for Jagger. A seeming jack-of-all-trades, Cammell had first gained attention for his art work, but had also written *Duffy,* a stilted comedy that starred James Coburn, James Mason, and James Fox. To Cammell's credit, the script for *Performance* not only presented a myriad of ideas, but was also surprisingly witty. When filming began, however, the script was far from complete, and both Roeg and Cammell continued working on it, as Roeg describes: "We would rehearse through the night sometimes and out of that would come changes, because it was, after all, a dialogue between two people who were finally one . . . both sides of the same: so you really couldn't script that. We would go away then and work on it all night. It came out of that evolvement."[2]

The central theme of the film is one long popular in fiction: the protagonist is exposed to a new environment or lifestyle and is altered because of it. Cammell's twist was to have the protagonist be a gangster encountering the milieu of a rock star. A primary source for the film's story line would be Herman Hesse's *Steppenwolf,* whose plot *Performance* closely resembles. Like Chas, Harry Haller is in the midst of flight when he is confronted by individuals he is unable to comprehend. There would be other literary influences, including J. W. Dunnes's *An Experiment with Time,* which hypothesized that past, present, and future coexist. The most obvious influence, however, would be writer Jorge Luis Borges, whose works are constantly alluded to in the film.

As is typical of Roeg's work, the meaning of the opening image has been lost on most viewers. A plane hurtles through the sky but is not seen again in the film until the conclusion. As Nic Waller has pointed out, the shot "lasts just long enough for us to register what is happening. Later on, one of the gangsters picks up the shiny model of a jet plane. We may make a conscious connection between the two. Probably we don't. Near the end of the film, Chas, the young gangster on the run from his own gang, looks up and catches sight of a distant plane through the trees. He has pinned his hopes on a flight to America and anonymity. But the plane, now tiny, drifts away like a phantom, and anyway he has already started on an inner journey of self-discovery. Planes now exist in a different order of reality for him."

Performance itself will exist on a different level for the viewer, with an opening montage where images move so fast that the viewer is left disoriented. Shots of a limousine moving down a country highway are juxtaposed with shots of a couple making violent love. Then the title song begins, briefly synopsizing the story, with references to demons, empty cellars, and trains, all important elements of the film. As his companion comes down on him, Chas Devlin lifts up a mirror to look at his reflection and the image freezes as the title is announced. Both the mirror and the word *performance* will be used throughout to comment on Chas's identity and his profession. The music abruptly ends and in the silence Chas begins to slap the girl, then seems about to strangle her, so that the act resembles murder more than lovemaking. Already it is apparent that Chas equates sex with violence. The images of the limousine continue to intrude until they begin to overlap, and the sequence ends with the closing of two doors: Chas's wardrobe door and the door of the limousine.

With the sex completed, Chas has little interest in his companion, Donna, and tries to hurry her off as he prepares for his day. Mirrors continue to predominate as the characters examine their reflections, but at this point their importance is more aesthetic than narrational. Having dismissed his companion, Chas straightens up his apartment, his propensity for order already apparent. There are no indications of livelihood, and as he gets into a car with two other men, he seems more a businessman than a gangster. In the front seat, Rosebloom and Wilson are bemoaning the violence children are confronted with on television. While their vehicle heads toward an unknown destination, another is arriving elsewhere. The limousine that opened the film returns as Tony Farrell emerges from it to enter a courtroom, initiating another complex montage. Close-ups of Tony and Chas hint at their physical resemblance. Chas and his colleagues have entered an automobile garage, while Farrell begins to speak in front of a jury, his words often seeming to refer to Chas's business: "What are really on trial here today are the ethics of a community. Our national economy, even our national survival, evolves upon the consolidation by merger of the smaller and weaker economic units with the larger, lustier pillars of our commercial economy."

Farrell's words become lost in the noise of a computer as Chas and his men enter the office of a garage, where they proceed to intimidate the employees. The sequence that follows, which contrasts the lawyer's summation and Chas's destruction of the office, is kinetic, almost hallucinatory. The intimation is obvious: the morals of the business community are no better than those of the gangsters. There is controlled mayhem to the latter's work as they knock office supplies to the ground and physically threaten the owner, who failed to take seriously a meeting with Chas's superior. The lawyer continues to talk, with the sound of the computers still overlaying the scenes. The meaning of this becomes apparent from his speech— "Words still have meanings in these days of computers." When Farrell refers to his client, Roeg cuts to a newspaper article with the man's picture and will do the same when Farrell mentions the man who should be on trial, Harry Flowers. Roeg is already manipulating our perception of film.

Roeg's films often break down the dimensions of time, as if the past, present, and future coexist, something Borges had long conjectured. The first instance of this temporal distortion occurs when Flowers is shown greeting Chas in his office, but a cut to the automobile garage shows Chas still involved in his destructive activities. When Chas does enter Flowers's office, he is asked about the trial and the plaintiff, Fraser. There is a quick insert of Fraser, but it is actually a flashforward to his meeting with Chas. Chas confidently tells Flowers the matter is being taken care of, and Flowers calls him a "nutcase like all artists." If Roeg is experimenting temporarily in this case, in the next sequence he experiments spatially. Farrell speaks of protecting the smaller businessman while the image of the jury changes in color and size. Inexplicably, members of the jury have become the audience at a pornographic cinema, further proof of society's moral decline. Chas is attempting to get money from the cinema's owner, while on the screen a woman is getting whipped on the buttocks.

The intimidation of Fraser and Farrell begins with the chauffeur ironically telling one of the men to "keep his hair on." As a shocked Farrell looks on, Chas tells Fraser not to involve Harry in his own trial, to "shut his hole." Behind him Rosebloom makes a gesture that is identical to the boy's attempt to communicate with the aborigine in *Walkabout*. Although Fraser seems to accept what is being asked of him, Farrell continues to try to regain control, insisting that Chas address his remarks to him. Chas seems agreeable to this and goes off, leaving Fraser and Farrell to go into their club. The confrontation Fraser has inadvertently brought on himself begins when his chauffeur is grabbed just as he is getting Farrell's limousine. Bound and gagged, the man is forced to watch as Chas pours acid along the surface of the car. At one point he acts as if he is going to pour it on the chauffeur's head, but the others remind him that they must not waste what they have.

Rosebloom and Wilson will often go about their work with an ironic attitude. Prior to their arrival at the car garage, Rosebloom had reminded his companion to put on his tie, as if to conform to some sort of protocol. When their attention turns to the chauffeur, they put shaving cream on his head and begin to shave him bald. The men then reminisce about their childhood experiences at the barbershop. In contrast, Chas's work often takes on an obsessive quality; he even reminds the men not to get shaving cream on the man's collar. He becomes irritated at his colleagues' dialogue and shouts for them to shut their mouths. It is the first intimation that his role is almost that of an outsider. His work completed, Chas holds a small mirror up for the man to see what has happened and leaves, telling him to inform Farrell that he will be "in touch."

Returning to the office, Chas overhears Flowers mention Joey Maddocks, whose betting office they want to take over. Chas volunteers to coerce Maddocks into capitulating, but Flowers wants him to remain out of it. Maddocks was Chas's boyhood friend, but their relationship changed when Maddocks began a boxing career. It is significant that the "change" is never brought out in the film, but it will anticipate Chas's own alteration. Roeg's use of inserts here often resembles the flash cuts in *Petulia*. When Maddock's career is mentioned, there is a shot of him boxing; when his business is discussed, there is a cut to the storefront. These vignettes seem more a gimmick here, providing neither essential information nor commentary, but they do anticipate Roeg's use of such flashes in *Insignificance*.

The true nature of Chas's relationship with Maddocks is often hinted at, in both the dialogue and the juxtaposition of images. Flowers tells Rosebloom to hire some men to redecorate the shop, and there is a cut to two men throwing a can into the window, as if the events are already predestined. Chas presses Flowers about taking the job, but Flowers grows angry, saying, "Don't you ever listen to a word I say? Keep personal relations out of business. Your relations with Maddocks was doubly personal." While Chas looks around at the men with him, their images inexplicably turn to black and white as he repeats Harry's motto "Let the death who's holding the sodding baby." The image of Harry jolts backward until he is only a small square in the center of the screen; this is another tactic that disorients the viewer. The sequence ends as if the proceedings had been a military debriefing, with Harry telling the men to be at ease and lifting the blind as if there had been a blackout.

As a symbol of status and position, property is often the target of violence in the film. The lawyer's limousine has been destroyed and so now is Maddocks's shop. As this occurs, Chas goes about straightening up his apartment; the expectation is created that it too will be the center of violence. Although angered by what has happened, Maddocks is unwilling to press charges against Flowers because he is aware of the further repercussions that could occur. The inspector warns him that he has a war on his hands, and the man's scarred face looks like that of a veteran. His line anticipates the war that will serve as a backdrop to *Eureka*. As Maddocks is cleaning up, Chas arrives to survey the damage. Tossing a startled Maddocks his coat, Chas tells him he is to meet with Flowers. Further evidence of their homosexual relationship occurs when, as Chas walks out, one of Maddocks's men asks if "he's the one."

Maddocks's first meeting with Flowers is on the stage of a nightclub, a significant reference to their being performers. In words echoing Farrell's speech, Flowers calls their relationship a merger, "not a takeover." Photographs are taken of Flowers with his arm around Maddocks, whom he constantly addresses as his son. Flowers's attention turns to Chas, who went against his dictum by bringing Maddocks to him. He asks if he fancies himself the Lone Ranger, but Chas confidently tells him that he knows who he is. To the others Flowers says that he has "known a few performers in my time, but I'll tell you this, he's got the gift." One of the men suggests that Chas enjoys his work, which Flowers admits is a good trait, but one that can go too far. His anger released, Flowers reminds Chas that he works for him, while in the background Maddocks is enjoying Chas's predicament. Accepting his role in Flowers's organization, Maddocks now stands at his side and even orders a round of drinks for everyone. Flowers's advisor, Wilson, tells Chas that their business is to push the buttons, but the latter remains confident, replying: "I'm alive and well. You push the buttons on that." Momentarily turning his back on Chas, Flowers looks back to see he has gone. He confides to Wilson that "that boy is in bother," pointing to his head. Wilson seems to agree, mumbling that Chas has become out-of-date.

While Chas is driving home, Roeg cuts to his apartment, where paint is being splattered on the walls. By the time he has entered his apartment, his walls have been covered in red paint, and Maddocks and his gang begin to beat him viciously. The beating will take the sexual paradigms even further, with Chas being held down while his pants are pulled down. Maddocks begins to whip his buttocks with a belt, recalling the earlier footage from the porno theatre. Further proof that the beating is sexually motivated is Roeg's inclusion of flashbooks to the sexual encounter which opens the film. Maddocks tries to get Chas to admit the truth, and there is a cut to the word "poof," which has been spray-painted on the wall. Chas seems on the verge of responding to the questions, when he passes out. One of the men tells Maddocks to give him the "kiss of life."

Chas has only feigned unconsciousness, and with one of the men out of the room, Chas fights back. Throwing his shirt over Maddocks's head, he kicks a second man into the bathtub. Another man attempts to drag Chas across the floor, but he manages to pull a gun out from behind a radiator. One of the men escapes, but Chas's attention is on Maddocks, as the music helps to focus the tension. Maddocks backs up from Chas, much like a frightened child, and pulls a cover over his face, while Chas repeats that he is a "bullet." Chas pulls the trigger, killing Maddocks, turning the screen red (a color which is predominant not just in this film, but in most of Roeg's films). He pays no attention to the other man, who escapes to the street outside. Quickly dressing, Chas also makes a fast departure, picking up the can of red paint as he leaves.

The murder of Maddocks segregates Chas from Flowers's organization, and with his departure the organization takes an obvious homosexual turn. Wilson comes into the room, throwing off his coat and waving his arms about in an effeminate manner, while Flowers sits on the bed reading a homosexual magazine. When Wilson moves into the bathroom, he is flanked by a man wearing only his underwear. Flowers reminds the others that he warned Chas, but he no longer seems in control and begins to hide under the covers as if he were hoping to escape the problems (echoing Maddocks's earlier movement). He does not even stir when the phone rings and only grudgingly accepts the call when he learns it is Chas. Chas's manner is more consolatory here as he tells Flowers that the murder was an accident. Learning where he is calling from, Flowers puts his hand over the phone, and the men argue what to do with him. Chas seems to anticipate his fate: he unconsciously draws a hangman on the paper in front of him and finally flees as Wilson and Rosebloom are sent out after him.

Having parked his car out of sight, Chas begins to dye his hair, using a cream and the red paint. As he does this, there are shots of Turner spraying a wall in his home. Even before they have met, the two men seem to have come together. The first shot of Turner occurs when Maddocks's men are vandalizing Chas's apartment. Most baffling is the scene when Chas murders Maddocks. He is photographed from behind, but it is Turner's head that is shown. The crosscutting between a pair of men continues in Roeg's films until such a pair finally merge with even greater emphasis in *The Man Who Fell to Earth.*

Chas's salvation comes seemingly through a chance encounter at a train station, not by his own actions. A nearby musician is saying goodbye to his mother and telling her of the boarder he has just left behind, who still owes him back rent. As Chas hurries off to the address he mentioned, the mother tells her son that Turner is "peculiar, a hermit, he can't face reality." If this meeting were simple happenstance, it would stretch credibility, but Neil Feineman has argued that it is anything but a chance encounter. In his book on Roeg, Feineman discusses how Flowers's words are often repeated verbatim in the second half by Turner and notes that as Chas starts off toward Turner's home, there is a brief shot of Flowers looking into the camera, as if he is aware of what is happening. Chas's later hallucination in which he envisions Turner as Flowers seems to confirm this.

Chas's arrival at the said address begins with an appropriately surreal conversation over the intercom outside the door. The woman who answers makes a peculiar attempt to mimic an answering machine as Chas tries to apologize for being too early. He identifies himself as a friend of the former tenant, saying he has brought with him the back rent owed. With the promise of money, the woman buzzes Chas in. In stepping into the home, Chas seems to enter a new world, a house decorated in various styles, with an accumulation of paintings and a clutter of knickknacks. The style of the film will also undergo a change. Prior to Chas's arrival at the home, the film has been kinetic in its presentation, with the editing constantly forcing the viewer to watch the proceedings attentively. Once Chas enters the house, however, the story is presented in a more linear fashion.

Chas is photographed from above, with the music recalling that of a horror film as he moves about. Pherber, the woman who had talked to Chas on the intercom, greets him as she descends in an elevator. Clad in a fur, she is put off by Chas's swollen face, which he attributes to an automobile accident. Taken to a room, he identifies himself as Johnny Dean, a name presumably taken from a nearby picture of James Dean. In contrast to Chas's ordered apartment, this room is littered with photographs, drug paraphernalia, and musical instruments. Even with his life in danger, Chas remains tied to his old values and is disturbed by Pherber's accumulation of charges he must pay. She lies on the bed, scratching the fur covering her crotch, already inviting him sexually. When asked about his profession, Chas tells her he is a juggler, another type of performer.

Leaving Chas, Pherber returns upstairs, singing, "people get ready, cause here we go," as she picks up a movie camera from the nightstand. Filming herself in the mirror, she laughs at Chas's reference to his auto accident, already skeptical of his story. Climbing onto the bed, the camera still in hand, she begins to photograph the occupants of the bed, Turner and Lucy. Both are asleep and after positioning their forms, Pherber begins to kiss first one, then the other. The three fall easily into making love, with the image slowed so that it has a romantic quality. This is one of the few instances of a sexual scene in a Roeg film in which another action does not intrude; thus it remains one of his more erotic sequences.

Downstairs Chas is awakened by a young girl, Lori, who wears a false mustache, so that even the child's sexual identity is modified. He sends her off to buy turpentine, while upstairs the three tenants are occupied in the bathroom. Lucy and Turner sit in a tub, where she is complaining about a government official who did not take her seriously. Neither Turner nor Pherber seem to pay much attention to her, but argue instead over whether to let Chas stay. Pherber tells Turner that Chas is a juggler and that he would love her, but then corrects herself to say him because Chas's sexuality is already confused. There is also an air of decadence about the place, not just the casual sexuality of its inhabitants, but the air of decadence surrounding the home itself. (One producer complained that even the bath water was dirty.) Pherber proves to be the most practical of the trio, arguing that they need Chas's money, but Turner seems unconvinced.

Hoping to escape the country, Chas contacts his friend Tony, who tells him he has become front-page news. Tony agrees to get him a passport, while Chas discloses that he has concealed himself in a "freak show," full of long hairs, beatniks, and free love. Lori comes down to tell Chas that Turner wants to meet with him, but when he enters Turner's room, it seems vacant. Turner's song "Wake Up Niggers" plays in the background, however, as Chas casually lights a cigarette and looks disdainfully around the room. Sitting down in a large thronelike chair, Chas looks up at the mirror on the ceiling, just as the music abruptly stops. Thus Chas's first view of Turner is upside down.

When Turner emerges from behind a partition, he seems more like a vampire than a rock musician; his costume is a long robe. His pale complexion and long thin fingers add to the illusion, as does his closing of the curtain to block out the sunlight. He tells Chas that the room is no longer for rent and attempts to return his money, but Chas will have no part of it. He tells Turner that he needs a "Bohemian atmosphere" in which to live. Turner calls him a performer of natural magic; he picks up a microphone as he begins to dance about Chas, who looks on with bemused condemnation. Chas tells Turner that he "performs," but when Turner throws three balls at him, he makes no effort to catch them; instead he ridicules Turner. After sarcastically asking him to sing, Chas calls him a "comical little geezer," and says, "You'll look funny when you're fifty." It will not be the offer of money which changes Turner's mind, but instead Chas's remark that he must fit in: "I've got to fit in, Mr. Turner."

Neither man seems to notice Lucy when she comes in, concealing herself behind a partition as Turner asks Chas what he would do in his place. In another reference to his own self-perception, Chas is asked if he knows who he is. Chas confidently replies that he does, and Turner agrees to let him stay, but only on a daily basis. Still hidden, Lucy is dwarfed by a giant mural on the wall which relates to the identities of both men: one of the figures is a gangster, the other could be a rock musician. With Chas looking on, she goes back out the door. At this point he remains a voyeur, constantly amazed and bewildered by those around him.

There have already been portents of Chas's future relationship and eventual union with Turner, and these continue throughout the film. Pouring turpentine over his head to wash out the red, Chas pauses as he notices his resemblance to the painting of Turner on the wall. It seems surprising that Chas is familiar with Turner's career, but dismisses him as not having been that important. Lori quickly disputes this assessment, listing the number of hits Turner has had and explaining that he has retired to write a book and some music. She discounts Chas's assertion that Pherber is Turner's secretary and boasts that their love story is world famous, saying, "You don't know nothing, do you, Dad?" In the kitchen, Lucy attempts to put two female receptacles together, a slightly obvious metaphor for the sexual preference she shares with Pherber. Already sensing that Chas's presence will only lead to misfortune, she wonders why Turner allowed him to stay. The women are preparing the mushrooms Pherber had earlier picked, while downstairs Chas is meticulously cleaning his suit.

To understand *Performance* is to realize the importance of the works of Borges to the film and Roeg's career. The first reference to his work occurs when Chas terrorizes the owner of the pornography theater. Waiting in the car outside, Rosebloom is reading a copy of *A Personal Anthology* by Borges, but the most direct reference comes when Turner quotes from the book. Turner reads to Lucy and Pherber the ending of Borges's short story "The South." The excerpt deals with a man who has left a sanitarium, but finds himself confronted by a gaucho who offers him a knife in anticipation of a duel. Before he can complete the story, a fly strikes Turner in the face, causing the book to fall to the floor. The fly is shown in close-up (à la David Lynch), as the life leaves its body. Although the short story is left uncompleted, it does prefigure the film's ending, in which a man is allowed to have a heroic death of his choosing, instead of facing death while locked away in isolation.

Pherber realizes that Turner is afraid of Chas, but Turner argues that Chas is also afraid of him. Turner's actions often seem without purpose, as when two artists arrive with a painting he has commissioned. Angered that they are late, Turner will not purchase the painting, but instead buys the empty frame. Needing a picture for his passport, Chas goes upstairs to find

Pherber and Turner preparing some mushrooms. Pherber quickly notices the change in his hair color, and he tells her he is having a laugh with his image. If Turner's and Chas's actions have often been presented simultaneously, here they seem to merge. The camera travels through the back of Turner's head to focus on Chas's face, just as Turner's face is superimposed over his. Even their voices intermix as Turner tells him he knows "exactly what he means." The intimation is that the two men's identities have merged, and this is confirmed when Turner seems to know the truth about Chas. He admits he prefers the old image, and he and Pherber try to decide where they witnessed his act, finally deciding it was in Tokyo. Already it is obvious they no longer believe in his story or his alias.

Having found a discarded photograph downstairs, Chas asks Turner if he has a Polaroid. He tells them that his agent has requested a photograph, and Pherber comes up to him, saying it is time for a change. The first photograph they take is of Chas in a suit and mustache, his resemblance to Tony Farrell now complete. Yet, if Chas still holds to the same ideals as the lawyer, Pherber and Turner will soon alter him both physically and emotionally. Turner worries that the photographs are for narcissistic purposes, while Pherber offers Chas one of the mushrooms, initiating his alteration. Chas is filmed through the lens of the camera, and the next photograph shows his image doubled, his personality coming undone. He is dissatisfied with the disguise, worrying that he looks "dodgy."

> CHAS We've gone too far.
> TURNER He means we haven't really got anywhere.
> PHERBER He means we've got to go much further out.
> CHAS We have to go much further, much further back and faster.

Chas is already disconcerted, something even Pherber notices. He goes behind the clothes rack to change, and as he takes off his shirt, they see the marks from his beating. He dismisses them as another result of his accident. Turner seems sympathetic, asking if he wants a passport photo; his knowledge of Chas is now complete. Pherber cleans Chas's wounds, while the mushrooms begin to affect him. He still holds to the identity of Johnny Dean, and Pherber muses that maybe he does not know who he is, a suggestion about Chas that has been repeated throughout the film. Turner is playing the guitar off to the side (his shadow on the wall like that of a demon), and he begins to sing, finally calling Chas the bogeyman. Half-stoned, Chas repeats his earlier remark that he is alive and well: "You push the buttons." Turner begins to sing, the words seeming to comment on what has occurred. ("Woke up this morning and opened up the door. And I said, 'Hello, Satan, I believe it's time to go.'" He tells Chas that they "push the button" and that he is the horror show. Turner's words begin to echo Flowers's: first he calls Chas a pro, then he says that he has got the gift.

A scene from *Performance*. Turner's (Mick Jagger) transformation of gangster Chas Devlin (James Fox) is nearly complete.

The effects of the mushroom have taken hold of Chas, and he becomes fascinated by the light of a candle, holding his hand over it. His attention turns to the mosaic pattern on a coffee table, but if he is experiencing new sensations, his values remain the same: he offers to purchase the table. The transformation continues even as Turner and Pherber uncover his true nature. At one point Pherber calls him Chas, his alias having been forgotten. When she offers him a mushroom similar to the one he has already consumed, the camera moves in on it, highlighting its shape and pattern. He calls it a horrible-looking thing, then screams that he had been poisoned. The camera spins as Chas falls to the ground screaming, the image freezing as his mouth is frozen in terror.

One of the obvious cinematic influences of the film is Ingmar Bergman's *Persona*, released just a year earlier. This film not only anticipated the transference of identities but also the use of nontraditional cinematic techniques which often distance the viewer by removing them from the story. The similarities in the film can be seen in Susan Sontag's analysis of the earlier work:

> The theme is that of doubling; the variations are those that follow from the leading possibilities of that theme (on both a formal and a psychological level) such as duplication, inversion, reciprocal exchange, unity

and fission, and repetition. The action cannot be univocally paraphrased. It's correct to speak of *Persona* in terms of the fortunes of two characters named Elizabeth and Alma who are engaged in a desperate duel of identities. But it is equally pertinent to treat *Persona* as relating the duel between two mythical parts of a single self: the corrupted person who acts (Elizabeth) and the ingenuous soul (Alma) who founders in contact with corruption.[3]

While Turner, Pherber, and Chas sit around a table, the dialogue begins to hint at the film's conclusion, particularly at Turner's fate. "The blood of this vegetable is boring a hole. This second hole is penetrating the hole of your face, the skull of your bones. I just want to get right in there, do you know what I mean?" says Pherber. She is dismantling Chas's gun to examine it just as they are attempting to analyze his mind. She wears a dark wig so that she resembles both Turuner and Lucy, further proof of their identities intermixing. They remind Chas that they sat through his act and now he must do the same for them. Turner admits he understands performing and Pherber tells Chas that Turner had the gift once. Turner emerges from behind the clothes rack wearing a black leather jacket and false sideburns that recall Elvis. He says the only real performance is the one that achieves madness. When he asks Chas if he is with him, Chas tells him he is.

Chas stands in front of a mirror wearing a wig and one of Turner's outfits, and as Pherber adjusts his clothing, she asks if he really has to leave. It is Turner, however, who gives the response: "Tomorrow he learns what's true and what's not." Turner's next words could also be used to describe Roeg's style: "Nothing is true and everything is permitted." These are the last words of "The Old Man on the Mountain," a story Turner begins to read, while Pherber and Chas stand in front of a mirror, their images coalescing into one. The story concerns a group of assassins who are drugged and taken into the forest, which they take to be paradise. When the king calls upon them to kill someone, they must perform the task with the knowledge that once it is completed they will be carried up into paradise. In a direct reference to Turner's story, Pherber asks Chas if he is in the garden and then says that he should not listen to old men.

As they lie in bed together, Pherber admires Chas's muscles and asks him to look at her body, as she lifts off her clothing. She compares herself to a triangle with male and female parts and then asks if he has ever had a "female feel." He grows angry, but she continues to question his sexual identity, even holding a mirror to his chest so that her breast is reflected on him. Next she positions the mirror so that her face is superimposed over his. He calls her and her friends weird, and she says that Turner is both male and female and that he has come to terms with his identity. Turner has entered the room but quietly goes on past the two. Chas calls her sick, and as they wrestle he asks her what Turner wants. Admitting that Turner has lost his demon, she tells Chas that Turner wants a dark mirror. Turner had been examining himself in the mirror when he realized that it was "time for a change, then immediately as he watched, the image faded. His demon had abandoned him." As she talks, Turner is shown looking up at a mirror and this image becomes the reflection in an amulet. Pherber tells Chas that Turner is trying to get back his demon and has been waiting for Chas for a long time. She then tells Chas that Turner is waiting for him downstairs.

Walking down the hall, Chas can hear music already playing. Going into a room, Chas finds Lucy is dancing about while Turner is adjusting his sound system. Turner attempts to dance, but his movements seem stilted and finally he sits down to watch Lucy. Then Turner suddenly begins to dance freely to the music, as Lucy is doing, and he picks up a light rod as he dances. He thrusts it out toward Chas, who seems lost in the music. At one point, Turner lets out a scream and the image freezes. There is a cut to Turner's likeness when he was at the height of his career, an intimation that his demon has returned. The camera and the music close in on Chas's ear, as if they were traveling through it, and the musical journey begins. The sequence anticipates the style of music videos, which were to come into vogue nearly ten years later with MTV, but it is not simply a musical montage. It takes the themes of transference even further, with Flowers and Turner now seeming to be the same.

A small insert shows Flowers at his desk, saying "right, again," but he is quickly replaced by Turner wearing a suit and sitting at the same desk. Around him sit the other men in Flowers's organization whom Turner questions about whether they consider it equitable. Listening to the music, he tells one man to turn it up, an echo of an earlier request by Flowers. Turner sings "Memo from Mr. T," a song whose lyrics will often evoke a response in the men. When Chas walks in to take his seat in front of the desk, Turner shines the light on him, singing that he remembers him from "fifty-six, a faggy little leather boy." The other men in the room are lost in their own conversations and take no notice of Turner as he begins to undress Wilson. Turner orders them to do the same, and Turner's outfit is now his own. Behind him, Flowers can be seen once again adjusting the painting, which alternates between the one in his office and the one Turner had earlier turned down. Dressed once again in a suit, Turner pulls out a drawer and dumps bullets onto a stack of homosexual magazines. In a reminder of Flowers's motto, Turner sings that the baby is dead and smashes the mirror, bringing the sequence to an end. The gangsters lie naked on the floor, exhausted.

Turner tries to wake Chas, telling him he must call his agent, while in another room Lucy and Pherber sit on a bed discussing Chas. Lucy asks

Pherber if she has had sex with Chas, and the two of them examine his gun because they find his profession fascinating. Remaining lost in his stupor, Chas calls Tony, while Turner stands behind him. After apologizing for calling so late, Chas tells Tony he can get the photo to him, but Turner suggests that Tony come there to get it. When Turner gives Chas the address to repeat to Tony, it once again seems that another person is being drawn to the house. From the scene of Tony nervously speaking on the phone, the camera pans to a shot of his wife, with Rosebloom and Wilson sitting near her. As Tony hangs up the phone, Rosebloom wonders why he has forgotten to call, "Forgot, but not forgiven."

Upstairs Lucy lies in a bed looking through a viewmaster at images of Persia. As Turner walks toward the bed, she asks him why Chas wants to go to America and says that he would do better to go to Persia. Pherber lies asleep beside Lucy as Turner asks if the mountains would be better without the bandits, returning to the story "The Old Man on the Mountain." Chas is asleep in his bedroom, and the camera pans across the room to show Turner silently observing him, while upstairs Lucy sleeps beside Pherber. When Chas awakens, he mumbles that he has been through a cement mixer. Beside him Turner rolls over and the two begin to kiss, but as they separate, Turner has become Lucy, although she is wearing Turner's outfit. Pulling off her robe, Chas describes her as being undeveloped, "like a little boy." In the other room Turner looks out the window, complaining it is a lousy morning. Lucy presents Chas with a rock, as well as a ring which she calls magical. She tells Chas he should not go to the United States, but should instead become a bandit in Persia.

Clad in one of Turner's robes, Chas stands in the bathroom where Lucy is bathing. As he wonders if Turner should not have retired, Chas adjusts the wig he has worn for his disguise; he is more comfortable now with his new identity. That his sensibilities have indeed changed is demonstrated by his willingness to go upstairs to get Lucy her shampoo, the first act he has done for someone else without expecting anything in return. Ironically, this action leads to the resolvement of his conflict with his past, for upstairs he finds Flowers's men waiting for him. Realizing he is trapped, Chas tells Rosebloom that he will leave peacefully, provided he can first go upstairs. Reluctantly, Rosebloom agrees to this, after first warning Chas that men are also stationed outside.

Chas goes into the bedroom and finds Turner in bed with Pherber. When he learns that Chas must leave, Turner wants to go with him. "You don't know where I'm going, pal," says Chas, but Turner confidently tells him he does. Chas stands by the window, wondering what to do, while Turner already seems aware of what is to happen. In an action already associated with death, Turner pulls the covers up to his face, while Chas walks to the foot of the bed. Quietly, with none of the malice he demonstrated in murdering Maddocks, Chas raises his gun and fires. The bullet is filmed entering Turner's head, passing through a photograph of Borges, and seeming to exit outside the building. Chas's earlier boast that he was a bullet has taken on a physical representation. The camera follows Chas as he is escorted outside, but significantly he is photographed from behind.

Downstairs, Lucy is calling for Chas, while Rosebloom explores the house. Without her seeing him, Rosebloom comes in and leaves a note from Chas saying he has gone to Persia. He continues to move through the house, while Chas is being escorted down the street. He opens a closet and finds Turner lying among the empty frames, for like the frames Turner's body serves no purpose without what it had contained. Chas gets into an open car, where he is greeted by Harry, but as the car pulls away it is Turner who looks out. The transformation that had been anticipated is now complete. Under the closing credits, the image of Persia returns as well as a shot of the Borges book, now lying discarded on the floor.

Performance is a stunning debut, which introduces the theme Roeg will continue to use in his other films: a protagonist lost in an unknown environment from which he or she can emerge only through self-knowledge. It also introduces Roeg's future format: he will begin most of his films with a sequence that announces the primary themes, which are to be examined in more detail in the second half. Thus Flowers's words in the first half will often be spoken by Turner in the second. The first section will culminate with a murder, as does the second and Chas's sexual confusion in the beginning will culminate in his finding his true self at the film's climax. Roeg explains this strategy by saying:

> I do like to set people against an unfamiliar background. I think the background can be used tremendously by the actor. It makes him stand out. I don't want the characters to meld with their environment. In an unfamiliar place they can't help relating differently, until all their sharpened concentration goes on with their own problems, which is the story.[4]

The film would also ironically foretell the fate of Roeg's other films. Once it was completed, the producers were bothered by what the directors had wrought and decided it was better to hold back the film than to be embarrassed by its release. For two years the film sat on the shelf before it finally received an unceremonious send-off. The critical response was not only negative, but often antagonistic in nature, as the following remarks by critic Paul D. Zimmerman show: "For even with its titillation truncated and some of its punches pulled, this sorded little story of a gangster tough who hides out in the house of three drug freaks is among the ugliest, most contrived and self-indulgent films of the year."[5] This theme would be echoed by many, and only a few years later would *Performance* be reexamined and discovered to be the masterpiece it was. At the time, however, Roeg had no way of knowing this, and the response the film received shocked him: "But after what I'd done, I thought, can people really imagine that someone who's spent so much time in film doesn't know what foot he's putting forward?" That he can't feel pride? I even had offers from people who said, 'I can help you out if you're in trouble' and 'It's difficult the first time.' That whole complacent attitude."[6]

Jack Kroll, writing for *Art in America* magazine, was one of the few who took the film seriously, and he seemed to understand the effect the film was having on people: "Apparently this film was able to peel away a layer of calloused epidermis from many sophisticated people and hit some fresh nerves. In doing so it raises, or resurrects, some basic points about the movie medium."[7]

At the time the supporters of *Performance* were often writers for smaller, less mainstream publications. They saw in it a document of the sixties, one of the few films from this period which still adequately presents the drug culture as critic Stephen Farber has noted: "*Performance* is the first film to render the drug experience imaginatively and compellingly; more than that, it is the definitive statement of the drug experience as mystical conversion, a radical assault on conventional values, and the key to the transformation of life."[8]

Even as Roeg was waiting for the film's release, he was beginning the film he had wanted to direct earlier, *Walkabout*. Thus, even though the response to *Performance* could have destroyed many a career, Roeg was only beginning his. Cammell would not be so fortunate. It would be nearly ten years before he would direct another film, the unsuccessful *Demon Seed*.

Notes

1. Jonathan Hacker and David Price, *Take 10*, p. 367.
2. *Cinema Papers*, April 1974, p. 175.
3. Susan Sontag, *Styles of Radical Will*, p. 87.
4. *American Film*, January 80, p. 26.
5. *Newsweek*, August 17, 1970, p. 85.
6. *American Film*, p. 25.
7. *Art in America*, March 1971, p. 114.
8. *Cinema*, Fall 1970, p. 20.

TWO

Walkabout

James Vance Marshall's novella *Walkabout* has become something of a children's classic, particularly in Australia, where the story is set. It concerns two children who survive a plane crash but then must travel through the outback to return to civilization. Near death, they are saved by an aborigine boy engaged in a walkabout, his society's test of manhood. The young brother begins to develop a relationship with the aborigine, even learning some of his language, but the girl grows fearful of him and interprets his actions as a sexual threat. Seeing her fear, the aborigine mistakes it for an ability to sense his death. As if resigned to his supposed fate, he gradually grows weaker, eventually willing himself to die. Alone again, the children continue and at last meet up with a group of aborigines. Changed by her encounter, the girl seems more willing to accept these aborigines and even attempts to communicate with them. She draws a picture of a house, and the aborigines react by gesturing that just such a structure is only a short distance away. Thus as the children walk off, they are presumably about to be saved.

It is hard to see why the book *Walkabout* deserves its reputation as a classic. The children come across as racist, and Marshall's tone seems to encourage this attitude. He creates the perfect Noble Savage, providing us with details of his life, but not of his personality. Roeg had long been enamored of the story, and of Edward Bond's script, however, which, though sparse, provided much with which Roeg could work. It was not the visual potential which attracted him, but the central conflict:

> It was that here were two people—two people in effect, since the little boy really acts as a chorus to the aborigine and the girl—who by this curious moment of fate were at a point where they could have been in love with each other. They had everything to offer each other, but they couldn't communicate and went zooming to their own separate destinies,

19

through the odd placement of identity, the identity that other people had
put on them.[1]

One alteration in the film was not due to a script change, but to natural
aging. Jenny Agutter had been thirteen when Roeg first chose her for the
part but was sixteen when filming actually started; her age helped to accentuate the sexuality of the story. The aborigine would be played by David
Gumpilil, who knew no English. Roeg would communicate to the actor
primarily through sign language. (It would not be the last time that Roeg
used an actor who spoke no English; he often cast such actors because the
confusion they conveyed added something to their role. The most striking
example would be Renato Scarpa, cast as the inspector in *Don't Look Now*.)
For the part of the boy, Roeg looked no further than his own family, picking
his son Luc to play the role. At first Roeg was uncomfortable with the idea
of directing his own son, but he soon became fascinated by Luc's response
to the experience. At one point he even thought of filming a video diary
of Luc's experience, to be titled *Luka's Diary*, but the project was never
completed.

"In Australia when an aborigine man child reaches 16 he is sent out
into the land. For months he must live from it. Sleep on it. Eat of its fruit
and flesh. Stay alive. Even if it means killing his fellow creatures. The
Aborigine calls it the walkabout. This is the story of a walkabout."

This introduction does not just serve as a definition to the film, it alerts
us to the thematic paradigms of the film. Three children are sent into the
outback, one by choice, the others by tragedy, but for all three it is a test
of sorts. For Roeg the central question is not survival, but the interaction
of characters whose responses have been conditioned by society. He has
called the film a documentary and his subject is the juxtaposition of two
cultures; the editing juxtaposes an event in the city to a similar act in the
outback and vice versa. The opening immediately indicates the dichotomy
of the city and the desert. The camera pans across a brick wall to reveal
the city; later the camera will again pan across the wall, this time to reveal
the desert.

The focus is not on the main characters, but on their daily routine.
They are never even named, so that we identify them by their roles instead
of their personalities: the father, the boy, the girl, and the aborigine. The
opening montage does not delineate their characters, but shows instead
how their environment dominates them. The father is anonymous among
the other businessmen, as is the girl in her own setting: her school uniform
unites her with her classmates. She is practicing her breathing exercises,
producing one of many sounds overlaying the images, sounds that include
aborigine music and the natural noises of the city. The father enters an
office building, but he is photographed from the outside, through the window,

a technique that distances him from us. When he emerges, he seems disconcerted and sits at the base of the building, looking up at the giant structure.

Of the family, only the boy shows signs of individuality, as he interacts with his fellow students or attempts to communicate with his father. On his way home from school, he leaves the sidewalk to cut through a park, but even here nature is more an exhibit then a natural environment. All of the trees are carefully tagged, including a large, spiderlike tree the boy passes, whose pattern will be duplicated by one in the outback. The identification of the characters simply by their role suggests an allegory, and many elements of the film resemble a biblical story. The motif of the tree also has its basis in religion and will come to symbolize not just life and death, but also sex. In addition, trees will be the site of two deaths that will resemble the Crucifixion.

The family apartment seems lost between the city and the outback, perched on the edge of the sea. The mother prepares a picnic lunch as she listens to the radio (that the first words of the film come from the radio is not surprising, considering the role it will play). In *Walkabout* we see for the first time Roeg's use of another medium to act as a commentator on the action. He explains this technique by saying:

> I'm interested in the split senses in engaging people's attention on more than one surface at a time. There'll be more of this in the coming genera-tions. Already people watch television and read a magazine at the same time, looking from one to the other. Kids are accustomed to doing two or three things at a time now. This is what I was trying to put into *Walkabout*.[2]

The radio announcer is talking of gourmet cooking, but his words allude to what the children will go through: "Birds pick desperately at the grain in the hope of penetrating through to the light, which he mistakes for the sun." Much later, the girl will search in the darkness for the light, an obvious metaphor for what she hopes to obtain. In the living room the father quietly walks by, looking at his wife in the kitchen, but saying nothing. Standing out on the patio, he remains emotionless, even as his son calls to him from the swimming pool. Although the children are interact-ing, the pool they swim in isolates them from their surroundings.

If the father shows any feeling toward his family, it is a silent con-tempt, and their picnic in the outback serves to delineate this. Having parked the car on the dry, barren ground, he begins to work on his papers, oblivious to either the boy or the girl until they disturb him. He ad-monishes the boy for talking with his mouth full and roughly pulls the girl's hand away when she tries to turn on the radio. When he starts the car again, a brief shot of the empty gas gauge indicates the trip will be one-way.

In driving into the outback, the father is taking the children away from civilization's influence. The car comes to a stop and the boy races off as the father says they will eat there. The girl looks at him with a confused expression, then starts to put out the blanket and the food. By setting out the food the mother has prepared, the girl is already assuming her role. Again, it is only the boy who seems to enjoy the environment; he races about the rocks playing with his toy soldiers and squirt gun. The girl has turned on the radio, and Rod Stewart's song is oddly prophetic, both in its title ("Gasoline Alley") and its words ("going home, running home").

The father has remained in the car reading over mineral charts and a book entitled *Structural Geometry;* he continues to ignore the boy, who struggles to make contact with him. Bringing over one of his toy cars, the boy tells his father that the "wheel has fallen off," but getting no response, he wanders off. It is only now that the father looks after the children, but it is through binoculars, which seem to distance them instead of bringing them closer. He watches as the boy puts the gun into his mouth, a morbid hint of what is to come. Although the viewer is aware of the father's estrangement from his family, the first bullet he fires at the boy catches us by surprise. This unexpected violence is typical of Bond's work, particularly the film *Saved,* which shocked many theatre patrons with the beating to death of a baby. Believing it all to be a game, the boy reacts by firing his squirt gun at the father. Thus when his sister tackles the boy to the ground to protect him, he criticizes her for ruining his chance to shoot. Even as the father continues to shoot, he calls out to the children, safely hidden by the rocks: "We've got to go now. I've got to go now."

Having reached a ravine, the girl attempts to look out as the father seems to lose patience, shouting for them to "come out now." After firing aimlessly at the picnic lunch, he takes out a gasoline can from the trunk. When a muffled shot rings out, the girl ventures to look out and sees her father fall back to the ground dead as the car becomes engulfed in flames. The image is repeated twice, from different angles, to prolong the shock (a technique Sergei Eisenstein has also experimented with). The car turns white from the heat, and the camera moves in on the father's papers and briefcase, which also burn. The viewer is left not just in shock, but also in confusion, unsure as to what motivated the father to do such a ghastly act. The film itself provides few clues, except that he seems burdened by something. One possible motive comes from the writer himself, not in reference to this work, but in an introduction to his play *Lear.* Bond suggests what can cause an individual to turn to violence:

> We respond aggressively when we are constantly deprived of our physical and emotional needs, or when we are threatened with this; and if we are constantly deprived and threatened in this way—as human

beings now are — we live in a constant state of aggression. It does not matter how much a man doing routine work in, say, a factory or office is paid: he will still be deprived in this sense. Because he is behaving in a way for which he is not designed, he is alienated from his natural self, and this will have physical and emotional consequences for him. He becomes nervous and tense and he begins to look for threats everywhere. This makes him belligerent and provocative; he becomes a threat to other people, and so his situation rapidly deteriorates.

Although most critics have taken the father's actions to be murderous, it could also be contended that his intentions are to save his children, not to kill them. Knowing what society has done to him, he forces his children out into the outback on his own form of a walkabout. This could account for his so obviously missing them as he fires and for his not going after them in an area which provides them little protection. Instead he destroys the only transportation available to them and the only guide they have. The film offers some proof of this, from the only outside source available to us, the radio. This evidence comes much later in the film, when the two take a break from their journey and hear on the radio the words: "The idea that man has passed through ten thousand years of trials and suffering in order that they might lapse into perpetual obsession and comfortable shopkeeping." The girl automatically shuts off the radio, before we can hear more of the announcer's argument, but the meaning is clear. Without some event to disturb the pattern, individuals will continue to travel down the road toward self-destruction. Roeg's analysis of the film seems to concur with this theory:

> The story offers an opportunity to start afresh — even explode the burden of manners to a degree, to put on a new footing the relationship between men and women of the same or different color or social background. All of these differences might stem from a whole history of the world that has been misunderstood. We must start again, not from sophistication but from total innocence.[3]

While the car continues to burn, the girl rushes back to gather up what few provisions they have, including the radio. Returning to her brother, she urges him into the outback, even as he worries about the father's reaction, saying, "He said I wasn't to go out of his sight." The girl tries to reassure her brother, but as they walk off, her actions already seem ill-advised. In the process of trying to save her brother from the sight of their father's body, she is taking him further away from civilization.

As the children begin their journey, Roeg cuts to a small reptile, which seems to hiss at them as they pass. He will incorporate many shots of animals during the children's ordeal, but his canvas is much larger than simply the area through which they travel. The regions the animals inhabit are often hundreds of miles apart and in locations the children will not even cross. This is the visual equivalent of a technique Marshall used in his novel when he cut away from the central action to incorporate many details of the outback. In the book these asides seemed an intrusion, but Roeg is able to incorporate the external material into the film more easily, creating a region as mysterious and threatening for the viewer as it must be for the children. Another technique Roeg employs is to use the natural landscape to indicate the emotions the children are feeling. As they settle down for the night, he superimposes a rock formation over the image of them falling asleep. Critic Anthony Boyle realized the meaning of this and similar shots:

> Roeg not only shows the landscape; he also uses it as a visual metaphor for the internal state of his characters. For example, when the children sleep, the camera superimposes their bodies on the bleak rocks, giving the viewer the conception that their internal situation is desperate. At another point, when Peter [Boyle takes the name from the novel] slides down a sandhill, the camera lingers to record the sand closing over his path. In this sequence Roeg uses the landscape as a device to fix for us the isolation and extremity of the children's position. They are in danger of being swallowed up by their surroundings.[4]

Another indication of this vulnerability comes the next morning when the boy admits he has had a bad dream. The girl continues to have difficulty with her role of leader, even losing what few supplies they have as she climbs a hill. "You're dropping everything," the boy tells her. "The ammunitions are falling out." Later they will find they have lost their can opener, so what food they do have is difficult to use. With no direction in mind, they climb the highest peak, hoping to see some landmark, but instead they see only how desolate the area appears. As they look out at the sea, the boy's words seem both questioning and hopeful: "It's the sea isn't it?" The boy's optimism will gradually fade, and the girl finds herself fighting his spirit as much as the environment. She encourages him to eat salt, believing it will help them get by without water, and she attempts to turn their ordeal into a game.

Lacking the girl's determination, the boy yields to his desires to give up, rolling down a dune to come to rest below. The girl comes over the top and attempts to get him to continue. "I can't go down there. It isn't fair," she tells him. Her face is covered in sand as she calls after him, making a quiet plea: "Oh, please make him come." The words apply not only to her brother, but to her hope for a savior. The boy lies in the sand, ignoring her words, which begin to sound like those of their father, as she says, "I'm going now." Finally giving in, she stumbles down the hill, picking up his discarded belongings as she goes. She arrives just as he closes his eyes, seemingly asleep, and the screen turns black.

Undeterred, the girl continues, carrying her brother on her back even when she suspects he is faking sleep. "You should try to help me. I'm tired too," she complains. As she begins to lose her grip on him, he points at something in the distance. As he slides off her back, he sees that it is a tree surrounded by vegetation, and he quickly walks toward it. The girl is more hesitant, standing back and watching the tree and her brother merge into one image. A choir begins, as if the discovery were a religious experience.

The boy's attitude may seem selfish, but we never lose our sympathy for him. He proves himself to be the more resourceful of the two: he discovers the oasis and he has the ability to communicate with the aborigine. The girl, however, clings to standards which have no meaning in the desert. When she comes up behind the boy as he begins to drink from the pond beside the tree, her first reaction is not one of relief, but condemnation: "You said you were too tired to walk." He eats the red fruit which floats on the surface, but only after she sees the birds eating it, does she feel it is safe to try it. The children bathe, but in the first indication of her sexual anxiety, the girl leaves her undergarments on, even in front of her brother. She tries to clean their clothes, telling him they "don't want people thinking we're a couple of tramps." Logically he asks, what people?

The death of the father is constantly brought back to the children. The radio announces a mass of remembrance, triggering a flashback of the father, and the next program contains the sound of a car crash, another reminder of his death. The boy asks if their car has crashed, which is the first intimation that he knows what has happened. Sitting in the water, he plays with a toy boat as his sister begins to dress. He asserts that in stories the hero always wins ("even Bugs Bunny always wins") and then asks if they are superheroes. She hopes that they are, and when he asks if they are lost, she tries to remain confident, replying, "Of course not."

The oasis will prove to be transitory, however. As the children sleep, the fruit is eaten by the insects and the animals which inhabit the area. The pond evaporates, leaving behind only mud, which the boy walks through as the girl looks on in dismay. Even the boy realizes they should have picked some fruit and picks up the empty lemonade bottle in which they could have kept water. With no direction in mind, the girl decides they will remain there, in the hope that the water will return. Their possible fate is suggested by the mud the boy dumps onto his toy boat and the dead carcass which buzzards fly over. With only the thin tablecloth as shelter, the children find their strength waning as the days pass. Roeg continually cuts to the sun in *Walkabout* so that it takes on a strange fascination. At times it seems like a solar transmitter as the image is overlaid with the sound of a computer.

The heat takes its toll, and the children lie on the ground, too weak to even sit up. Thus the aborigine's appearance at first seems like a mirage, and the boy's words are significant as he calls out "Dad." Startled, the girl sits up, and as the figure moves closer, it is apparent he is an aborigine boy. Unaware that he is being watched, the aborigine dances about and spears a reptile, but on seeing the children he comes forward, speaking to them in his language. The girl watches him from the protection of the tree, very much aware of his nearly naked body. He gestures to the ground as if questioning them on the water, but when they make no response he walks on. Only now do the children seem to realize what is happening, as the boy shouts for the girl to ask about water. They chase after the aborigine, but the girl proves ineffective in communicating with him. First she says they are English; then she asks where Adelaide is. The boy must remind her that water is their first priority, but she continues to disappoint the viewer, saying to the aborigine: "You must understand. Anyone can understand that. We want to drink. I can't make it any clearer than that." With a simple gesture, however, the boy makes their needs perfectly clear to the aborigine. As the boy gestures toward his mouth and makes a gulping sound, the aborigine smiles and says "guapa," his word for water.

The aborigine walks the children back to the oasis, where water is still available; it has only gone underground. Using a hollow stick, the aborigine brings the water back up to the surface, and the boy and the girl drink from it. This done, the aborigine leads them off into the distance as a bird looks down at them from a tree. The next day they continue to walk, the boy acting as an intermediary between the other two as he takes each of their hands in his. Further into the desert they come across a herd of camels. The boy fantasizes about the camels being driven by men, but the aborigine is more pessimistic. He imagines their dead bodies, some covered in insects. It is the first indication that the aborigine is haunted by death.

Roeg is one of the few commercial filmmakers who consciously experiment with film grammar in presenting their stories; he does this particularly in his early films. It is most evident in his editing style, but it can also be seen in his use of techniques that break with the traditional rules of cinema. In *Performance* his experimentation was evident in his use of black and white, in his imbuing some sequences with a particular color, and in the exchange of characters without warning or apparent reason. In *Walkabout*, it can be seen in the inclusion of still photographs in three sequences of the film. The first occurs when the aborigine begins to hunt down some kangaroos the image freezes to emphasize the joy of the aborigine. When the images finally move, they seem speeded up as the aborigine chases after a kangaroo, his spear only bouncing off it. One of the kangaroos stops, and the aborigine moves stealthily up to him. This time the spear finds its target, and the animal falls dead. As the aborigine begins to cut up the carcass, Roeg cuts to a butcher cutting up meat in his store.

The girl (Jenny Agutter) and the boy (Lucien John) decide to follow the aborigine (David Gumpilil) in hopes that he will lead them to food and water in *Walkabout*.

The butcher carefully weighs the meat before laying it on cellophane, unlike the aborigine, who pulls apart the meat and eats from it. The montage serves to contrast the manner in which the two societies obtain their food and is typical of sequences Roeg will use throughout his films. In their presentation, these sequences resemble the theory of montage that Eisenstein first put forth, but the results, as Michael Dempsey has pointed out, are markedly different:

> Roeg's montage does not say that two shots are connected; it says that they might be. Eisenstein's editing aims at certainty, Roeg's for uncertainty. With Roeg, A plus B does not necessarily equal C; it may equal D or Q or nothing, and plus may be minus. When his rapid juxtapositions outrun our ability to sort them out, we tumble into an uncertainty that, in the hands of a hack, would be merely cheap but that, in his, becomes genuinely metaphysical. He uses them to undercut our allegiance to reason, our dogged confidence that we are standing on solid ground.[5]

Having eaten the meat, the three sit around a fire as the aborigine proudly displays his spear. The boy takes his toy soldiers from his satchel, while the girl tries to convince him to share them with the aborigine, saying, "Don't be mean. I'd expect he'd like to play. He's never had any toys of his own." If her intentions are well-meaning, they also indicate her inability to understand the aborigine's culture. She believes that because he lacks material goods, he is lacking in basic needs or emotions. The aborigine quickly proves this assumption to be false as he begins to wrestle playfully with the boy. The girl joins in as the boy is lifted onto a tree, and there is a shot of some aborigine children laughing, as if they were observing the trio. In fact, they are part of a group that has come across the father's body and the burnt-out car. Roeg cuts between the two activities, the aborigines exploring the car and the children playfully climbing the tree. The girl is at ease, the only time she will be when she is with the aborigine, but she still modestly pulls down her skirt. The contrast to the aborigine women, who walk about topless with no sense of shame is evident.

If the sequence is marked by optimism, its ending is filled with foreboding. The aborigines have placed the father's body in a tree to keep it safe from the animals, and the camera closes in on the father's face. Having taken over the father's role in the care of the children, the aborigine is also doomed to the same fate. The exploration of the car comes to an end when the radio is accidently turned on. The aborigines walk off as the announcer is telling his listeners to turn their cars in for cash. That night the girl rubs her leg as the aborigine looks on. He speaks to her and she seems to understand, replying, "I'll be all right in the morning. It got a bit sore from . . ." Unable to finish her sentence, the girl recalls how they played on the tree, but now realizes how vulnerable she was. The limbs of the tree are white, like her skin, and to further this analogy, the girl's legs are photographed against the branches. "Oh, dear," she says. The aborigine picks up his spear while he is talking to her, then goes off alone. Coming across her belongings hanging from a branch, he stands beside them, motionless, with one foot in the air.

Earlier the girl had warned the boy not to go without his shirt, but he had ignored her because her authority was already undermined. Now the sun continues to beat down on them and seems to result in delirium. As Roeg photographs the sun, the sound track includes the father's voice calling for his children, the shot which killed him ringing out, and the radio, which has become their companion. Walking along a white forest devoid of vegetation, the aborigine goes up to the carcass of a kangaroo to pull out a handful of animal fat. The boy lies across the girl's lap, his back burnt from the sun. As the girl is trying to comfort the boy, she cannot help but remind him of her earlier warning.

Roeg's experimentation with traditional techniques continues as the three walk in a forest. The boy begins to tell the aborigine a story, despite his sister's argument that he will not understand. This opinion does not prevent her from correcting various points of his account, however (an autobiographical touch from Roeg, whose sister often did the same to him).

The story concerns a boy who lives with his mother, who never speaks to him. He believes she is physically unable to talk, until he comes home one day and hears her talking to herself. When he enters the house, however, she inexplicably stops. Determined to hear her voice, he climbs a ladder one night to listen at her window, but though he can see her lips moving, he is still unable to hear her. Moving closer to the glass, he loses his footing and the ladder falls. Hanging precariously from the ledge, but not wanting to give himself away, he tries to get down on his own, only to fall to his death.

As the boy is telling his story, Roeg has the image turn back like the pages of a book to reveal a new frame. This frame is repeated throughout the story, as if to indicate that the film itself is a story. When the boy comes to the climax of his story, he turns directly toward the aborigine as he says that the boy "broke his neck." Although the story could be taken as an allegory of the aborigine's fate, Roeg mitigates this effect by having the boy continue with the story even though his sister says, "I told you he doesn't understand." The story is left unfinished, however, when the boy becomes distracted by an airplane flying overhead. At this point Roeg intended to include another interlude that would show the passengers of this plane coming into physical contact with each other, but otherwise paying no attention to one another. It would have furthered his discourse on the emotional distancing of individuals.

The girl's attempts to communicate continue to fail as the three become involved in painting. The aborigine has painted animals on the boy's back and some designs on the girl's arm. She in turn has drawn a house on a rock formation, but even the boy cannot tell what it is. The aborigine's drawings are more detailed, but also more obscure. To the boy they look like dinosaurs and spaceships. "I think he might take us to the moon," he remarks. The girl, however, is less interested in the aborigine's drawing than in the fact that she does not have the proper tools to work with, such as crayons.

Roeg cuts away from the central action to a group of meteorologists conducting experiments in the outback. One of the scientists is watching a red weather balloon through binoculars, while his female colleague is worrying about losing another one, saying, "They're expensive and I don't like to waste expensive things." She is seated at a table making notations, while at a small table in the distance, three laborers play cards (the faces of the cards are naked women). Opera music plays in the background. When the woman crosses her legs, the three men turn in unison, their image frozen. All the men seem to be looking at her, although she fails to notice. One scientist offers her a cigarette, glancing down at her breasts as he does. When she adjusts her blouse, the men again all stare. When another scientist walks over to the woman, the three laborers watch carefully, having forgotten their game. As the man begins to kiss and suck her fingers, one of the laborers cuts loose one of the balloons. The scientists chase vainly after it, while the woman repeats how expensive they are. Except for the missing balloons, which the children later find, this episode seems to have no relation to the main story. Even its presentation is different; it almost seems a humorous homage to Fellini. The scene seems slightly out of place in the many prints that are missing a second sequence which John Izod believes works as a companion piece to the first:

> Later there occurs another incident which embodies the idea of dead sexuality, and which does touch one of the group. The black boy on his own approaches an encampment where frantic whites harass aborigine workers as they attempt to produce plaster kangaroos for a distant tourist market. A white prostitute invites the boy (in English) to go with her. He refuses (in his own tongue, but he has understood her well enough), and leads the others, who have not seen the encounter, back into the safe desert. One of the foremen goes into the prostitute's house.[6]

One of the most erotic scenes in the film is also one of the most innocent: this is the scene in which the girl swims nude in a lake. As she glides through the water in slow motion, Roeg cuts away to the aborigine and the boy, who are catching fish with the spear. The two seem united in their tasks, whether they are getting food, gathering wood, or simply playing. The scenes of the girl swimming are extended so that her activity seems to be not just a simple respite, but an achievement of harmony with the landscape. She emerges from the lake to dress, her image reflected in the water below. Rain begins to fall and lightning is visible in the sky, like portents of doom. The boy walks along the water and mud, the aborigine beside him. That night the aborigine gets up from the ground, unable to sleep, and goes to the girl's clothing. After gently touching it, he turns on the radio, a symbol of her civilization.

The next day the children come across the lost weather equipment. The aborigine holds out the balloon to the girl, but she walks past him without acknowledging his offer. Instead she tells her brother to ask him how much longer it will take before they reach civilization. Before the boy can do this, however, the balloon the aborigine is carrying explodes and he falls to the ground frightened. This sequence is the first indication of the girl's callous treatment of the aborigine: she smiles slightly at his embarrassment. The boy holds his fingers up, and the aborigine smiles, holding up one. "We will be there today," the boy exclaims. The music soars as the balloon floats up, creating a sense of release. The balloon is more than just their first contact with civilization; it also points to the differences in the way the girl and the aborigine think, as Marsha Kinder and Beverle Houston have noted:

The Aborigine responds to the balloon iconically associating it with the sun. The red, round ball of the sun is an image that occurs throughout the film and appears just before we see the red balloon for the first time. The Aborigine offers the balloon to the girl as a gift, as if he were offering her the sun, but she misperceives his gesture. Then the balloon suddenly bursts, suggesting metaphorically the Aborigine's bursting hopes and foreshadowing that he will be the one to suffer as a result of the misunderstanding. The exchange is reversed in the scene where the Aborigine rejects the toy soldier offered to him as a gift by the white boy. Failing to discover any indexical or iconical meaning and not knowing the code by which it might be a symbolic sign, he tosses it away as a worthless object. Yet the toy has considerable iconic value for the white boy; it is a visual representation of a man who fights with strength and prowess. In offering the gift, he attempts to repay the Aborigine for teaching him some of the skills of manhood within the "primitive" culture.[7]

The boy's words about finding civilization prove prophetic as they come across a fence. The girl walks backward, running her hand along the fence just as she had in the opening of the film. When she touches a wooden pole, she turns in expectation. Seeing a house in the distance, she runs toward it, only to find it deserted and half-destroyed. Silently she walks through the ruined house, the camera panning across a room to give it a slightly distorted look. All that she finds of the occupants are some photographs on the wall and a group of makeshift graves in the backyard. As she stands by the graves, the aborigine comes up with a dead bird in his hand, not aware of the pain she is feeling.

Having sent the boy on an errand, the aborigine talks to the girl in words she cannot fail to understand. The two are framed by a mirror as he makes gestures that disclose his love for her while a smaller mirror shines on their eyes. Then the boy returns and the moment is broken; the girl wanders off, exploring the house as the aborigine silently watches. She looks at the photographs of the occupants of the house, but as she begins to cry, the aborigine turns away. This is the most tender scene of the film, as the girl longs for the civilization she has been cut off from and the aborigine realizes he has lost her. Whatever emotions these two have felt, it is obvious a change has occurred in their relationship. They pass in and out of the shadows of the house without seeming to notice one another. In fact, she begins to treat him more like a servant, ordering him to get some water. For the first time he speaks a word in English, "water," but she is uninterested. As he walks away, she watches a butterfly land on her arm and seems to give it more notice than she had the aborigine.

The aborigine runs up to the boy and gestures for him to follow, leading him to a road. Before the boy can react to the discovery, the aborigine picks him up and carries him back into the forest. He instructs the boy to pull up some small trees, while he goes off alone. He comes across a buffalo and begins to wrestle with the animal, until both are nearly struck by a jeep. The next scene does not occur in the present (or else the children would hear the shots), but is actually something from the aborigine's past, perhaps his first contact with whites. He looks on as the driver begins to fire at the buffalo, but his bullets seem to miss and the animal does not react to the sound. When the animal is finally hit, it falls to the ground, and the image is distorted by the grainy stock. The sequence seems to fuse memory with fantasy, particularly as the aborigine's attention turns to the boy, who also seems to be the subject of his anger. A spider bites the boy and as he spins about, the animals around him stop in their tracks. When the animals do move again, Roeg cuts to the dead buffalo, which seems to rise back up. The hunter continues to fire indiscriminately, then goes up to the carcass to cut it open. His actions are not based on needs, as the aborigine's are, but on sport.

This scene allows the viewer to understand the aborigine's fears that the whites are encroaching upon his environment. Disturbed by his remembrance, he returns to the shack, passing by the girl without speaking. Even the girl seems to notice he is troubled. She stares after him as he heads out into the outback. The sequence ends with a view of the carcasses of the animals lying on the ground, decayed and covered with insects. The camera begins to pan across a pile of bones, indicating how much destruction has occurred. Among the bones lies the aborigine, his body painted to appear like a skeleton, with only a few feathers to serve as a costume. As the camera pans across his face, his eyes suddenly open.

When the aborigine later comes upon the girl in the house, her first reaction is that he poses a sexual threat, an interpretation many critics have also made. This interpretation seems more related to her being topless at the moment, than to any action on his part, however; the dance he begins around the house is a dance of death, not of love. He had already declared his love when he had talked to her in front of the mirror; here he seems to be acknowledging his fate. She ignores all of this in her attempt to get away, as she quickly throws on her blouse and shuts the door to block him out. When the door begins to open, her worst fears seem realized, but it is her brother who comes through the opening, not the aborigine. She asks where he has been, her courage beginning to return. She follows the boy as he walks through the house, even as he goes up to the aborigine to offer him the leaves he has gathered. When the aborigine makes no response, the boy asks her what the dance means. In the first of many interpretations she gives of the dance, she tells him the aborigine is dancing because they have found the house.

The dance continues on through the night, as the aborigine pushes himself beyond endurance. Having finished their own activities, the children settle down to sleep for the night. The final image of the aborigine occurs as he stumbles about and the flowers he has carried fall to the ground. When the children wake the next morning, the aborigine is no longer present, and the girl relaxes. She shows no remorse for having rejected the aborigine because she believes she did the proper thing. She is still unable to verbalize her real fear. ("Suppose he wanted to do something or something happened, suppose he tried to . . . suppose he went up and left us.") She believes he has gone home, now that he has led them to the road, and she thinks that they must be near a town. The children bathe in preparation for their return to society, and the girl gives still another interpretation of the dance: it was the aborigine's way of saying good-bye.

It is only after the two have dressed that the boy tells his sister the true fate of the aborigine, that he is dead. He leads her outside to a tree where the aborigine lies hanging, his position recalling the final fate of the father's body. Neither of the children seem to acknowledge his loss, but only stare at the body in confusion. The girl gathers fruit from beneath his body and gives it to the boy before sending him away. Only when she is alone does she even reach out to the body, gently brushing away some insects (echoing her incidental touching of him on their first meeting). This slight gesture is the only indication that the girl did indeed have feelings toward the aborigine. Like the father's actions which opened the film, the aborigine's death leaves the viewer wondering about motivation. Only if we realize the implications of the sequence that precedes the dance do we realize that the aborigine's death is a sign not just of his defeat, but of the defeat of his entire culture.

A semi-truck goes by on the highway, pulling three trailers, but when the children arrive the road is empty. After they have walked along it a while, the boy remembers the radio, which they have left behind. The girl reminds him that the batteries no longer worked, but Roeg cuts back to the radio still sitting beside the deserted homestead. It comes on as the camera moves about the grounds, focusing on the remains of their stay: the white cloth the girl had carried, the bird the aborigine had killed, and the well from which he drew water. In Roeg's films nothing is what it seems.

The road does lead to a town, and while the two look down at it from a distance, the boy finally asks what has happened to the father. "Did he shoot himself?" he says, indicating he is aware of what occurred. The girl tells him it was an accident, but he is not convinced and wonders why he did it. When she says, "I suppose he thought he was doing the best thing," he replies, "That's silly." Her only answer is "I said I don't know."

Continuing on into the town, the children are disheartened to find it seems to be deserted. Only some water sprinklers that are operating indicate that someone still lives there. In a scene that recalls the aborigine's initial appearance, the children look dumbfounded as a man walks past them, casually greeting them before going into his home. The girl races to the door, but as she tries to tell the man what has happened, he keeps his distance. Only when he notices the boy picking up a sprinkling can does he finally emerge, showing more concern for his property than for the children. When he mentions a mine in town, the boy innocently asks what was in it. "Nothing. That's why they shut it," the man replies.

The man's actions are in direct contrast to those of the aborigine. Instead of helping the children, he returns to the safety of his house, offering them no aid. Giving up on him, they head off to explore the town. Despite the man's behavior, the children seem to believe their ordeal is almost over. As the girl looks on, the boy takes some blocks out from under a tractor, causing it to roll forward and crash into some debris. Marshall's novel had ended in the outback, with the children on the way to being saved, but Roeg includes a coda to his story. As the tractor crashes, there is a swish pan which returns the action to the city.

The closing of the film mirrors its opening with a scene of people hurrying through the streets. Among them walks a young businessman, whose manner is much like that of the father. He has married the girl and many years have passed since her time in the outback, but she still inhabits the same apartment, where she works in the kitchen much as her mother did. She is slicing up kangaroo meat, pausing only long enough to take a drag from her cigarette and to recall the aborigine cutting up a kangaroo's carcass. In contrast to the father, who ignored his wife, the young businessman immediately greets the girl and begins to tell her of a shake-up at the office. One of the men has lost his job, and it takes little imagination to see that this is what could have happened to the father to set him off. As the man talks excitedly, the girl remembers the outback, but her memory is of something that did not occur. She and her brother are sitting naked on a small island as the aborigine dives into the water. They quickly join him, and the three frolic in the water as the camera pans to their clothes hanging from sticks like scarecrows. A male narrator begins to read the A. E. Housman poem "Into My Heart an Air . . . ." The film ends with the words "rien ne va plus," as if a game of chance has ended. If the ending seems pessimistic, with the girl missing her chance to avoid her mother's fate, Roeg's interpretation is decidedly different:

> At the end there was hope, even if it was a subjective thing for the girl. It had touched the girl. It wasn't going to be the same. If I'd shot it that "oh, yes darling, isn't it wonderful that you're going to get that promotion" and she hadn't thought at all of the past, there would have been absolutely no hope. But the stain had been left on her . . . . She sees in her husband the same route that her father went, but the mother had never had her experience, so she's finding out things which could be transferred to the children.[8]

Ironically, *Walkabout* would be popular with many of the same critics who had so disliked *Performance*. If the film seemed less threatening to them, they still failed to realize how detailed it really was. *Walkabout* is indeed one of Roeg's most accessible films in terms of plot. In terms of themes and motifs, however, it is one of his most intricate. If *Performance* introduced many of Roeg's most persistent themes, *Walkabout* serves notice of his more lyrical side. It is also his first film in which the focus is on a female protagonist. The pointed obscurity of many seemingly crucial plot elements would also run throughout Roeg's work. Although he found *Walkabout* flawed, John Russell Taylor considered it a "curiously haunting film, with moments of real power when myth seems to take on flesh and be reenacted convincingly before our eyes. The attempt is on a grand scale, and if it does not always succeed there is still enough there to make it much more worth seeing than many a modest, moderate success, and to give us very high hopes for Mr. Roeg's subsequent work."[9]

In the summer of 1971, Roeg attended a rock festival in England near Glastonbury, long reputed to be the site of King Arthur's court. Five thousand people attended events spread over a 150 acre region to hear David Bowie, Traffic, and a handful of other musicians. Using much of his own money and a camera crew at his disposal, Roeg shot a tremendous amount of material for what he thought would be more than the simple recording of an event:

> What I'm trying to begin to show is that fashion and generation gaps and all those things are irrelevant. None of it really exists. All that exists is the human being. And in the film we see human beings — very young ones, getting older. And old ones too. Fashion is inconsequential. Human beings have always been the same. I'm using a lot of engravings in the movie — to show the link in time. The crowd there interested me because I'd worked on films like *Knights of the Round Table* and *Ivanhoe* and I never thought they were very well done: they'd just looked up history books and dressed people up, but they didn't behave as if they belonged to the period — their movements were related to the way crowds behave today. But at Glastonbury, because of this extraordinary equation of space and people, I could see that people behave according to the way they are positioned. There was the look of a medieval fair to it. They had mummers and jugglers and religious sects. It was a melting pot of human beings, much more than just a show.[10]

What could have been one of Roeg's most challenging works instead became another in a series of disappointments, however, as he recalls: "We got it into a sample shape, which we tried to sell, but we ran out of money and the other people who had put money in wanted to get out. So another company took it over, they bought all the footage, and I know it was some marvelous footage we shot. They rushed it together and I've never seen the finished film."[11]

Few people have seen the resulting work, which was credited to Peter Neal. The film, *Glastonbury Fayre,* was given a limited release in 1972, but has since disappeared.

Notes

1. *Sight and Sound,* Winter 1973, p. 7.
2. *Film Criticism,* Spring 1976, p. 27.
3. Ibid.
4. *Film Literature,* Spring 1979, p. 71.
5. *Film Quarterly,* Spring 1974, p. 41.
6. *Sight and Sound,* Spring 1980, p. 115.
7. Marsha Kinder and Beverle Houston, *Self and Cinema,* p. 378.
8. *Cinema Papers,* April 1974, p. 175.
9. *The Times,* October 8, 1971, p. 20.
10. *Millimeter,* March 1981, p. 174.
11. *Films and Filming,* January 1972, p. 24.

THREE

Don't Look Now

If *Performance* and *Walkabout* were not commercial successes, they did solidify Roeg's reputation as a director. What that reputation was, however, would be debated throughout the rest of his career. He was still thought of more as a director noted for his images than for his content, despite the complexity of his first two films. He was also criticized for being too confusing for the average viewer. Thus for his next work he wanted to direct a film in which the story was more accessible to audiences, as he explains: "I wanted to keep it within a story form that *Performance* and *Walkabout* hadn't taken. They were yarns too, of course, but they were different movements. One was a film of emotions and ideas; and the other I wanted to make — I hate to use the word because it always conjures up another connotation — a documentary using a story form. Now I wanted to make another film developing a similar idea and not to lose sight of the yarn. To stick to the yarn."[1]

"Don't look now," John said to his wife, "but there are a couple of old girls two tables away who are trying to hypnotize me."

So begins English writer Daphne du Maurier's novella *Don't Look Now*, the source for Roeg's third film. Du Maurier is perhaps best known for the works Alfred Hitchcock adapted for the screen: *Rebecca*, *The Birds*, and the less successful *Jamaica Inn*. In adapting this work, Roeg and his screenwriters took an approach similar to Hitchcock, incorporating many of the landmarks of Venice into the story and creating protagonists the public could easily identify with. They even included a scene which nearly duplicates a classic scene from *The 39 Steps*. In that film, Hitchcock had cut from a woman's scream to the scream of a train whistle. Here Roeg will cut from Laura Baxter's scream in England to the scream of a jackhammer in Venice.

Du Maurier's story concerns a couple on vacation in Venice, where they are trying to get over their daughter's death. The wife is contacted by a pair of sisters, one of whom claims to have seen a vision of her dead daughter. This sister also believes the husband has second sight, an idea he will not accept. Later the sister predicts a tragedy, and when the couple's other child is injured, the prophecy seems fulfilled. The wife returns to England to be with the son, while the husband stays behind. While traveling around Venice, he believes he sees his wife with the sisters, and when she does not respond to his calls to England, he thinks the worst, particularly as Venice is plagued by a series of murders. He contacts the police, only to learn that his wife has been in England all along. Confused, he goes into the streets and spots a young child who seems to be in trouble. When he goes to the child's aid he discovers that he is in fact a midget and the serial killer. As the husband lies dying from a knife wound, the "hammering and the voices and the barking dog grew fainter, and 'Oh, God,' he thought, 'what a bloody silly way to die.'" The image of his wife and the two sisters had in fact been their appearance on his funeral barge.

Roeg and his writers deleted little from the book but did add several things to the story. John Baxter is not on vacation, but is instead in Venice to restore a church (Roeg can thus fill the film with Catholic imagery). Roeg also includes the daughter's death, creating a haunting sequence both we and the protagonists carry through the picture. Starring in the film would be Julie Christie (her fourth film working with Roeg) and Donald Sutherland, both recognized box-office attractions. For the first time Roeg turned over the duties of cinematographer to someone else, Anthony Richmond, who had worked with him on *Walkabout* and would serve as director of photography for his next two films.

The film opens with rain falling on a lake, and the camera moves in on the scene as the title is superimposed. This image fades into one that is harder to discern; only later do we realize that it is the window of the hotel John and Laura will stay at in Venice. Already the present and the future coalesce. The montage that follows begins with scenes whose very banality suggests a hidden terror: a girl pushes a wheelbarrow by a lake as a white horse runs past and her brother rides his bike in the distance. Moving closer to the lake, she holds tightly to her doll (a soldier in a gas mask who talks when his string is pulled), as she throws a red ball into the water. At one point she leans over the lake and her red coat is reflected in the water; the reflection fades into a fire burning in the fireplace inside the Baxter home. Laura is looking through some books, while her husband, John, examines slides of a church he is to renovate. He comes across one containing a figure in red sitting in a pew, and he seems drawn to it, taking it from the tray to examine it closer. When he asks Laura what she is looking for, she tells him that she is searching for the answer to a question their daughter posed: "If the world is round, why is a frozen pond flat?" She

John Baxter (Donald Sutherland) looks up from his work, sensing something is wrong, while his wife Laura (Julie Christie) looks on in a scene from *Don't Look Now*.

believes she has found a possible answer, but he is not convinced and his statement is relevant not just to this film, but also to Roeg's career: "Nothing is what it seems."

The opening sequence will delineate many recurring motifs of the films: the figure in red (and the prominence of this color throughout the film), broken glass, and water, as well as indications of John's special gift. The image of the red figure in the slide becomes the reflection of the girl's red coat in the water, the resemblance already uniting them. John Jr. rides his bike over a mirror, and his father looks up as if hearing the sound. Christine, however, is aligned with her mother through a simple gesture each performs. In his haste, John knocks a glass of wine over, and the red liquid spreads across the table and onto the slide. The liquid begins to turn the image red, as if it were bleeding. John Jr. runs toward the house, and his father's uneasiness causes him to stop what he is doing. As John moves to the door, there is an insert of Christine lying in the water.

The girl's death is among the most haunting scenes in cinema. The scene does not only contain John's futile effort to save her, it also intimates his own fate. As he instinctively runs to the lake, Roeg cuts to the slide, the liquid continuing to envelope the image. John leaps into the lake, as his son stands behind him with a shard of glass in his hand, another portent of what is to come. Laura still sits inside, oblivious to what is occurring, and beside her lies a book John has written, *The Fragile Geometry of Space.* The title could easily summarize Roeg's attitude toward time and provides a fitting title for Joseph Lanza's examination of his career. The actions of the characters are slowed down, heightening John's emotions as he goes under the water to bring up his daughter. This action is repeated two more times, a device Roeg had already used in *Walkabout.* John lets out a long, mournful scream which sounds like that of an animal and holds Christine tightly in his arms; meanwhile the slide has become completely immersed in the red liquid. John makes his way to the shore and puts his daughter on the ground, attempting to resuscitate her. When this fails, he tries to pick her up, but stumbles in the mud. As he makes his way to the house, Laura finally emerges, still unaware of what has happened. When she does look up at John, she lets out a long, piercing scream which becomes the scream of a jackhammer in Venice.

Roeg was particularly interested in the contrast between the Baxters' position and the tragic events that overtake them: "The tragedy I wanted to show was that although there is what appeared to be privilege — they were the golden people — even golden people can't escape life. You know life actually deals the blows. The Kennedys — the most golden people of all — have tragedies coming out of the blue like some terrible sickle sweeping away."[2]

The only indication of how much time has passed is that John is now at work on the renovation. He emerges from the archaeological site, the water in the canal behind him serving as a reminder of his daughter's death. Laura is sitting in a restaurant writing to their son as John comes up to her. He is disturbed by the way the work is progressing and her words are doubly significant: "It's incredible you can't change your course." She begins to read the letter, which details John's work, but stops short, admitting it is simply another boring letter. If the death is not alluded to in either the letter or their conversations, their impersonal manner indicates it has not been forgotten. John constantly fidgets, and when he first sees the two sisters sitting across the room, he is inexplicably disturbed by the one woman's glances. If John already seems to sense something wrong with the women, he will also unwittingly set into motion the events that will lead them to him. Complaining he is cold, he closes a nearby window. This action causes a door near the women to blow open and a cinder blows into one sister's eye. As her companion tries to free the object, John returns to the table to order his food. The two women stumble into the Baxters' table as they are trying to make their way to the bathroom and then start out the wrong door. Noticing their difficulty, Laura goes to the women's aid, guiding them to the bathroom, while John glances at the letter she has written.

In the bathroom, the women apologize for staring, something Laura had not noticed. In the background the restroom attendant quietly looks on as the one woman continues to try to help her companion. The composition here is important, for while the women's faces are multiplied in the mirrors on the wall, only when Wendy tells Laura that her sister is blind is Heather's face fully revealed. There is a close-up of her face, before Roeg cuts back to John, who is still sitting at the table. John thinks back to their departure from the house following Christine's death and remembers the lake where she died. The piano music that will be associated with their personal life begins to play, but the remembrance ends on the face of Heather, as if she shares the memory. Laura has finally freed the cinder from Wendy's eye, who tells Wendy she reminds her of her daughter. "If only I had a daughter," Wendy remarks. Without warning, Heather tells Laura she has no reason to be sad, and Wendy explains that her sister is psychic. "I've seen your little girl, sitting between you and your husband and she was laughing," says Heather. Laura begins to break down, and as Heather mentions her daughter's raincoat, Laura remembers Christine running along in her red mack. Outside, John is once again examining the slide containing the red figure.

The two sisters start out the door, but Laura, shaken by Heather's words, grabs out at her sleeve. When Laura asks if Christine was really there, Heather smiles, saying she was. Laura is left alone with the silent observer (the bathroom attendant) and her own reflection in the mirror. In the restaurant the women prepare to leave, and Wendy tells her sister: "I felt you were right. I felt we should." John watches as they leave, but it is a while before Laura returns and sits down, looking tired and weak. As he is speaking, she begins to stand, then falls forward onto the table in a faint. Once again events are slowed down as he tries to grab at her, but instead tips the tables so that its contents fall onto her unconscious body. Among the debris is some broken glass, and their wine drips onto this glass. Using the technique he employs for the father's death in *Walkabout*, Roeg presents Laura's accident subjectively, in the manner in which the participants perceive it.

Laura is taken by boat to a hospital, and when John goes to her room, he finds she is more relaxed and is even making faces at the children in the next ward. She tries to tell him that Christine is still with them, but his response is typically blunt, carrying no trace of sympathy: "Christine is dead." She tells him of Heather's vision, and even though he tries to comfort her, it is already apparent that he wants no part of the women or their beliefs. Taking the boat back to their hotel, the Baxters find their way blocked by a group of policemen in the midst of a murder investigation. Watching from above the canal, a police inspector eyes John with suspicion as they turn around. Laura's query is equally baffling: "I thought this was . . . isn't this the place where you. . . ." but John quickly cuts her off. While other directors would have made the murders taking place in Venice more prominent in the story, Roeg keeps them in the background so that we are aware that they are occurring, but our attention remains on John and Laura. There are no newspaper headlines announcing the murders, nor do the characters give them much notice. Only later will the murders take on more prominence, as they converge with the Baxters' personal tragedy.

On an impulse, Laura asks to stop at a church they are passing, another action John seems to greet with condescension. He agrees to go in, but his attention is focused on the architecture ("I don't like this church at all"), while she lights a candle, not for their daughter, but to signify the miracle she believes has occurred. He begins to explore the building, but on seeing the sisters in a tour group he kneels down and covers his face to evade them. He is startled when Laura comes up to him and laughingly calls him a hypocrite. He reminds her that they are late for their meeting with the bishop, and as they depart, Roeg cuts to the six candles, one of which blows out, as if to foretell a death.

Laura greets the bishop by kissing his ring, thus seeming to unite herself with him. Even the bishop is aware of the change in her and says she looks much better. John tries to turn the conversation to his work, but the bishop shows little interest in the renovation and says: "The church belongs to God, but he doesn't seem to care about them. Does he have other priorities? We have stopped listening." Turning to Laura, the bishop asks her if she is a Christian. "I don't know. I'm kind to animals and children," she replies. John seems to enjoy her predicament as the bishop tells them that St. Nicholas is the patron saint of "children and scholars. An interesting combination, don't you think?" With the bishop's departure, Laura wonders why he asked if she was a Christian, and John reminds her that she had kissed his ring. As they walk toward their hotel she tells him the bishop makes her uncomfortable, and John seems to agree: "He probably makes God feel slightly less than immaculate."

The notoriety surrounding the ensuing lovemaking scene has sometimes overshadowed its importance not just to the story, but also to our understanding of the characters. It begins with their return to the hotel room. Laura is for the first time at ease with her daughter's death. As she opens a suitcase and sees the ball Christine had with her at her death, she smiles to herself. They prepare for their night out, their actions constantly emphasizing their familiarity with one another. She takes a bath as he showers, and she teases him about his weight. In the bedroom the two lie beside one another as she reads a newspaper article he has recommended. She says that it is a miracle that she did not get hurt when she fell, but John is not surprised, noting, "An unconscious body always reacts faster than the mind ever can." The two begin to read the newspaper together while Laura starts to stroke his naked body, initiating their sexual encounter.

The sequence that Roeg is most identified with is the succeeding one, in which the couple's lovemaking is interspersed with their subsequent dressing. The sexual content is among the most frank in mainstream cinema, but the eroticism is diluted in the montage so that the attention is on the participants. Laura is relaxed because she is not only freed from the guilt of her daughter's death, but is also anticipating the birth of another child. (As she dresses, she rubs her stomach and smiles to herself.) Roeg experimented with this sequence by presenting it in a linear form, but found it lacked the impact he was seeking:

> Without that love scene, you never see them get happy together; they're always rowing; they're always rowing, Julie's always grumbling and running beside this tall chap saying "You don't understand." They seem so miserable all the time! But most people do seem miserable: Love is a very miserable affair. And when I put that scene back in, suddenly you can't get confused about them. They're like a married couple.[3]

This fragmented approach also prefigures the dissolution of John and Laura's relationship. Although they are united in sex, they are photographed separately as they dress, as if they are already moving toward their separate destinies. Roeg describes this technique:

> Because we see the sex in flashes and because the emotions of the sex also suffuse the dressing, the intercutting makes the sequence doubly erotic — yet also melancholy. For we sense that, no matter how intense their love or how satisfying their sex may be, John and Laura still cannot save themselves. The splintered editing imposes a feeling of desperation on their thrusting and caressing. And since the two scenes are shown simultaneously although they presumably happened one after the other, we get lost with the characters as past, present, and future merge into a single evanescent mirage.[4]

The Venice that Roeg portrays is not the city one would find in a travel brochure. The holiday season is over, and the hotel John and Laura stay in is preparing to close; white sheets already cover the furniture. As the couple make their way to the restaurant, they seem totally alone because the streets are empty. An oppressive atmosphere adds to the tension of the story, so that the city itself becomes a character. Losing the way among the labyrinth of streets and alleys, John seems drawn to one of the exits. He stands by the water, but Laura is frightened off by rats crawling along the edge. Looking around, he seems to experience a case of déjà vu, saying, "I know this place." Laura believes she has found the way, but the stillness is shattered by a scream and shutters going up. Now confident that he knows where he is, John leads her out of the alley, only to discover they had been close to the restaurant all along.

The next day John is putting a hooded figure into place on the outside of the church while Laura looks on. Glancing down, John is startled to see the sisters watching from a distance, but is relieved to see that Laura has not yet noticed them. When they move off without speaking, John's attention turns back to his work. Laura, however, wanders off around the corner and thus meets the sisters. Heather stands behind a metal gate, a position that foreshadows her later incarceration. Eager to learn more from the women, Laura begins to walk off with them; for the first time she is willing to talk about what has happened. On hearing of John's actions at the time of his daughter's death, Heather realizes he too has second sight. "It's a curse as well as a gift," she says, and she takes exception when Laura asks if she can contact Christine for them: "They all want mumbo jumbo about ectoplasm and holding hands. Second sight is a gift from the good Lord who sees all and I consider it an impertinence to call back his creatures from their rest for our entertainment." Nonetheless, she agrees to meet with John and Laura to attempt to contact Christine. Her protestations thus seem more an act than a serious conviction.

As expected, John is scornful of the sisters' motives, and Roeg seems to confirm this with a brief insert which interrupts their discussion. When John ridicules the sisters, calling their beliefs mumbo jumbo in an ironic echo of Heather's earlier comment, Roeg cuts to a brief shot of the two women laughing. The implication is that the sisters are laughing at Laura, but as Roeg has pointed out, there is nothing to indicate this directly. Only because their reaction is juxtaposed with the Baxters' discussion does the viewer assume their motives are false. This linkage was intentional because Roeg was concerned the sisters were becoming too predictable. If the love scene had shown the couple at their closest, the argument here shows them at their most distant. Laura even intimates that it is John's fault Christine died (because he allowed her to play by the lake), and the two go their separate ways.

In the sisters' hotel room, Laura is fascinated by the portraits of Wendy's children and in particular, a small bust of a child. It is a bust of Wendy's son, who has died, but she is quick to point out that she still has her other two children, as Laura could still have other children. Heather, however, seems to feel the loss of life more, saying, "Nothing can take the place of one who's gone." In preparation for their séance, the sisters turn off the lights and the three women gather about a small table, while John sits alone in a restaurant drinking. He gets up from the table to go off in search of Laura, but on entering the hotel lobby, he finds it deserted. Despite their being in different locations, Heather seems to look across the room at John. He walks through the halls, while Heather clutches at her chest, calling his name. Coming to the sisters' room, John leans down by the door to listen, only to be confronted by a man speaking Italian. Earlier he had been able to converse with his workers in Italian, but here he seems unable to understand the man. As he flees out of the hotel, Laura holds tightly to Heather, who has begun to cry.

When Laura is reunited with a drunken John, they return to the hotel, where she worries that he will become sick. He boasts that it has been ten years since he has drunk so much. He seems anxious as he constantly moves about, while Laura tells him that Heather has warned that his life is in danger. Instead of responding to the prophecy, John races from the room to throw up something, he'll admit later, he's never done before. If his mind cannot accept the information, his body already has. Although he seems more sober, John is still disoriented by what has happened. When Laura argues that they should leave Venice, he loses his temper, shouting that Christine is dead: "She does not come peeping from the fucking grave. Christine is dead, dead, dead." Stunned by his outburst, Laura quietly walks away, playing with her wedding ring. She seems to give in and says that maybe the sisters did influence her and that she should go back to taking her pills. John is quick to go along with this intention and even gets her a glass of water to take them, but in fact, she has not given in. She quietly asks if they can take some time off, and when he agrees, she discreetly takes the pill from her mouth and hides it in her sleeve.

That night John and Laura are awakened by a call from England with the news that their son has been in an accident. Laura prepares to take a flight to England, sure that this is the danger the sisters had warned them of. With John promising to ask the bishop for time off, Laura leaves on a boat as the music associated with their lovemaking returns, but in a slower, more elegiac form. Although we do not realize it, this will be the last time the two will see one another, and the camera rests on Laura as the boat sails off. With her departure, John's isolation is complete; only his fate awaits him.

John returns to the church, where the bishop is examining a cross. The film is filled with religious artifacts but they remain objects which are examined, but not necessarily revered. Even the bishop's faith, while not seriously shaken, will be questioned. He approves of the work that John has done, but he realizes John is troubled by something. John tells him of the accident and admits that there have been "complications since Christine's death." Saying he will pray for them, the bishop concurs that John should have gone with Laura. Their attention returns to the mosaics which make up the artwork on the wall, and the bishop boasts that the craftsmen have worked with his family for generations. Wanting to compare a new piece with the original, John starts to climb the ladder to the scaffolding above. As he climbs to the top, Wendy's image can be seen in the light, once again laughing. This shot seems a cheat, serving no other purpose than to implicate the women, but this is the only severe flaw in the picture.

Standing on the swaying platform, John is comparing the pieces when a beam falls from the ceiling. It crashes through the scaffolding, smashing through glass and severing the lines which hold the platform. John manages to hold onto the dangling scaffolding, while the men below hurry to save him as broken glass and pieces of mosaic fall about them. The bishop looks up at him, his arms outstretched as if he were attempting to break his fall, while one of the men holds out a pole to John. Instead of drawing him in, it seems to push him further out, and the man drops the pole, which nearly strikes the bishop. After taking hold of a nearby rope, John manages to swing close enough to one of the workers for the man to grab hold of him. Below, the bishop seems to give thanks, then walks off, inadvertently crushing the mosaics which had once seemed so important.

Outside the church, the bishop tells John he should sit down, but he prefers to walk. John admits he is shaken not just by what has happened but by the way it seems to confirm Heather's prophecy. For the bishop the fall is a reminder of his own father's death, which had occurred under similar circumstances. He also proves sympathetic to the idea of second sight, saying, "I wish I didn't have to believe in prophecies, but I do. But I wish I didn't have to." The men have made their way to the canal, where another body has been discovered. The police and a large crowd have gathered to look on as a woman's body is pulled from the water. The sight reminds John once again of his daughter's death. The bishop will constantly be associated with death, from John's near fatal fall to his appearance at the conclusion of the film. It is even more disturbing that he seems to sense the moment of John's death. Like the other characters in the film, he will be implicated in John's fate, as Neil Feineman has pointed out:

> The bishop is tied to the sisters and to the film's events visually as well as thematically. Wendy wears a semi-circular gold broach with three globes hanging from it. The camera emphasizes the piece just before Wendy bumps into Laura in the restaurant; Laura notices it when she goes to the sisters' first hotel room. The shape reappears on the mosaic that John is restoring; the rest of the face of the original design has worn away, leaving only the shape. While trying to restore the face, which will alter the shape, John is almost killed. Later, the shape will reappear, although in a more elongated form, as an icon on the bishop's office wall. At the end of the movie, John's blood will coagulate into the same shape. And through a flashback to the introductory montage, we realize the shape was introduced when the slide bled the same way at the beginning.[5]

Returning to his room, John begins to gather up his belongings, including a discarded picture of Laura, which he pockets. In the bathroom he picks up both his and her toilet articles, reminders of their lovemaking. Having left the hotel, John is riding on a boat when he is shocked to see

Laura standing on a boat passing by. With her are the two sisters, and he shouts her name, but she shows no reaction as her boat goes off into the distance. When his boat docks, John races off down the street, returning to the hotel to look for her, but he is told she has not come back. There is a forlorn quality to the scene as John walks along the streets and alleys, unsure about what is happening. Beside the steps leading into the water, he finds a doll, whose stiff form is like that of his daughter.

John seems to be in a constant state of confusion and even loses his way inside the police station. Having given a description of the two women, he takes the resulting sketches upstairs, but seems unsure about what office he should enter. The inspector he meets with is the same man who is investigating the murders. Accepting the drawing of the women and a photograph of Laura, the inspector muses how women come to look alike after a while, but continue to have their own characteristics. "The skill of the police artist is to make the living appear dead," he says. John begins to tell the inspector how his wife met with the sisters and how she fainted when one of them told her about seeing their daughter. "When she came round, she was totally changed. She was happy, she had come to terms with the death. She was her whole self again," he tells the inspector.

Even John seems to realize that he has misinterpreted the situation and says that he and his wife had argued over the sisters. Glancing outside the window, the inspector can see the sisters walking past, although he may not be aware of who they are. He cannot fail to notice, however, that one is leading the other or that the blind woman seems to hesitate a moment before going on. Discussing their son's accident, John tells the inspector that he saw Laura off on the boat when she left for England. When asked what it is that he fears, John seems confused, pausing a few seconds before saying that it is the "killer on the loose." He intimates that Laura is not a well woman, and the inspector seems to understand. He begins to doodle on the sketches in front of him, filling in the eyes on the drawing of Heather. "My wife got something from these two women, something that doctors couldn't give her, I couldn't give her, and that she needed so she went with them. Where I don't know," says John. The inspector advises him to continue with his search, but John's disconcerting manner causes the inspector to have him tailed.

John begins to walk the streets, retracing his steps, unaware that a man is following him. Looking out from a pedestrian bridge, John can see the reflection of the figure in red, but the image is lost as a woman throws water into the river. John returns to the sisters hotel, but his difficulties in communicating continue. He tries to talk to two hotel workers in English, but only when he gestures to his eyes do the women seem to understand and lead him to the sisters' room. John is shocked to find the room vacated, the bedding rolled up, and the furnishings gone. He tries to ask the women what has happened to the occupants, but gets nowhere until the man who has followed him comes in. As he introduces himself to John, Roeg cuts to the sisters, set up in a new hotel.

John returns to the bishop's office, and as he waits to see him, he puts in a call to his son's boarding school. The woman on the other end tells him that John Jr. is all right. The woman then mentions Laura's name, and a stunned John suddenly hears his wife's voice. As Laura tells him she will be home soon, he tries to say that he thought he had seen her in Venice. The two seem to be involved in their own conversations, with neither appearing to hear the other. She agrees to meet with him for supper that night after her return flight and then hangs up before he can tell her of his vision. If John and Laura are already isolated from one another, the son is equally alone, for once again his mother leaves him to join his father.

Arriving at the police station, John finds Heather sitting in a room with another woman guarding her. Identifying himself as Laura's husband, he tells Heather that Wendy has gone to the British consul. The woman is terrified, but John tries to apologize, saying there has been a mistake. He escorts her from the building, as the inspector silently looks after them. Meanwhile, Laura has arrived at the airport, where she is greeted by a man holding a sign with her name on it. As John walks Heather toward her hotel room, she tells him how safe she feels in Venice. She likes the sound echoing off the water, but Wendy hates it. Heather explains her reaction by saying: "It's like a city in Aspic left over from a dinner party and all the guests are dead and gone. It frightens her. Too many shadows." She also tells John that Milton always loved the city.

Laura learns her escort is a policeman and that he intends to take her to the station, even though John has already left. If John's fate had been the result of one person or one action, it would seem the result of happenstance. Instead a variety of factors and individuals unite to insure that the inevitable occurs.

Heather confesses to John how reassuring it is to be escorted by a man and admits that they had changed hotels because of her sister's fear of prowlers. Again their conduct has a credible reason, but it is the presentation of their actions that calls them into question. In another disturbing scene, John and Heather arrive at the hotel only to be greeted by Wendy, who presumably left the police station after them, but arrived at the hotel first. Despite Wendy's evident hostility toward him, John remains in the sisters' room, looking over the photographs that had fascinated his wife. Offered a drink, he instead asks for water, an act that coincidentally links him to the lead character in Roeg's next film.

At the station, Laura is told John has already gone and then is handed the sketches of the women. "It doesn't look like her," she says. Handed her own photograph, she smiles in remembrance. Only when Heather goes into a seizure does John leave the sisters, but once he is gone, Heather tells Wendy to bring him back. From the street, John can still hear Heather's screams, but he is gone by the time Wendy runs out. Instead she runs into Laura, but rather than having her go after John, she takes her up to Heather. Her convulsions over, Heather walks toward Laura, stretching her hands out like a zombie as she tells her that Christine has warned her: "She told you. She told you to leave Venice." Her words continue to reverberate as Laura runs down the stairs. In his bedroom, the bishop mysteriously awakens, sitting up in bed. Roeg closes in on the red candle burning on a shelf.

Walking along the water, John hears voices shouting in the distance and looks to see the figure in red hurrying off. Taking it be either the spirit of his daughter or simply someone in trouble, he gives chase. He follows the figure through a gate and locks it behind him, keeping the others out, but also inadvertently trapping himself. The ambiance becomes even more foreboding: fog gathers about his feet as he searches for the small figure. Laura races through the streets looking for him, while John is confronted by a vision of Heather in the mist. The sound track adds to the tension, as mysterious noises echo in the darkness. Seeing the figure above him, John starts up a flight of stairs, while Laura is impeded by the locked gate. She reaches out to him through the fence.

Coming upon the figure, whose back is to him, John tries to offer comfort, saying he has come to help. It is only now that John recognizes the figure as the one he had seen in the slide. The person who turns to face John is not a child, but a hideous dwarf, who begins to walk toward him. When the dwarf removes his hand from his pocket to reveal a knife, John understands that this is the killer the police have been seeking. The knife strikes out at him, and John falls to the ground, the blood seeping from the wound. As his feet kick out a window, the sound recalls his son's bike striking the glass in the opening scene. While John lies writhing in pain, images from his past return: the scaffolding, Heather, his daughter, and making love to his wife. The montage continues, so that we see how the events had foreshadowed his murder, while church bells in the background toll his death. The sequence ends with the slide becoming completely suffused with red.

The film concludes with John's casket being carried by a boat through the canal, followed by a boat carrying Laura and the sisters, the action he had earlier envisioned. As the camera holds on Laura's face, a slight smile comes to her lips. Although the shock of the murder remains, this slight expression gives a sense of optimism. Her husband and daughter are dead, but Heather's earlier words give her solace ("and she was laughing"). Their boat comes to a stop and as the three women get out, they are greeted by the bishop and another priest. The final credits roll as the women walk away.

Don't Look Now remains one of Roeg's most well-received films; many consider it one of the best horror films of modern times. The reviews were genuinely positive, but even some critics who liked the film dismissed it as an exercise in terror. Moira Walsh, for example, wrote, "The verdict: a great deal of skillfully created atmosphere and professional acting competence has been expended on a finally meaningless project, though I suspect that meaninglessness is director Roeg's quite deliberate message."[6]

Roeg's first goal may be to entertain, but he remains committed to other objectives. If the film were simply an exercise, it would not have retained its forcefulness. Witness the case of the *Exorcist,* which not only does not seem as frightening as it once did, but is actually quite boring. As Tom Milne has pointed out, *Don't Look Now* works as a companion piece to *Performance:* "We are back again, as with *Performance* and to a lesser extent *Walkabout,* in a Borgesian world where the natural and the supernatural coexist, and where life is a dark labyrinth through which man is impelled to run towards an encounter with his 'demon.' Don't look now, Roeg might be saying, but every time you hear or see something, your mind is drawing connections and conclusions from depths of which you know nothing."[7]

Following *Don't Look Now,* Roeg considered filming Joseph Conrad's *Victory,* with Donald Sutherland again playing the lead. This project was quickly forgotten as Roeg began preparations to film W. D. Richter's *Deadly Honeymoon.*

The story deals with a newly married couple who are terrorized by two gangsters. The couple eventually plot their revenge on the men, inadvertently becoming the men in the process. With Richter having adapted his own work, Roeg began preproduction work, but just five days before filming was to begin, MGM canceled the project. The reasons were never made clear, but undaunted, Roeg turned to another project, an adaptation of Isak Dinesen's autobiographical story, *Out of Africa.* Dinesen's account of her life intrigued Roeg:

> It's her life and she interests me as a woman because she seemed to be a marvelous example of total truthful womanhood in terms of her position in society, in her marriage and in love and literature. She's an extraordinary example for men and women in the world today. She's passionate and understanding and forgiving and vulnerable. It's quite an interesting attitude and that's why I wanted a woman to work with me on it.[8]

In the end it would be Sydney Pollack who would direct the film, but the episode suggests that Roeg was turning toward a more feminine perspective for his characters.

Notes

1. *Sight and Sound,* Winter 1973, p. 3.
2. *Cinema Papers,* April 1974, p. 177.
3. *American Film,* January 1980, p. 25.
4. *Film Quarterly,* Spring 1974, p. 41.
5. Neil Feineman, *Nicolas Roeg,* pp. 89–90.
6. *America,* February 23, 1974, p. 134.
7. *Sight and Sound,* Winter 1973, p. 237.
8. *Cinema Papers,* April 1974, p. 177.

FOUR

The Man Who Fell to Earth

The story of *The Man Who Fell to Earth* is emblematic of many science fiction films: an alien arrives on earth and assumes a human form. On paper, *The Day the Earth Stood Still* story line closely resembles that of Roeg's film: a visitor from a distant planet arrives and seems to possess skills much more advanced than ours. For a time he loses himself among the population of Washington, D.C., only confiding his secret to a woman with whom he boards. The aesthetic differences in the two works seem to remove any comparison, however. Gort's spacecraft makes a dramatic appearance in front of a crowd of witnesses, the alien comes with a specific purpose, and the story ends with a dramatic warning to the audience. Although many similar elements had been contained in their source material, Roeg and screenwriter Paul Mayersburg eliminated them in the film. Not only are the motives of the protagonist obscured, but many of the science fiction elements have been deleted, so that Roeg could later argue that the film might all take place in the mind of a wealthy recluse. In fact, it was not the science fiction elements which attracted him, but the sense of isolation surrounding the central character:

> What drew me to *The Man Who Fell to Earth* is a real story that happened to a friend of mine who was with the Egyptian Army. He had a nice family and was well situated, but he had to leave Egypt after Farouk was overthrown and everything changed. He went to America and had to leave the wife and children behind. He lived in New York City virtually as a beggar until he got himself an accountant's job. During his seven year stay, he eventually lost touch with his family and developed a relationship with this woman. Then, his wife traced him and implored him to get her and the kids out of Egypt. At that point he had to make this decision. The night before his family arrived in America, he left the woman and the pain he went through was incredible. Mr. Newton reminds me of that special person who got away and left someone behind.[1]

The source was a 1963 novel written by the author of *The Hustler,* Walter Tevis, a work Roeg had come across in the early seventies. For the script he turned to English film critic Paul Mayersburg, whose screenwriting career had so far been unsuccessful. Much attention has been paid to Roeg's use of singers to play the leads in many of his films, but he has also shown a willingness to work with first-time screenwriters. Mayersburg, Yale Udoff, and Terry Johnson all received their first film credits with Roeg. In his previous films, Roeg's contributions to the screenplay had come after the screenwriters had first completed their version. With Mayersburg, however, Roeg found a writer whose sensibilities mirrored his own. Mayersberg's primary task was to translate Tevis's extended time frame into film form, which proved difficult. The novel begins in 1972 and concludes four years later in the midst of the presidential campaigns. Mayersberg resolved the dilemma by approaching the material in a non-linear format, and his plans were ambitious to say the least:

> Nobody talks of the non sequiturs of a circus because the plot isn't clear. The reason is that everybody knows the form as a circus. *The Man Who Fell to Earth* is a movie where we hope to introduce another form, or an interesting variation of an existing one, into the cinema. I don't know if there is a true antecedent of this film. Certainly there was none either in my mind or, as far as I know, in Nic's. That's to say there was no single antecedent. I would like to think that the nearest film to this one was perhaps *Les Enfants du Paradis,* which was fundamentally a simple story, but it stretched out through time and space in which characters were joined in their memories and thoughts and fears and loves.[2]

All science fiction films begin with a journey across either time or space; *The Man Who Fell to Earth* does both. The first frame shows four lights against a black background; these lights suddenly ignite. In the montage which follows, footage from a NASA mission is intermixed with vistas of a landscape which may or may not be Earth. The camera hurtles across a forest, before seeming to crash into the lake. We never see the visitor emerge from his spacecraft, and later scenes will hint that he simply fell from the sky. Instead, the first glimpse of the visitor is from a distance; he is a small figure hidden in the shadows of a dilapidated mining shack. The camera moves in to show the man stumbling on the rocky surface, then the camera pans up the hill to show his arrival has not gone unnoticed. A man dressed in a suit stoically watches the visitor, but makes no effort to communicate with him. This character, who will briefly return later, is the most prominent example of what Roeg calls the "watcher," a person who sits in attendance on the action, much as the audience does. These watchers often influence the dynamics of his compositions: two characters confront one another, while a third sits silently in the background, as if representing the audience.

The first man passes an abandoned train, while on the sound track can be heard a train whistle that indicates he is passing through the past and present. There is a sense of isolation in these scenes that will continue throughout the film. The only signs of civilization he passes are abandoned ones, which recall some scenes of the outback in *Walkabout*. Just as water was the central need of the children in that film so is it for the alien, who stands looking out at the river and constantly returns to it. But his manner is more like that of the aborigine, for when he is confronted by civilization he seems both frightened and confused. Stepping back from the bridge, he is nearly struck by an automobile, an incident that confirms how dangerous the environment can be for him. He passes a sign for the town of Haneyville, but his first contact is with a hot air balloon made up to look like a clown. The balloon seems to move menacingly toward him, while a drunk shouts from the basket of the balloon, offering alcohol (the first of many such temptations). It is with some relief that the alien lies down to sleep on a bench in front of a shop, waiting for it to open.

The opening of the shop effectively delineates Earth from the perspective of an alien, as even simple details take on a new fascination. Awakened by the store's alarm, the man goes to the door and seems surprised that it pulls open (a detail Roeg will later use for Martin in *Track 29* and Alexandra Del Lago in *Sweet Bird of Youth*). The camera pans around the interior of the store, which contains an accumulation of antiques and collectibles lost in the shadows, as well as a television. The alien's eyes focus on the shopkeeper, an old woman whose arms are encased in turquoise jewelry. He tells her he has come to sell a ring, a gift from his wife. Noticing the initials inscribed inside, the woman learns that the man is Thomas Jerome Newton, an Englishman (with a passport to prove it). Newton accepts her offer of twenty dollars, but when he returns to the river it is clear he has no need to sell the ring, because he takes out a roll of thousand-dollar bills and a string of rings identical to the one he sold. The return to the river is almost a religious experience: the sun bathes the images in its glow, while Newton lifts a cup of water to his mouth as if it were a chalice.

From *Performance* on, Roeg has demonstrated a strong interest in the sound track, experimenting as much with sound as with visual effects. As Newton sits by the river, the music turns ominous, as if forecasting danger, but in fact the sound emanates from the stereo of Oliver Farnsworth, a patent lawyer Newton visits. Roeg will frequently overlap sequences, as if Newton's attention is already focused on what is to happen. There is no indication of how much time has passed, but Newton's suit and manner indicate he is no longer the wanderer he was in the previous sequence. He remains, however, uncomfortable with his surroundings; he ignores Farnsworth's outstretched hand, mispronounces the word *patent*, and seems so fragile that Farnsworth worries about his health. He has also developed a wariness of others. Having offered Farnsworth $10,000 to look over his patents, he is reticent to leave the files overnight. "It's not that I don't trust you," he says, with emphasis on the final word.

Any clues to Newton's background at this point are often obscured. Farnsworth reads over the file, but what it contains is kept from the viewer. Instead, the camera follows Newton as he goes to the window to look over the city. In a subjective insert, Newton sees fireworks exploding in the sky, then watches as dawn arrives and the city comes to life. The sequence closely resembles the opening of *Walkabout,* even to the businessmen who walk the streets. In the apartment, Newton stands beside a television which is broadcasting images of violence, but at this point it is of little interest to him. When Farnsworth informs him that his inventions could be worth up to $300,000,000, he is shocked to hear that Newton thinks it is not enough. "I need more, he insisted. There is an urgency in Newton's manner which will not be present later, and Farnsworth's reply could easily be that of the viewers: "I'm trying to adjust my mind to all this." Farnsworth agrees to work for Newton, remarking, "perhaps you're not so different after all, Mr. Newton."

The resemblance between Farnsworth and Newton will continually be brought out in the film, from their appearance (both men wear glasses and seem physically fragile), to their intellectual capacity, to their willingness to trust others. Farnsworth is also a portent of a series of startling relationships which make up the film. He is involved with his male secretary, Trevor, while Newton will live with an Earth woman. There is also a relationship between a black man and a white woman, and relationships between a college professor and his students. If these relationships do not seem as shocking as they did when the film was released, they still create comment. None of these couplings are found in the book, where most of the relationships were strictly platonic, almost maternal in the case of Betty Lou. Farnsworth also gives the film an ironic commentary not found in the book, as in his observation to Trevor: "My father used to say, Oliver, when you get a gift horse, walk up to it, pat it, quiet the animal down, then using both hands force open its jaws and have a damn good look in its mouth." Trevor considers this good advice, as does Farnsworth, but the latter worries that his father was always wrong.

Rock music is used to introduce college professor Dr. Nathan Bryce, who will become Newton's opposite. Newton and Bryce will not meet till much later in the film, but the editing constantly juxtaposes their activities, taking even further the process Roeg employed in *Performance.* Bryce is at home grading papers while Newton sits in a Japanese restaurant watching a Kabuki play, but Newton's reactions often seem to respond to Bryce's actions. A female student walks in and casually undresses as Bryce marks her paper, promising a good grade. Their sexual encounter is as violent as the Samurai fight Newton is watching; Bryce charges at the woman like a crazed animal, tearing the rest of her clothes from her and dragging her into the bedroom. The sounds of their lovemaking overlap Newton's scenes, and he grows uncomfortable with the proceedings. As the couple nears a climax, Newton rushes out of the restaurant and the Samurai swordsmen fall to the ground as if spent. Bryce's actions already hint at his duplicity and indicate that he approaches sex as nothing more than a diversion. Even as the girl lies beside him, he starts grading papers again.

The sequence is also the first indication of the growth of Newton's company, World Enterprises. During the lovemaking scene involving Bryce and the girl, she had photographed their activity, and now she reveals that the film has already been developed. Examining it closer, Bryce notices the logo for World Enterprises and later will come across the same symbol in a book of art his daughter has sent him as a birthday gift. Opening the collection of poems and paintings, he looks at Brueghel's "Fall of Icarus." Beside the painting is an excerpt from a poem by Auden, "Musée des Beaux Arts." As the camera pauses on the poem, the sound of the ocean and sea gulls can be heard.

The poem predicts the fate of the alien, how he falls to earth and how everyone turns away to leave him isolated. In the book the references to Icarus are more pronounced and Tevis also includes allusions to Jesus Christ and Rumpelstiltskin. Roeg will use visual metaphors for the image of falling, particularly in filming the murders of Farnsworth and Newton. Images of falling also appear in the dialogue; Farnsworth describes the company's growth by saying: "It happened literally overnight. When Mr. Newton came into my apartment, my old life went straight out the window. In no time at all I got a brand new life and I like it. Maybe I'm not my own boss the way I used to be, but so what. Oliver, you're the president of one of the largest corporations in America. I'll tell you one thing. It's never too late. I didn't think a man could change at my age. I still can't believe it."

Bryce's life has become lost in indiscriminate sex and a career which no longer seems challenging, but he too will change. Called into Professor Canutti's office to defend his students' declining test scores, Bryce instead turns the topic to World Enterprises, which he boasts is dumping computers. "You want to know why?" he says. "They want to bring back human error because that's the way you get new ideas. By making mistakes. Back to man. His imagination." That Canutti fancies himself an intellectual is apparent not just from his condescending attitude toward Bryce, but from the furnishings of his office, with its ultramodern bookshelves carefully arranged and its white walls lacking in personality. He demonstrates his hostility toward the company, dismissing the dumping of the computers as a publicity stunt, then turns to Bryce's extracurricular activities. Aware of

Bryce's affairs with coeds, Canutti calls him a novelty freak, but Bryce counters that the education system has already dulled them. "They're already middle-aged, because that's what they're taught."

The action shifts west, as World Enterprises' base of operation is moved from New York to New Mexico. (One of the chief difficulties with the film is that the natural environment does not create an ambiance which mirrors the protagonists' feelings, the kind of ambience which helped to make Roeg's previous films so successful.) Newton's arrival is marked by suspicion (the police immediately check out his limousine), reminders of the past (a train passes through town), and continual fears of discovery (he checks in under an alias). He also shows that he has not yet acclimated to his environment, for when he finds himself caught on an elevator, he grows faint and falls to the floor. Believing he is dying, the elevator operator, Mary Lou, frantically struggles to stop the elevator, then drags Newton out into the hall. In a demonstration of both her anxiety and his vulnerability, she picks him up in her arms and carries him to his room, a sight that is simultaneously comic and pathetic. She lays him on the bed in his room and stays with him even as he proceeds to vomit. There is a genuine sense of concern in her voice as she cares for the stranger, in marked contrast to Bryce's actions.

As Mary Lou is cleaning Newton up, Roeg cuts to Bryce in bed with a coed. An intricate montage begins, involving Bryce with first one coed and then another, as well as a sleeping Newton, watched over by Mary Lou. Roeg juxtaposes the coeds as they make similar comments about Bryce, so that they become interchangeable. Bryce's lovemaking often seems incestuous: the first girl he made love to had held onto a photograph of his daughter during intercourse and here the coeds contrast his body with their fathers' bodies. The lovemaking also subtly comments on Newton's disguise (the girls examine organs Newton will later prove to be lacking). The sequence concludes with Bryce's words becoming distorted, as if they were being transmitted over space to Newton, who awakes with a start, Mary Lou still at his side.

Newton's second encounter with Mary Lou underscores her loneliness as she gradually grows drunk and shows no sign of leaving despite the late hour. She offers him alcohol (which he again declines), while warning him that the water is unsafe: "You know this is a very unhealthy place. The water here is all polluted, they put all kinds of chemicals into it to keep people from getting sick. It's a very unhealthy place." The place will indeed be unhealthy for Newton, but not because of the water, and here he remains optimistic: "I think it just takes getting used to." When she does finally leave, it is at his request, and as she walks out into the city she narrates her own feelings about Newton: "They always seem to lead such interesting lives, people who travel. People who write stories must lead kind of interesting lives too. I know I'll never be like a character in a story. I'll just be like everybody else. But maybe, maybe, why, I don't know. Maybe someday."

Roeg and Mayersburg will only outline the relationship between Mary Lou and Newton, as they move in with one another, build a home, argue, separate, and eventually betray one another, a format Roeg will use more effectively in *Bad Timing*. Their first lodging is a small apartment, presumably Mary Lou's, and the room is crowded with the three television sets Newton constantly watches. On one he monitors the activities of World Enterprises, while talking to Farnsworth over the phone. Farnsworth warns him that "the more secretive you are about your life, the more it arouses people's interest." He tells him of Bryce's interest in the company, which has turned into an obsession that the next sequence further delineates. Bryce is leaving a campus building loaded with books as he speaks of his personal life and World Enterprises: "For a whole year I concentrated equally on two things—fucking and World Enterprises. It was neck and neck." This is the first indication of how much time has passed and also the first direct affiliation between Newton and Bryce, as the latter is finally offered a job with the company. Bryce admits that his interest in young women soon waned as his "mind had developed a libido of its own." He travels to New Mexico, where Farnsworth confesses he has come to "like it out here. It's got a lot of space. That means freedom."

The televisions have multiplied in Newton's room, and the images begin to comment on the action. In the beginning there had been a sense of urgency about Newton's work, but it has now become lost in his dependence on television and alcohol for stimuli. Mary Lou arrives with more alcohol, but he takes no notice of her. "You know, Tommy, you're really a freak. I don't mean that unkindly. I like freaks." Among the images on the TV screens, the most dominant is one from *Love in the Afternoon*, and Gary Cooper's dialogue seems to echo Newton's feelings. ("Trouble is people get too attached to each other. Things drag on, scenes, tears, everything gets so maudlin. I think people should always behave as though they were between planes.") Mary Lou speaks back to the television, saying that's not enough. She tells Newton that they will go to church the next day, but her words immediately call her faith into question ("Lord, I love gin"). She explains her religious feelings by saying: "Everybody needs that, a meaning to life. When you look out at night there don't you feel that somewhere out there, there's got to be a God. There's got to be." Roeg cuts to the television set as the musician discretely leaves Cooper's room, but Newton's attention is on the trains outside, as he marvels that they are "so strange here."

The differences between Mary Lou and Newton often lie in how they interpret things. Newton confesses to Mary Lou that he is already married, but when he admits she and his wife are nothing alike, Mary Lou takes this to mean she is inferior. "Well, I guess I'll do for now," she says. The scene resembles something out of *Performance;* she sits in a bathtub applying conditioner while he examines himself in the mirror. Like Chas, Newton is examining his identity, wondering who he really is and struggling with what he is becoming. Ironically, the first reminder of his past comes as he and Mary Lou are being driven in the country. The sight of a white horse running past triggers the first flashback of his planet (if flashback is really the operative word here). Accompanied by the sentimental pop tune "Try to Remember," the sequence resembles a commercial, suggesting that television already influences his memories. He walks with his family along a grassy plain, but in a sudden sweep, the vegetation disappears, leaving only a dry desert. His true appearance is as a hairless, seemingly sexless, humanoid. Instead of seeming advanced, his civilization often seems backward. The train he boards is like a giant clay triangle with a sail, which explains his continued fascination with the vehicles on Earth. Trains also hold memories for Mary Lou, who recalls riding on them as a child; as she grew older, however, her fascination turned to disillusionment. Although the scenes of the planet would seem to confirm Newton's identity, Roeg's interpretation is different: "You in the audience think perhaps he's from outer space. I don't think that's definite. Perhaps he's from inner space. All we see is what's in his mind."[3]

Newton's nostalgia continues, as he returns to the hill he had stumbled down in the opening scene to take a picture of it. He demonstrates an ability to see across spatial and temporal distances as he looks out the window of his limousine and suddenly sees a pioneer family, who are equally startled by his appearance. It is Roeg's reminder that the past is always present, and the next scene seems to continue this discourse. Looking out over the lake he had crashed into, Newton's memories seem to overpower him, and he goes into a trance. Instead of crashing into the water, he imagines himself emerging from it, as if he is wishing he could turn back time. Mary Lou and his chauffeur return the unconscious Newton to his car, and the episode seems to renew his determination. He calls Farnsworth to tell him to sell off his holdings and invest everything in a space project. On the other extension Farnsworth is the first illustration of Roeg's experimentation with the aging process. It is a noticeably older Farnsworth who is talking to Newton, who seems not to have aged at all. During the film, the characters will age at varying rates, with the exception of Newton, who remains eternally youthful. Roeg describes his interest in the question of aging: "I'm fascinated by the interchange between aging and time. People age at different speeds. Bowie didn't age at all. Perhaps aging begins when people betray themselves in one way or another, when they start living by other people's lights."[4]

Even as the project moves forward, Newton seems to be settling down into his new milieu in a house he has built overlooking the lake where he first arrived. He presents Mary Lou with a telescope, creating the expectation he will finally confide in her; instead the gift initiates a sequence patterned after the lovemaking scene in *Don't Look Now*. As they go about setting up the telescope, Roeg intercuts the two of them making love, but the sequence lacks either the resonance or the meaning of the earlier work. It ends with two images which serve to disorient the viewer. The first is a shot of the two of them in profile that emphasizes the resemblance between them. This profile shot was modeled after the famous shot from *Persona*, and Roeg would reuse it in many of his films. It would most often show the protagonist's doppelganger, or double, but here it serves to emphasize the resemblance between two species. Following this scene, Mary Lou and Newton turn toward the camera, looking directly out at the audience, as if they are aware we are examining them. The viewer has become the watcher.

The presentation of the telescope and the resulting sexual intercourse is the moment when Newton and Mary Lou are closest, and in Roeg's films sexual contact is always a precursor to misfortune. In *Don't Look Now*, the lovemaking preceded the boy's accident; in *Walkabout* the aborigine's declaration of love is followed by the girl's rejection of him and his remembrance of the white hunter; in *Eureka* Tracy's break with her father comes after she makes love to Claude; and in *Insignificance* the actress's miscarriage follows her decision to have a family with her husband. In the present film, the lovemaking anticipates the dissolution of Newton and Mary Lou's relationship. He sits in front of a stereo system created by World Enterprises, where the disc has been replaced by a small sphere. Drunk and unimpressed by the music (background music from the film), he orders Mary Lou to put on some music with singing. She asks what is happening to him and puts on Roy Orbison's "Blue Bayou" as he sits down in front of a dozen television sets in a chair which incorporates TV controls. She wants to talk, but is unable to compete with the music or the images, and his response is to grin foolishly at her. Orbison's words capture Mary Lou's feelings of loneliness as she begins to cry, finally retreating to another room.

In the central image of the film, Newton is left alone with his televisions. The camera moves from one set to another as each seems to comment on Newton or the film. On one, Elvis is singing with some beautiful women (he is another musical performer turned actor like Bowie), while on another, Billy Budd is about to be hung (an innocent sacrificed for the state). A scene from *End of the Game* predicts Newton's incarceration and interrogation, and a shot of two lions copulating continues the discourse on sexual relations. One image also comments ironically on Roeg, featuring his first wife (Susan Rennie) with an actor from his next film, Denholm

Elliot. A scene of a lizard eating an insect is related to Bryce: he is later photographed playing with an insect and he helps to destroy Newton. Even a seemingly innocuous scene such as a pilot in flight relates to the film's perspective, as critic James Leach has commented:

> On one of the sets at one time a brief extract from David Lean's *Breaking the Sound Barrier* is seen and heard, and we pick out the moment at which the pilot successfully breaks the sound barrier by pushing the stick forward instead of pulling it back to come out of a dive. He can fly faster than the speed of sound because he reverses the conventional procedure; technology breaks through the apparent limits of time and space by breaking out of the conventions which were taken to be natural laws.[5]

Newton begins to scream out at the screens: "Get out of my mind. All of you. Leave my mind alone. Stay where you belong. Go away, back where you belong. Back where you came from." The scene culminates with an explosion on one of the screens.

Roeg takes the spatial relationship already established between Bryce and Newton even further. Having been told that Newton will arrive in town the next day, Bryce finds himself confronted by Newton's image. Dressed in the clothes in which he arrived, Newton tells him not to be so suspicious and then quickly disappears. There is a cut to Newton asleep with Mary Lou, presumably hundreds of miles away. When the two do meet, Newton does a double take, asking if they have not already met. Ignoring the query, Newton says his interest is in energy, "the transference of energy." During their conversation Newton admits to Bryce that he has thought about him "once or twice."

Arriving at Newton's factory, the two men walk about his craft, a small, glowing sphere. When Bryce recognizes it as a space vehicle, Newton tells him to "think beyond that." Their interest in the vehicle is superseded by Bryce's interest in Newton, which the latter seems to recognize, saying, "Ask me . . . the question you've been wanting to ask me." Bryce surprises us by asking if Newton is a Lithuanian; then he worries that the craft is a weapon because he believes it is too small to carry someone. He recalls seeing astronauts who went insane after their missions, but Newton advises him against believing everything he sees on television: "The strange thing about television is that it doesn't tell you everything. It shows you everything about life on earth. The true mysteries remain. Perhaps it's in the nature of television. Just waves in space." Bryce confesses he does not trust Newton completely and admits to being a disillusioned scientist, a stereotypical description that resembles the phrase "spaced-out spaceman." Bryce quotes a Latin phrase and expresses surprise that Newton does not recognize it, because it is the logo of the British Air Force: "Through difficulties to the stars."

The products of World Enterprises help both to serve Newton and to bring him down. Its economic dominance attracts the attention of the government, which seems fearful of its growth. A black federal agent, Peters, tries to enlist the aid of Farnsworth, but he proves uncooperative. Peters warns him that "the world is everchanging, like our own solar system." In contrast to Farnsworth, who is dedicated to Newton, Bryce is already moving away from him. He lures Newton to his home in order to photograph him with an X-ray camera, which is triggered by a television remote control. Newton is engrossed in watching the latest commercial for World Enterprises, in which he is prominently featured, a commercial which is actually a message to his wife (she views it on a small receiver on her planet). Newton seems to sense something as Bryce triggers the camera; later we will learn he can see the flash of an X-ray. At the same time Peters is meeting with his superiors, who tell him he must take the next step: "We're determining the social ecology. This is modern America and we're going to keep it that way."

From the time Newton pushes the button on the remote, his true identity becomes known. Not only does Bryce learn the truth, but Newton will finally confide in Mary Lou. The relationship between Newton and Mary Lou continues to disintegrate, and in her anger she calls him an alien, another word that has different meanings for each. To her he is an alien because his visa has expired, but her next words also comment ironically on his identity: "You don't understand how we live here." The argument begins to turn violent as she pulls at his clothing, only stopping as the oven timer goes off behind her. She removes a tray of cookies, but as she offers them to him, he slaps away the tray, sending the cookies into the air, where they are photographed falling in slow motion. The close-up of the broken cookies recalls a similar confrontation in *Petulia,* but the emotions here seem artificial compared to those in the earlier film.

Alone in the bathroom, Newton examines his image in the mirror on the wall, while a smaller mirror seems to enlarge his features. Having dirobed, he runs his hand along his body and then takes a pair of tweezers from the medicine cabinet. As he moves the tweezers toward his eyes, Roeg cuts to Mary Lou, who stands outside the door, aware that something is happening. When Newton does not respond to her calls, her anxiety grows until the door opens and he emerges in his true form. Screaming, she backs away, as Newton silently moves past her into the bedroom. Standing frozen against the wall, she urinates onto the floor in total fear. With great effort Mary Lou moves into the bedroom, where he lies on the bed, a hairless figure with neither nipples or a penis. Disrobing she climbs in beside him, her eyes closed as she kisses him, whispering that she lifted him up once. Newton tells her she must believe in him.

The focus of this scene is split between what Mary Lou is feeling and what Newton is imagining; thus we are left confused about whom we should empathize with. She is fighting back her revulsion to prove her love, but their contact is intercut with scenes of Newton and his wife making love, an act which seems to be as much an aquatic experience as a sexual one. Newton's lack of a sexual organ further hampers their efforts, and finally Mary Lou runs screaming into the kitchen. Huddled naked on the floor, she moans, "why?" as he returns to the bathroom to reapply his costume. Later she finds him standing on the wharf, and even as she apologizes we realize she has failed the perverse test he has put her through. He continues to stress the resemblance between his family and that of an Earthman ("they're like children, exactly like children"), but the obvious differences have resulted in the dissolution of their relationship. Newton stands beside a blue light, which, along with his house standing on the lake, recalls Gatsby's home in Fitzgerald's novel. In fact, Newton's predicament is not unlike Gatsby's, as Fitzgerald's narrator, Nick Carraway, describes it:

> And as I sat there brooding on the old, unknown world, I thought of Gatsby's wonder when he first picked out the green light at the end of Gatsby's dock. He had come a long way to this blue lawn, and his dream must have seemed so close he could hardly fail to grasp it. He did not know that it was already behind him, somewhere back in that vast obscurity beyond the city, where the dark field of the republic rolled on under the night.

Roeg continues to play with our perceptions as we see a truck driving down a desert highway and veering off the road at the sound of a gunshot. Hearing the sound of approaching horses, we assume the truck is under attack, but the sound actually emanates from Newton's television set. He has escaped to a shack in the middle of nowhere (as if he were returning to his own barren environment), and Bryce now visits him at this shack. Bryce wears a cowboy hat, an object which unties him with the setting, while Bryce remains out-of-place in his suit, like the eastern traveler so often ridiculed in Westerns. Stepping outside, the men discuss Newton's true identity. "I realize you've made certain assumptions about me," says Newton. He gives some clues to his planet: it is drought-stricken and its inhabitants have viewed Earth through its television transmissions, facts already apparent. He also remains pointedly obscure, however; he only gestures off into the distance when asked where the planet is located and he gives little information on his plan other than to say that his intention is not hostile. By contrast, in Tevis's novel his clearly stated mission is to obtain water for the inhabitants of his planet and also to take control of the planet. As critic James Leach has noted:

> The omission of the details of Newton's mission is typical of Roeg's attitude to all aspects of the novel's science-fiction framework. While such

omissions may create confusion with regards to the narrative, they do help to overcome one of the basic problems of the science fiction genre. The creation of an alternative world is a central concern of literary science-fiction, but the application of this idea to film often results in the merely spectacular. Since the film medium is not a conceptual medium, the visual details of the alternative world tend to drown out the ideas that this world might be intended to represent. Science-fiction films thus balance precariously between spectacular evocations of the unknown and verbal explanations.[6]

Newton does admit that he is not the first visitor to have come to the planet, saying: "I've seen them. I've seen their footsteps and their places." These statements recall the pioneer family he had earlier seen, but his words lack the significance they would have if Roeg had kept to his original intentions. The script had included references to ancient carvings, sculptures, and landing strips, which would have been in keeping with Roeg's fascination with other cultures. Traces of other cultures appear in *Performance, Walkabout, Eureka,* and other Roeg films.

In the exchange between Newton and Bryce, the latter says: "I've seen those things, we've all seen them. That's for theorists, I'm a scientist." Newton then replies, "I'm not a scientist, but I know all things begin and end in eternity."

Roeg cuts to the sun radiating heat, and Newton imagines that his family is dying. He confides to Bryce that he trusts both him and Mary Lou, but it is only Farnsworth who remains loyal to him. His companion, Trevor, warns him to get out of the company, but Farnsworth admits that he feels sorry for Newton, that he "can't help it." Trevor is setting out some cards, but when Farnsworth asks him what he sees, he tells him nothing, aware that their own future is finite.

A circus-like atmosphere surrounds the launch site of Newton's spacecraft as a large crowd struggles to see Newton and newsmen fight to interview him. To heighten his secrecy, he wears a blue body-stocking which covers his face. In his study, Farnsworth attempts to pay off Mary Lou, but she grows hysterical, crying that she only wants "Tommy." A further indication of how much time has passed is found in their appearance: Farnsworth's hair is completely grey and Mary Lou is older and much heavier, closer in spirit to the character in Tevis's novel. A newsman recounts the success of not just World Enterprises, but also its founder: "Where he has come from is as mysterious as where he's going." Newton is greeted by real-life astronaut James Lovell, then is pulled along by the crowd. His chauffeur helps him to his car, and he speeds off while Farnsworth is thanking Mary Lou, a scene which suggests he may have learned the truth.

Critic Tom Milne is intrigued by the associations scattered through the film:

Although never more than two of the four ever meet at any one time,
they are all indissolubly linked together by association. By the ginger cat
in Newton's room near the beginning, the (same?) ginger cat in the apartment shared by Bryce and Mary Lou at the end, the portrait of a cat with
the Anthean's eyes that hangs over Farnsworth's desk. Or, more elusively,
by Bryce's sudden hesitation on the pier as he arrives for his first encounter with Newton: he has just passed a hanging mobile whose form
echoes the glass chandelier in Farnsworth's apartment, and foreshadows
the form of the candles which Mary Lou lights at the end of her last fren-
zied love-making with Newton.[7]

The painting Tom Milne refers to is one of a series of paintings which
are found throughout the film that anticipate later events or serve as
reminders of the past. In one of the first meetings between Newton and
Mary Lou, there is a painting of a house overlooking a lake which presages
their future home. Professor Canutti is flanked in his office by a mural of
the universe, a reminder of Newton's journey. Finally, there is the photograph of Brueghel's painting, which predicts Newton's fate.

His superiors have warned Peters that they are not the Mafia ("we're
not some archaic joke"), but their tactics come across as the same. Newton
finds himself trapped in his own limousine with a driver who is actually a
government agent. As Newton is escorted to prison, Farnsworth is visited
by other agents of the government, who resemble Rosebloom and Wilson
in *Performance* in both their manner and appearance. Farnsworth's murder
is a small essay in black comedy. The two murderers put on motorcycle
helmets before they knock, only to find they have exchanged helmets by
mistake (echoing a famous Laurel and Hardy routine). Farnsworth does
not seem surprised by their arrival ("It had to come, didn't it"), but still puts
up a struggle, losing his glasses in the process. He shouts that they are his
eyes, a statement that indicates another bond to Newton. Farnsworth's
words are often absurd: he apologizes to his attackers when the window
they have tried to throw him out of does not break the first time. The second effort proves successful, and his body seems to float downward while
choir music plays. Trevor is found lifting weights, and his barbells are
thrown out the window, with he himself following close behind. The shot
of Trevor falling becomes that of Peters diving into his pool and emerging
with his wife in his arms. His muscular body is often on display in the film,
offering a marked contrast to Newton's frail physique. That night as Peters
prepares for bed he questions his wife about whether they "do and say the
right things." She assumes he is referring to children, but we are aware of
his true concerns.

We are introduced to Newton's prison in a long, tracking shot of a man
in a suit pushing a trunk through various rooms, all of differing styles. The
setting recalls the conclusion of *2001*, a film that could be considered the

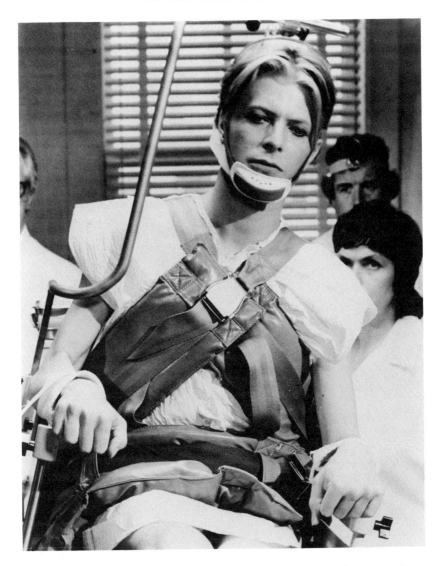

Government doctors work on Thomas Newton (David Bowie) to determine where he has come from in *The Man Who Fell to Earth*.

inverse of this one. Instead of an earthling arriving at another planet, in this case it is Newton who has arrived on Earth. If the two cultures coalesce in Kubrick's film, however, here they remain distinctly separate.

Finally stopping at one wall, the men with the trunk looks through a dart board, while on the other side can be heard an interview with Professor Canutti, whose words echo those of Peters. In discussing the failure of World Enterprises, Canutti argues that it "relied too heavily on that two-headed monster innovation. Now the American consumers can assimilate only so many new products in a given period of time and then no more." Newton lies on a bed watching a giant screen, not acknowledging the entrance of the servant, whose effeminate manner is stereotypically homosexual in contrast to the demeanor of Trevor and Farnsworth. Shutting off the television, the man pulls open curtains on the ceiling, and Newton's reaction indicates he is still not adjusted to sunlight.

Like the father's actions in *Walkabout,* Bryce's reasons for betraying Newton are never identified. Throughout the work on the project, Bryce expresses doubts, thinking that the craft may be a weapon or that it lacks a recovery program, but nothing indicates his future betrayal. When he meets with Peters, we see that he now works for the government, but Peters's warning to him is on a personal level: "I'm not sure if you know how all of this might affect you." Bryce observes Newton as he is being operated on by surgeons, but flees when Newton begins to shout his name. Not only does he ignore Newton's plight, he also tries to obtain Mary Lou's assistance in betraying him. As the two meet in a restaurant, Roeg intercuts their conversation with scenes from *The Third Man.* In his prison, Newton is watching Carol Reed's film, and the dialogue from the earlier work seems to comment on the present action.

It becomes apparent that Newton is equally guilty of deception, albeit unknowingly. While he is watching the film, a group of scientists come in to examine him. He tells them that he came alone, that no one saw him, but Roeg reminds us of the man who witnessed his arrival. If Newton's misstatement comes across as innocent, his next actions show how jaded he has become. When Mary Lou is allowed to see him, his first action is to check the doors, which remain locked. He looks at her through a drunken haze as the two of them hold tightly to their drinks. He is stirring his with a gun, which he begins to point at Mary Lou, circling her as he speaks. Talking like a gangster, he tells her that she "knows too much" and that if he killed her, his captors would take away her body and supply him with another girl. She becomes frightened when he puts the gun against her, but he smiles as he pulls the trigger. The screen goes black, and the song "Hello, Mary Lou" begins.

As the two have sex, Newton holds onto the gun, a phallic symbol whose blank bullets remind us of his lack of a sexual organ. The act is photographed as if it occurred in a shooting gallery: the lights flash as the music plays and the gun continues to fire. Newton and Mary Lou have lost any feelings for one another and have in fact become Bryce and his companion, even in the way Newton rips off Mary Lou's clothing. Roeg incorporates reminders of their past encounters to indicate how innocent they once were. For Roeg this flashback, along with the gun, comments on the changes in their relationship: "They aren't young people any more. As they get older, the likelihood of extra aids to eroticism is brought in. Newton has become totally human."[8]

The next scene seems to confirm this, as the two play ping pong in costumes which make them look like two bored socialites. The walls are decorated to look like a forest, and leaves are even sprinkled on the floor (one of the few times the background serves as a commentary on the action). Mary Lou is trying to convince Newton to tell the truth, saying that if he does, he can return to his planet. Although she tries to convince him that he is better off on Earth, she realizes what his real concern is. Chiding him, she says that even if he could return, his family would most likely be dead. Telling him he must prove who he is, she begins to unbutton his shirt, but he pulls away, saying, "I've proven everything I'm gonna prove. I've gone as far as I'm going." Completely distanced from him, Mary Lou admits she no longer loves him, and although he says the same, he offers her a ring, the last thing that is his to give. She takes it, but when it does not fit she hurls it to the floor. The ring begins to glow, and Roeg shows a scientist examining it. At best, Newton's offering of the ring was symbolic, but in throwing it down, Mary Lou has forever severed their relationship and the ring becomes another artifact to be examined.

Most of the alterations Roeg and Mayersburg perform on Tevis's novel can be justified, but one change serves no apparent purpose and in fact detracts from the film. During the testing he undergoes, Newton realizes that the doctors are going to use an X-ray on him and implores them not to because it will hurt his eyes. As they try to placate him with alcohol, they notice his lenses and want to take them out. Having convinced them to let him try, Newton is unable to remove them because of his nervousness. Instead of attempting to remove them, they go on with the X-ray. As the flash occurs, he screams and we assume he is blinded, just as he is in the novel. Instead, in a disappointing sequence, he surprises us by shouting that now the contacts are permanent. With the exception of alcohol, Newton's primary stimuli had been visual ones; blindness would have been the ultimate tragedy for him and would have explained his turning to an audible medium at a later point. It would have also completed his association with Farnsworth.

Left alone in his prison, Newton imagines a successful return to his planet, but in reality his spacecraft has been destroyed and even he is left with the knowledge that his family has probably perished. As he lies asleep on the bed, he is visited by the watcher, a scene which indicates the authorities have known of his identity all along. Inexplicably, these same authorities lose interest in Newton, and he finds the door unlocked. As the clocks begin to tick loudly, he hurries down in an elevator (no longer bothered by its movement), and it opens out into a lobby. The prison had

seemed like a mansion, but in fact it is only a floor in a cheap hotel. On
the sidewalk, Newton hurries off into the distance.

The question of where Newton flees to or how he gets by is left
unanswered as Roeg concentrates on what has become of Mary Lou and
Bryce. As Christmas nears, the two step into a liquor store to stock up on
alcohol, with Bryce mysteriously dressed in a Santa Claus suit. In their
apartment, Bing Crosby sings "True Love," while they remove their
costumes—he the Santa suit and she her false eyelashes. Bryce's life has
gone from rock music and coeds to old ballads and middle-aged women.
While he muses that Christmas has become less commercial, Mary Lou
looks out the window, remembering Newton, first with his wife, then with
her. (It is significant that the shot emphasizes the resemblance between
the two.) This act repeats the closing of *Walkabout,* in which the girl looks
wistfully back at her adventure and wonders what might have been.

Newton has recorded an album, the "Visitor," in hopes that his wife
will one day hear it, and this album enables Bryce to track Newton down.
(Although Bryce listens to the album, he wears headphones, so that once
again we fail to hear Bowie sing.) Drinking alone in an outdoor cafe,
Newton is not surprised when Bryce appears, "Strangely enough, I was just
thinking of you the other day," he says in a statement which recalls their
first meeting. Bryce admits he does not care much for the album, even
though "we hear most everything on the radio these days." Newton asks
about Mary Lou, but Bryce tells him he has not heard much of her, leaving
us to wonder if he is lying again or if they really have separated. When
asked if he is bitter, Newton admits, "we'd probably treat you the same if
you'd come over to our place." Even now Newton remains optimistic about
returning ("You must know there's always a chance") and asks if Bryce
needs any money. When Newton accidently knocks over his glass, the
waiter comes over to clean up the mess. Looking at Bryce, the waiter
remarks that "Mr. Newton has had enough." Bryce agrees with him, and
Newton bows his head as his hat engulfs the frame. Over the credits the
song *Stardust* is played, a reminder of another persona Bowie created,
Ziggy Stardust.

Roeg had suffered through negative reviews before, as well as censorship, but with *The Man Who Fell to Earth,* he was to confront something
else: the mutilation of his films by his American distributor. Donald Rugoff
purchased the American rights to the film, but was disturbed by the split
response the film received from a test audience. He decided the film needed
trimming, and although he received advice from various individuals, it was
primarily the influence of a professor of psychiatry, Dr. Richard C. Sim-
mons, which determined the final cut. The main deletions were Bryce's
sexual encounters with the two coeds, Newton's final sexual encounter
with Mary Lou, Bryce dressed in a Santa suit, and Mary Lou urinating on

the floor upon seeing Newton as his real self. The deletions trimmed the film by twenty minutes, but did little to help its commercial success. Instead the episode only showed how vulnerable Roeg's work could be. The plight of the film is well documented in a *New York Times* article in which Roeg comments on the fate of not just this film, but all of his works:

> I've been dogged with different versions. Before everything was cut on the grounds of censorship. That's a dying cause, so now things are cut on cultural grounds; certain things accepted in Europe are not considered acceptable for Americans. Having tried to push the structure of film grammar into a different area, I find myself explaining it, the reason why different things are in. Whenever one plays with film grammar, it offends people.[9]

Despite the fact that two versions of the film were being released, *The Man Who Fell to Earth* was Roeg's most eagerly anticipated film. It would also be his most debated, with most critics conceding that Bowie was perfect in the role of the alien, but wondering how to take the rest of the film. Jay Cocks wrote: "In *The Man Who Fell to Earth*, his newest and least successful effort, there is little to spell out anyway. The movie is about equally dazzling and disappointing, but where it goes wrong is in substance, not in style. Roeg's exuberance and invention are compromised here by a yarn that carries dank traces of 'Twilight Zone.'"[10]

Ironically, Roeg's film anticipated a new revival in science fiction films and would be released at the same time as *Logan's Run* and *Star Wars*, the latter of which overshadowed all films for the year in popularity. In contrast to these films, Roeg's work is more introspective and thought provoking, but in the end it falters and fails to hold the audience, in contrast to these other films. It has been accused of trying to do too much, but that hardly seems to be a sin. In fact, the problem is that the film is too erratic. Brilliant passages are overshadowed by static scenes that tell us nothing and cause the film to drag at times. A more critical flaw, however, is found in Roeg's treatment of his lead character. We are emotionally detached from Newton, just as we are from the girl in *Walkabout* and Alex in *Bad Timing*. With these films, however, our attention is held by the central story: will the children survive? did Alex commit rape? In *The Man Who Fell to Earth*, we gradually realize Newton will not return to his planet; once this realization occurs our interest quickly wanes. William Van Wert has decried the approach Roeg took to the film, one he felt was symptomatic of many directors, including Jean Luc Godard, Stanley Kubrick, and Robert Altman:

> Possessed of Romantic sensibilities, these filmmakers do battle with the Modern Age in film after film, a battle lost before it has begun, because their expertise is in the very technology they despise. There is a sense of

nostalgia for the past, a sense of lost innocence and time remembered in their films, a relentless self-destruct intuition in their themes, alleviated only by a sense of comic urgency, heavy-handed irony and self-parody bordering on nihilism. These are artists out of step with their time: advanced in the technical know-how, retrograde in their world view.[11]

The failure of *The Man Who Fell to Earth* marked an end to the first phase of Roeg's career. *Performance* introduced the themes which would obsess Roeg throughout his career, while *Walkabout* introduced more humanistic elements. *Don't Look Now* had been a genre piece, but it had continued the exploration of a nonlinear format and the idea that the future is already present. *The Man Who Fell to Earth* seemed to be the culmination of Roeg's work, but instead it pointed out its possible failures, as Neil Feineman has observed:

> When then, Roeg fails not just to fill us in on causes, effects, and the gradual unfolding of events or character motivation, but also fails to impose a recognizable visual consistency on the film as well, he is only pushing the refusal for an adherence to rationality to its logical end. I am not trying to apologize for Roeg here, nor am I trying to make his every shortcoming or action a virtue. However, almost everyone has criticized the movie for its failure to develop a consistency that directs and focuses our responses. And we do seem to need that direction in order to be involved.[12]

Roeg perhaps sensed this problem and decided his next film would deal more with emotions, saying: "I'd like to think it will be something about obsession. Obsession and fear go hand in hand."[13]

Notes

1. Joseph Lanza, *Fragile Geometry*, pp. 153–54.
2. *Sight and Sound*, Autumn 1975, p. 239.
3. *Interview*, March 3, 1976, p. 35.
4. *American Film*, January 1980, p. 27.
5. *Film Literature Quarterly*, Fall 1978, p. 371.
6. *Film Literature Quarterly*, Fall 1978, p. 372.
7. *Sight and Sound*, Fall 1978, p. 147.
8. *New York Times*, August 22, 1976, p. 11.
9. Ibid.
10. *Time*, June 14, 1976, p. 66.
11. *Western Humanities Review*, no. 2, 1979 pp. 141.
12. Neil Feineman, *Nicolas Roeg*, p. 140.
13. *New York Times*, August 22, 1976, p. 11.

FIVE

Bad Timing:
A Sensual Obsession

The difficulties in getting *The Man Who Fell to Earth* made and the problems in getting it released did not seem to deter Roeg from this genre. Among the unrealized projects that followed was a film based on the comic strip *Flash Gordon*, which Roeg found fascinating:

> Alex Raymond was a kind of genius you know. Really, he was an extraordinary man. The strip cartoon, I suppose, is the closest link of any other form to the cinema—I mean in technique, not in emotional terms—and he was, in the strip cartoon, doing extraordinary, advanced, clever things in the thirties. People allowed their children to read Flash Gordon because they weren't reading the pictures very much; they just looked at the bubbles. "Oh goodness Flash, you are wonderful. Thank goodness you saved me, Flash." The bubble was from a literary culture. In the thirties they weren't used to reading the pictures, and in the back of the pictures two girls are lashing each other with chains. Passionate and wonderful stuff, and Raymond was getting away with it with the bubbles, because they were saying "That's all right. That's very good for the kids." If the bubble had said what the back picture was doing ("Take that, you bitch, I'll lash your ass off"), they would say, "What kind of strip is this?"[1]

Roeg spent a year working on the script for producer Dino De Laurentiis, but in the end De Laurentiis was unimpressed. Instead he turned the project over to director Mike Hodges, who made it into something of a *Star Wars* rehash with little to recommend it. Another project Roeg spent time on was an adaptation of Joseph Gore's biography of Dashiel Hammett. This project too would go nowhere, which was probably fortunate for Roeg. German immigrant Wim Wenders was given the project, but in the end Francis Ford Coppolla proved ineffective in the capacity of producer. The final product pleased neither Wenders nor most critics.

Having already worked in a variety of genres, Roeg turned to one that seemed particularly suited to his vision. Film noir had sprung out of the American cinema during the Second World War and presented a pessimistic view of human nature. Often the central characters were men who were searching for answers and were involved with women who seemed deceitful. If the stories were sometimes routine, the manner in which they were presented definitely was not. The characters were hidden in shadows and the streets were wet with rain, while the stories were often told in flashback. For his material Roeg chose an obscure Italian novel *Ho Tentato di Vivere* by Constanzo Constantini. Working with film critic turned screenwriter Yale Udoff, Roeg kept little from the novel except its premise. His original title had been *Illusions*, but the film was ultimately released as *Bad Timing: A Sensual Obsession*. Although the phrase is found in *Petulia*, it actually occurred to Roeg one night as he was sleeping. He felt it was appropriate not only for the film, but for his career.

Bruno Ganz and Sissy Spacek were originally cast for the two leads, but when these two were involved in other projects Roeg was forced to look elsewhere. For the role of Dr. Alex Linden, he chose singer Art Garfunkel. This was the third time Roeg had chosen a rock singer to play the lead, and like Bowie and Jagger, Garfunkel was an inspired choice. Garfunkel, however, was not the novice these two men had been when it came to acting. He had already won critical acclaim for his performance in Mike Nichols's *Carnal Knowledge*, another sexually frank examination of relationships. For the pivotal role of Milena Flaherty, Roeg chose an actress who had first attracted his attention three years earlier. Theresa Russell was only twenty when she won a role in Elia Kazan's *The Last Tycoon*. She followed this with equally strong performances in *Straight Time* and the television miniseries "Blind Ambition." The choice of Russell was to prove fortunate not just for this film, but for Roeg's career and personal life. During filming the two would become lovers, and they eventually married. Russell would also go on to become Roeg's consummate actress, appearing in four more of his films.

As always, Roeg encountered difficulties in getting his film to the screen. The project was canceled twice, and producer Jeremy Thomas agreed to make it only if Roeg could get half the financing on his own. Production of the film was relatively trouble free, although Garfunkel soon realized his character was taking on many of Roeg's characteristics. When Garfunkel confronted Roeg about this, he agreed, but also said that the character of Milena contained an equal amount of his personality. For Roeg, it was not the characters or even the climax which worried him, but the central relationship:

> The ground that makes me nervous in *Bad Timing*, the thought that makes me tremble, is that I don't want to see in this love affair that

sentimental middle area that I think we all know. It's a real, very painful love affair. When one's in love, the moments of lyrical love are to me implicit in people's behaviors. It's actually something in that other, public manner that makes you understand that they have those moments of lyrical love.[2]

Bad Timing is the culmination of Roeg's fascination with time manipulation. Its storyline is simple—one found in many mysteries. A detective tries to unravel the events of a night which ended in tragedy. Like all of Roeg's work, however, nothing is quite so simple. Events from the past intermingle with the present as the detective tries to learn what part a college professor played in the tragedy. Then there is the difficulty the viewer has in separating fact from fantasy and determining in whose mind a given fantasy exists. It is a complex work, which is open to a variety of interpretations. By the time the film has concluded, the mystery itself will be called into question.

Under the opening credits we see a couple walking among the art works of Gustav Klimt. Although the man is clearly visible, the woman is hidden in the shadows, and this sets the aesthetic tone for the film. Dr. Alex Linden will constantly be examined, while Milena will remain something of an enigma to us. Roeg's use of Klimt's work throughout the film has a twofold purpose. Klimt is Vienna's most famous artist, but he also has much in common with Roeg. Like Roeg, Klimt's work was vilified in its time for its emphasis on nudity and its seeming disregard for the traditional rules of art. As Roeg's camera pans around the gallery, Tom Waits sings of Cagney and Hayworth (two film noir actors) in *Invitation to the Blues*. Like all the music in *Bad Timing*, the lyrics either comment on the action or on the characters. The mood of this scene is immediately shattered by the sound of an ambulance.

As the ambulance races through Vienna at night, attendants inside work on Milena, who is struggling to breathe. Sitting beside her, Linden views the action with a detached gaze. While Milena is fighting to survive, Linden calmly adjusts her clothing, a telling point about a man who will be shown to be more interested in details than in people. As the scene ends, Milena is heard to say softly, "Oh, Stefan, I'm sorry." As always, Roeg presents us with a detail we cannot comprehend on our first viewing. Although Stefan is shown in the following scene, we can only guess at his identity.

It is raining slightly as Stefan drives Milena across the bridge from Czechoslovakia into Austria. Having passed the border, Stefan pulls the car over and the two get out. This scene, which has very little dialogue, is the most poignant of the entire film. After taking out a suitcase, Stefan pulls out a cigarette, and Milena wordlessly lights it for him. He removes the

Alex Linden (Art Garfunkel) waits nervously as doctors work on Milena (*Bad Timing*).

wedding ring from her finger, and she then takes it back, hesitating slightly. The relationship between Milena and Stefan here is almost paternal, not just because of the age difference, but because of the way they relate to one another. At one point he brushes his finger down her nose, much like a father would playfully tease his daughter, and reminds her to call. She tells him that it really is not the end, but his eyes tell us that it is. Denholm Elliot's role as Stefan is a small one, but his performance will give it an impact that belies its size. His pain is barely held in check and finally he can only walk quietly away. Milena gets into the car and begins to drive off, the bridge acting as a metaphor for her journey to the unknown. A quick cut to the ambulance's arrival at the hospital tells us her fate will be a tragic one.

This prologue for *Bad Timing* is typical of Roeg's manner, which seems designed more to confuse than to enlighten; once again he presents material in a haphazard way. The scene in the art gallery actually occurs in the middle of the story, and the ride in the ambulance is at the conclusion, while the meeting with Stefan is the beginning of Milena's story. Sometimes Roeg will discard this disjointed manner once he begins the story proper, but with *Bad Timing* he uses this technique throughout and it is integral to our understanding of the film. He will also distort certain scenes to incorporate the memories or the fantasies of the protagonists. This technique is best exemplified by the phone call Milena makes to Alex on the night she attempts suicide. We will hear the call four times during the film, and each time it will be modified slightly. Here Milena seems to be pleading with Alex, but he has a detached manner. Ironically, the call has been recorded (on Alex's answering machine), but even this recording will prove unreliable.

At the hospital, attendants try to determine what has happened to Milena. Because they speak in German, most of what we hear is indecipherable, like the Italian spoken in *Don't Look Now*. Alex gives them an empty pill bottle, but he has no way of knowing how many she has taken. As the doctors begin to work on Milena, Alex walks around the hospital, smoking a cigarette and thinking back to their first meeting. At a party, Alex sees Milena across the room and their eyes meet. She boldly walks toward him as he plays with a small knife, an object whose significance is only late apparent.

> MILENA   We're gonna meet. It might as well be now.
> ALEX   Could be right, then again why spoil the mystery.
> MILENA   Mystery?
> ALEX   If we don't meet, there is always the possibility it could have been perfect.

Before Milena can respond, Alex is called away. The scene returns to Alex in the hospital, where he is still smoking a cigarette and carrying a trenchcoat, which gives him a look reminiscent of Humphrey Bogart in forties film noir. Alex, however, lacks Bogart's force (more often than not, Alex seems more like a blank slate offering no decipherable emotions). Indeed, it is Milena who often seems to be the one who takes action. As Alex is about to leave the party, his way is blocked by Milena, who holds her leg up in front of him, both blocking and inviting him. Uncomfortable with her blatant sexuality, Alex can only make weak entreaties for her to let him by. She tells him she will not let him pass until he agrees to call her, and she hands him a match box with her number on it. She keeps her leg in place, however, and a vanquished Alex if forced to walk underneath it.

At the hospital, Alex tries to minimize his relationship with Milena, saying he is only a friend. Alex seems to be distancing himself not just from the events of the night, but from Milena herself. He tells the anonymous policeman that when Milena called to say she intended to kill herself, he hung up on her. Roeg immediately shows this assertion to be a lie by again playing Milena's phone call, which ends with her hanging up. He also damns Alex by showing him looking at his watch following Milena's call. The time is 10:18 P.M., but when the policeman asks what time she called

Alex will not even make an approximation. All that is known for sure is that he called for the ambulance at 1:30 A.M. What occurred in those three hours lies at the heart of the mystery.

Roeg will often omit events other directors would consider crucial to the story. We never see Alex call Milena (from their conversation it sounds as if Milena had again taken the initiative); we only see them on their first date. The setting for this scene is in marked contrast to the rest of the scenes in which they appear. They are out-of-doors during the daytime, among other people. Most of their scenes together are at night and indoors, with the two of them isolated from those around them. The two are relaxed with one another (this will not be the case later). When he realizes he has received a parking ticket, they can laugh at the humor of the situation, but the incident prefigures his later problems with authorities.

Inspector Fredrich Netusil is introduced as he looks at Milena through the operating room glass, much like Alex will often look at her through windows. He walks down the corridor as Alex is talking to a female doctor, and the two stare at one another wordlessly, a hint of suspicion in both their expressions. Some reviewers have criticized the use of American actor Harvey Keitel to play an Austrian detective, but this choice is consistent with Roeg's style. As with all his films, his characters function in an alien world, whether it be our planet, Vienna, or Venice. This separates them linguistically and emotionally from those around them and isolates their conflicts. Thus such obvious casting flaws as the choice of Keitel here and Rutger Hauer and Joe Pesci in Roeg's next film actually serve a purpose. A loner who ridicules his associates and flaunts his intellectualism, Netusil will form an immediate bond with Alex despite their antagonistic relationship.

As the relationship between Alex and Milena continues to advance, he takes her to a bookstore to purchase a parlor game which examines a person's personality through his or her preferences in color. Her choices, however, are kept from us, and Alex only jokingly shakes his head, saying she should not be left alone. It is at this point that Milena and Alex tour the art gallery, admiring Klimt's works. Gazing at one painting, *The Kiss,* Milena decides the couple portrayed is happy, but Alex's reply is atypical as usual: "That is because they don't know each other well enough yet." Milena glances at a scratch on Alex's neck, a mark presumably left from their last sexual encounter. He gradually learns more of her as she tells him about two abortions she has had. In typical fashion he is concerned with the fathers' reactions, but there is no sense of condemnation in his attitude as there will be later. Milena anticipates the other women Russell will portray, who are either unable to have children or have aborted one.

The first indication of difficulty in their relationship occurs when Alex watches Milena kiss a male friend. Alex seems uncomfortable and ineffectual, as he did when first confronted with Milena's sexuality. When the man (Konrad, an actor friend of Milena's) walks away, Alex can only weakly call him an asshole. To assuage Alex's ego, Milena sits on his lap and begins to kiss him just as passionately, to the cheers of her friends. There is a quick insert of the pair making love, which seems to emphasize the fact that the two are airing their feelings in public. In his own environment, such as his office or his classroom, Alex seems more in control. He is lecturing a group of students on curiosity ("through the gratification of curiosity one acquires knowledge"), when he is told Milena is waiting for him in his office. He finds her lying on his couch, as if she were a patient (which she may be). She asks him if there is hope for them, and he jokingly replies no. As the two begin to laugh, Alex falls onto the couch beside her. This blissful respite is shattered by a shot of Milena going into cardiac arrest on the operating table.

In another flashback Alex arrives at Milena's apartment to find her drunk. There has been no setup for this scene, but it is the first intimation that their relationship has problems. She is listening to Moroccan music (which will often accompany tragic scenes) and is reading *The Sheltering Sky* by Paul Bowles (which concerns the difficulties of a couple in Morocco). In the manner in which he mocks Milena, Alex seems destined to take on the dominant role (until now they had seemed to be equals), while her future dependence on alcohol is already apparent. At the inception of this scene, there is a quick shot of Milena on the operating table, a shot that subtly hints this could all be her recollections. Often the most painful scenes are accompanied by scenes of Milena either going into cardiac arrest or having trouble breathing. During one of the more pleasant memories, the shot of Milena shows her smiling. Ironically, these scenes tend to distance us from Milena, as does the way in which she is often photographed through other objects. We have gradually been drawn into the men's conflict and tend to ignore Milena's struggle.

As Netusil begins his questioning of Alex, there is an immediate animosity between the two. Alex seems to realize this and even apologizes at one point, but his conciliatory attitude is short-lived. There is, however, an indication that the two are more than just antagonists, because they are framed so that the resemblance between them is brought out. Gradually Netusil will become Alex's doppelganger, or double. Characteristics of one man will be given to the other, and gradually the line between the two will disappear. This is a return to the theme of *Performance* and points to the central conflict of *Eureka*. In this film, however, the theme will also influence our response to scenes. By the film's end we will not be sure whose remembrance of events we are really seeing.

Also crucial to our perception of the film is the cinematography of Anthony Richmond. He had worked with Roeg on *The Man Who Fell to Earth* and, as in that film, the framing here is exceptional. The camera constantly moves, but in an untypical manner so that characters who are standing at the side of the frame abruptly shift to the center. At other times the camera will zoom in on the characters to emphasize their reactions. This technique draws us into the film and implicates us in the action. Richmond's mis-en-scène is also important, particularly in the next scene. As Alex lectures in an auditorium, he is dominated by his background. When he speaks of isolation, he is shown against a plain blackboard, and while he speaks on spying, the image of Stalin is displayed behind him.

"I must first know who I am before I can know what I am capable of," Alex asserts. "How we come into this world and how we go out is different for every one of us. We are constantly in isolation — watching, spying on everyone and everything around us." Alex's lecture is supposedly on secrecy and spying, but it is really about his philosophy of life. This is a hypnotic scene as Alex shows slides of a child on one wall and a couple making love on the opposite wall and then calls the child the first spy. He exhibits slides of famous men he calls spies: Freud, Stalin, and J. Edgar Hoover. The students react as if they are watching a tennis match by looking back and forth as images are flashed on each wall. When asked by a student whether he too is not a spy, Alex tells her he prefers the word *observer*.

It is as an observer that Alex relates to Milena. He is unable simply to exist with her, but must place her under some sort of microscope. As they make an attempt at a reconciliation, he cannot help but observe a German translation of a play by Harold Pinter in her car, and he immediately assumes she is still seeing Konrad. With Alex's jealousy again aroused, the two leave the car, but their surroundings provide little comfort. The environment is gloomy, with its barren trees and grey skies, and a metal fence seems to encircle them. Alex tries to convince Milena to move in with him, but she puts it off. In the end she walks off, while Alex flicks her cigarette ashes off of his car seat.

What follows next has no place in time and makes little sense when examined objectively. Alex places a photograph on a wall and immediately afterward Netusil is shown taking the same picture down. It is significant that the picture is of a maze, a two-dimensional representation of the film's labyrinth-like exploration. Netusil is also shown in his home, surrounded by his family. The viewer cannot easily determine whether this is a flashback or a portent of the future. The sequence does at any rate further strengthen the bond between the two men. For Alex, Netusil will become his conscience, questioning his actions and motives. For Netusil, Alex will become a figure of his imagination and obsession. The scene ends with Alex picking up the phone to call Milena.

The two meet in a place of Milena's choosing, a nightclub which features a stripper who gyrates on a trampoline (the cagelike quality of the trampoline echoes the fence in the earlier scene). Alex sees Milena among her friends, but backs into the shadows to watch as she kisses a male friend. She comes up behind Alex and holds his face so that he must watch the stripper, another act seemed designed to embarrass him. As usual, Alex is upset that they are not alone, but Milena assuages him by leaving with him.

With Milena still in critical condition and having signed his police statement, Alex goes outside to avoid Netusil's questioning. Looking out from a bridge and smoking a cigarette, Alex thinks back on Milena. He sees her image in the water and remembers the two of them making love. Once again the scenes of Milena in the hospital break in, and she begins to gag, the sound carrying over into the next scene. The two are making love and Alex kisses Milena's neck, while on the operating table blood spurts out from the same spot. This film received an X-rating on its release for its sexual content, but there is no eroticism to any of the scenes because of the context in which they are presented. This treatment serves to heighten the viewer's awareness that their relationship is devoid of love.

More pieces of Milena's life are presented (her brother and mother died when she was young; her father was in the military and was unable to cope with the family's losses). Her actions continue to be confusing, however. She tells Alex she has never married, but Roeg cuts to a scene of her with Stefan. Although we first assume this to be a flashback, it becomes apparent she has gone to visit Stefan just before she is to move in with Alex. The two have just made love, and "Someday I'll Get Over You" by Billie Holiday plays over the scene. Like their scene together on the bridge, this one is filled with sadness as Stefan realizes Milena has only returned for a visit. The sequence is devoid of dialogue, which adds to its poignancy. As the scene ends, however, Milena does something unusual. She is walking away from Stefan, her suitcase in hand, when suddenly she breaks into a smile. Is she mocking Stefan (as Alex mocks her) or is the smile simply a sign of her happiness?

Once again Milena must cross the bridge from Czechoslovakia to Austria, but this time her way will be blocked. Upset because she is late, Alex becomes more angry when he sees her kiss another man (not Stefan). "Just do one thing for me Milena," he says, "never force yourself to be different from who you are." This is what Alex is really asking of her, however. He often seems childlike in his reactions, either pouting to gain Milena's sympathy or ridiculing her. He is the male equivalent of Linda in *Track 29*, whose childlike characteristics will be even more pronounced. As Milena starts to leave, she says she had something to tell him, but the viewer is left wondering what it was. Alex shouts after her that he is sorry, but by now we realize these words have no meaning for him.

In his home, Alex checks the messages on his answering machine. A military official has called about some work and one of his old girlfriends has also left a message. Alex goes to the window and looks out, playing once more with the small pen knife. In film noir, fate often takes control of events, and here it comes in the form of the U.S. military. Alex is recruited to prepare psychological profiles on some men, but in typical Roeg fashion, the reason for the work is unstated. Asked to do a profile on two Czechoslovakians, Alex opens the file on Stefan Vognic and immediately learns that Milena is his wife. Unable to understand why Milena would have married Stefan, Alex talks about him with a colleague in a cafe (the man is either familiar with Stefan or with the file). His colleague, who could represent the audience, makes a remark in jest which is actually the film's theme: "Everything I say has to be taken in the context of who I am." On the sound track, zither music plays a melody which is reminiscent of the theme from *The Third Man*, indicating the deceit that is occurring.

Although we expect a confrontation between Alex and Milena, instead we find them in bed together calmly discussing the situation. Milena does not believe that she lied when she said she was not married; she tells Alex her denial was only words and words have no meaning. As Alex lies on Milena's chest, he starts to repeat the phrase "to whom," his voice gradually getting louder while Alex is still shouting the words, Roeg cuts to a shot of Milena in the hospital being jolted as the doctors attempt to start her heart. There is a quick cut to a scene of Alex violently shaking Milena, then a switch back to the hospital, and finally a cut back to Alex lying once more on Milena's chest, quietly repeating the phrase. Milena's blissful expression tells us that what we have seen has not occurred, but is actually Alex's fantasy.

Alex continues to read over the file surreptitiously, while Milena tries to explain to him her attraction to Stefan. She admits she tried to change for Stefan, but that the more rules she created for herself, the more difficulty she had. The conversation foreshadows her problems with Alex because Alex cannot be satisfied with the way she is, but must try to change her. His distrust of her increases when he inadvertently finds pictures of her with Stefan and with another man. She is in the other room, discussing a play and asking his opinion of it. Looking at the pictures, Alex silently says, "the drama?" before there is an abrupt cut to a shot of him seated on a bus still looking at the photographs. The overlapping song is "Who Are You?" by the Who (which could be Alex's plaintive cry to understand Milena), but Roeg will cut away before we hear the words of the music. Alex looks around the bus at the male passengers, fantasizing that they are Milena's lovers as his obsession turns into paranoia.

At the hospital, Alex has been awakened by Netusil and his associates, who then hurry off to question the doctor. Dazed, as if he were still asleep, Alex looks at a red fire extinguisher. (Roeg often focuses on objects to precede a fade-out or, as he does in *Eureka*, to give the sense that the camera is looking about. Alex then imagines Milena once again lying on the couch asking if there is any hope for them. Her appearance has been altered (she now looks Madonna-like). There is no laughter in the scene, and Alex has changed his response to yes as they kiss.

Roeg crosscuts between scenes of Netusil trying to learn the facts and Alex trying to learn the truth about Milena. Hesitantly, Alex goes to a government building to inquire about Milena getting a divorce. His awkwardness is intensified by an unidentified woman who sits in the room staring silently at him. The male official does not take the problem seriously and does not even believe the problem concerns Alex. Later Milena seems to agree with this when she complains to Alex that he could have caused trouble for Stefan. Alex says she cannot have it both ways — either she is married or she is not — and then he criticizes her for keeping her apartment messy.

Netusil's work takes on an obsessive quality as he retraces Alex's route to the apartment. Ironically, his relationship with his associate mirrors Alex's with Milena. He often ridicules the man even when the latter provides him with important information. In entering Milena's apartment, Netusil seems to enter her and Alex's world. Alex arrives at her apartment, which she has cleaned up in another effort to please him, and he is immediately aroused. Alex wants to make love, but Milena puts him off, wanting to talk. Like a child, Alex grows distant and hostile, and Milena realizes he is only interested in the physical aspect of their relationship. Making an excuse to leave, Alex starts down the stairs, but Milena follows after him, taunting him with her body. She literally invites him to rape her on the stairs, which he does, in an act which is quick and violent, almost masturbatory. When it is over, Milena races off in tears, shouting that he can't just love her for who she is. Standing in the doorway of Milena's apartment, Netusil mumbles, "right again." Has this sequence been something of Netusil's conception? This possibility is reinforced as Netusil walks around the room and imagines the two making love. As he looks at prints of Schiele's paintings, he seems to confront a naked Alex, his body strikingly similar to the forms Schiele created. As critic Harlan Kennedy has noted:

> If Klimt is a taking-off point for the film's style, the paintings of his pupil Egon Schiele add force and meaning to its content. Schiele's swirling expressionist couples, bound in a morbid frenzy of lovemaking, were an offspring of art nouveau, and it is no accident that Schiele's work is constantly glimpsed in the background of Roeg's Vienna-set meditation of love and death.[3]

Netusil's discovery of a colored rock among Milena's belongings triggers another sequence. As he pours the sand inside the rock onto his hand, the action shifts to Alex and Milena's trip to Morocco, a tirp already anticipated by the copy of *The Sheltering Sky* displayed earlier. When their vehicle breaks down, they are forced to flag down an oncoming truck. Although the driver speaks no English and we have no idea what is being said, his look is enough to tell us what he is thinking. He glances down Milena's blouse, focusing on her breasts, and agrees to let her ride up front, while forcing Alex to ride in the back. During the ride, Alex is reduced to looking in through a dirty window at Milena and the Moroccan, unable to hear or even see what is happening. Even when they arrive at their destination, the couple has trouble shaking the Moroccan, who trails after them into the hotel lobby.

The isolation of the couple is intensified by their incongruity with the surroundings, another instance of Roeg's leitmotif: a stranger in a strange land. They ride a motorcycle through the streets teaming with donkeys and women in traditional clothing. In Milena's apartment Netusil is handed a note in which Milena pleads with Alex to understand her less and love her more. This note relates to the next scene, in which Alex asks Milena to marry him, while they are still on their vacation. Once again she puts him off, saying they should enjoy the moment. As the two discuss the matter, Roeg constantly cuts to a street scene involving Moroccan merchants and a snake charmer. On the flight back, Milena plays with the rock which Netusil has found in her apartment. Some critics have even argued that the entire Moroccan scene is actually Netusil's fantasy, as Susan Barber suggests:

> In his fantasies about the couple, he seems to enjoy making Alex look foolish, as if it makes Netusil feel superior. This tendency is most powerfully demonstrated in the Morocco fantasy, which can be interpreted as generating from Netusil's point of view. The sequence begins in Milena's apartment as the inspector is looking through her things; he pours sand from a rock into his hand, which dissolves into a shot of Alex walking on a sand dune in Morocco. Further evidence that this is Netusil's fantasy is the fact that the room in the hotel where Alex and Milena stay is strikingly similar to her apartment, only the decor is different.[4]

Milena has come across the file on Stefan, as well as the instruction book from the parlor game she and Alex had earlier played. Again, we never learn the meaning of the game, but Roeg focuses on a sentence on the back of the book: "It is not a parlour game, and most emphatically it is not a weapon to be used in a general context of one-upmanship." Milena leaves, tossing her keys to the apartment onto the desk beside the book and file. Alex's attempts to call her are unsuccessful, and he is forced to contact Stefan. Alex seems helpless as Stefan grows hostile, bitterly telling him that he hopes Alex finds Milena, so that she will grow bored with him.

Netusil begins questioning Alex about Stefan, continually referring to

Milena as Mrs. Vognic, to emphasize the adulterous nature of Alex's relationship with her, which Alex continues to deny. When Alex next sees Milena, it is, as usual, through a window. Alex is in a diner when Milena taps on the window to catch the attention of a university student sitting nearby. Alex catches up to Milena as she is talking to the student, his jealousy and his desire for her in conflict. When the student leaves, Alex talks to Milena, but both prove unable to communicate what they feel. To heighten our sense of their anxiety, Roeg uses voice-overs, so that we can hear their thoughts. As usual, however, the tranquility is broken by Alex's suspicions. When he confronts Milena about the photo he has found earlier, she tells him it was of her brother. Alex does not believe her and tells her she will never change. "If you weren't who you were, I wouldn't have to change," she tells him.

Milena runs off, while the student, who has returned, stares blankly at Alex. Then he too runs off, leaving Alex alone with his books, the cold academician who seems somehow impotent. Realizing what he has done, Alex goes to Milena's apartment, hoping to find her, and instead must wait all night for her to return, only to discover she is still angry and now drunk. He tells her that he cannot bear to think of her with anyone else, something which has already been made obvious. Milena seems unsettled: she still loves Alex, but is unable to see what can make the relationship work. In this scene she lets loose all the bitterness she feels towards Alex because of the way he treats her: "What do you want me to do? What do you want me to say? Do you want me to kill myself? Would you know then?" The outburst anticipates Milena's later actions.

Milena tries to break away, but Alex continues to press her, with the close proximity of the stairs adding to the sense of their being entrapped and serving as a reminder of the earlier rape. Often their faces are hidden in shadows, so that we are forced to concentrate on what they say. In frustration she tells him that she did sleep with the student, and he reacts with violence, slapping her across the face. To emphasize the violence, Roeg freezes on Milena's shocked reaction before quickly cutting away. This technique returns to the experiments Roeg had conducted with freeze-frames in *Walkabout*.

Netusil questions Alex about Milena's drug dependency, then brings up a police report concerning a complaint filed against Milena for being drunk and disorderly. The "subject" of the outburst had been Alex and Netusil demands to know the reason: "How, Dr. Linden, do you account for a young girl getting into a state of drugs, depression?"

Alex is in the middle of having sex with another woman, when Milena calls. Just as he will later deny his relationship with Milena, here he denies the existence of the woman, although Milena can plainly hear her. The Moroccan music again plays as the two again argue over the file he has kept on her. If his actions seem repentant, he remains callous to those around him, not even caring that his present companion is forced to listen to his pleas. Milena hangs up on Alex and his response is telling: "I hate to be hung up on." Alex needs to be in control, to dominate, and his inability to dominate Milena is part of what attracts her to him.

The relationship between Alex and Milena has taken on a masochistic nature. Although it has dragged on long past any hope of reconciliation, they are still inexplicably drawn to one another. Worried that Milena may try to kill herself, Alex goes to her apartment, only to have her jump out at him dressed in an outlandish costume. Wearing a wig, white makeup, and a strange outfit, Milena is celebrating the death of the Milena whom Alex cannot love, while she is instead becoming the Milena she thinks he wants, one who is willing to have herself chained up. She looks hideous, pitiful, as if this is her death mask. Disgusted, Alex starts to leave, while Milena grows violent, first shouting at him from the stairs, then from the window. When this fails to have any effect, she resorts to throwing bottles. Still trying to remain in control, Alex walks about with his hands in his pockets gingerly dodging the glass missiles.

Alex still cannot break away from Milena, even though love is no longer his motive. At times it seems as if he is trying to see how far he can push her, gauging her reaction. He silently watches her from across the street while "Who Are You" is heard on the sound track again. This time Roger Daltry's vocals serve to echo Alex's thoughts. As is so often the case, Alex looks at Milena through a window as if she were under a microscope.

When Netusil returns to the question of the time Milena called, the events of the previous night begin to unfold. After taking a handful of pills, Milena calls Alex to say good-bye. Her words are slurred and the conversation appears brief. Once she hangs up, however, Alex plays back the tape on his answering machine. We hear Milena's final words, but instead of ending Milena continues on. She tells him she has done something stupid (just as she had prefaced her other phone call). If the opening sequence of the film is accurate, then Alex has no reason to believe she has attempted suicide. This would account for his first going to a nightclub and then waiting outside of her apartment, listening to the radio. If the later version is true, then the earlier scene may have been Alex's attempt to block out the truth.

Alex and Netusil begin to recreate the night in question, but no mention is made of Alex's going to the nightclub. He tries to evade questions about which radio station he had on (the station his car radio was tuned to went off the air at midnight) and finally explodes over Netusil's continued use of the phrase "Mrs. Vognic." Upstairs in Milena's apartment, Netusil tells Alex that Milena was in an advances stage of coma when she arrived at the hospital, so it would have been impossible for her to have called Alex after 1:00 A.M. Indeed, Alex finds Milena slumped in a corner, the pills already haven taken effect. Instead of helping her, Alex can only ridicule her, and Milena realizes she has gone too far in her efforts. Unable to lift herself, she can only crawl over to the phone, but aware of how powerless she is, Alex unplugs it, cutting her off completely from the outside world. It has come down to the two of them, with Alex finally having dominion over her. "We don't need anyone else. Just you and me," he says. As she slumps deeper into a coma, Alex lifts her up and places her on the bed.

What the viewer can see, Netusil can only hypothesize about, and his questions now sound desperate: "Detection. What is it if not a process of elimination. Why I chose this profession. A puzzle. Certainly the law doesn't interest me." His name itself foretells his failure. It is a Czechoslovakian name which means "man who does not know something." Netusil seems to drift off as he runs things through his mind, admitting that what he needs is a confession from Alex. He agrees that attempting suicide is not a punishable offense, but ravishment is. Alex carefully positions Milena on the bed, as if he were arranging an effigy. In the background the Moroccan music plays.

Unsure of what he wants, Alex walks about the room examining the objects and photos which make up her life. There is a quick shot of him naked, as if he were already contemplating the act of rape. The Moroccan music gradually grows louder, until Alex finally takes the needle off the record. He quietly tells Milena to wake up, but there is no response. He has been playing with a knife (the one he had when they met), and he now uses it to cut her undergarments. The cutting sound has been amplified and seems to momentarily awaken Milena. Her eyes are open, but she can only stare vacantly at Alex as he caresses her body. As Alex cuts her underpants, there is a quick switch to Netusil violently pulling back a blanket from the bed. To emphasize the suddenness of the act, there is a loud scream on the sound track.

By now Netusil's questions begin to take on a sexual nature, as if Alex had lived out one of Netusil's fantasies. He demands to know the answer, saying no one is around. When he asks Alex to explain to him about ravishment, it appears that the subject titillates him. He will continually repeat the word as if he were contemplating the act: "Ravishment. It has to do with, well, in a sense, in a sense, you take advantage of someone's love. You disguise your feelings of hatred." When Alex says, "Somehow, I have the feeling we're talking about you," Netusil replies, "We're not that unalike."

Netusil begins to talk of superior people and lower species who spread diseases as if he is carrying on the Nazi principle of a greater race. These ideals also seem in keeping with Alex's superior attitude. Alex's rape of

Milena is a rape without violence, but one which is abhorrent nonetheless. He is almost tender as he desecrates her, repeating that he loves her. Following the act, Alex once again takes on the persona of a professional, carefully dressing Milena and straightening the room. He examines Milena's pupils, puts fire to her feet, and checks her pulse to determine the state of her coma. Finally, after having spent an hour and a half in her apartment, Alex calls for the ambulance and the story comes full circle.

The viewer has seen a possible solution, but for Netusil there is no such solace. His failure to learn the truth is symptomatic of his career. He admits he is a poor detective and holds Alex's arm as if they have developed a bond, pleading, "Confess. Please, Dr. Linden. As a personal favor." Netusil insists a confession could help, but Alex wonders whom it would help. Netusil crouches beside him like a confessor, but the moment is broken by the appearance of Stefan, who tells them that Milena will survive. Netusil reacts like someone caught in an obscene act: he quickly stands up and nervously paces about the room, saying, "Thankful news. Even if for me it's arrived a little bit too early."

Netusil and his assistant leave, presumably to question Milena. Alex may be free from Netusil's condemnation, but Stefan remains angry, saying: "What did you get from her, Dr. Linden? Not enough, I would think. You must understand, you see, it's not enough to love a woman when she is difficult. You must love her tremendously. More even than one's own dignity. Don't you agree?" Alex looks back at him, but Stefan suddenly fades from the room as if he had been a mirage. Has this too been an illusion?

Disheartened, Alex returns home, having neither proven his case nor even learned if his theory was correct. What follows is either once again his imagination or simply events from the future. Alex is shown getting into a cab from which a woman has just departed. As the cab begins to pull away, Alex realizes the woman is Milena, her hair now short and blond and a scar visible on her neck from the surgery. Milena turns to glare at Alex, as he vainly shouts her name. In the middle of this scene, there is a quick shot of Netusil standing in front of his bathroom mirror banging his fists. Has this been a figment of his desire to see Milena finally free of Alex, or is it simply a coincidence that the two should run into one another in a city the size of New York? The film ends with Billie Holiday singing, "it's the same old story only new to me."

Bad Timing is a film which seemed to have an unusual effect on the participants. Tragically, it paralleled the events in Garfunkel's own life. During filming he would receive a call that his girlfriend had killed herself, and like Alex, Garfunkel would be questioned by the police concerning his relationship with her. Even during the filming, Roeg seemed to realize the film had a power of its own:

More than anything else I've done I let this film happen to me. It was like some bolting horse and I was trying to stay on it. It had a momentum all of its own. When that happens you can sense it if you are lucky, then if you can hold on to your nerve you can let it go. You are always in danger with interfering with it, yet, if you do, it's all over. Letting it happen is quite frightening and it doesn't necessarily mean it's going to be any good in the end.[5]

As usual, the critical response to Roeg's film was sharply divided. It won the top prize at the Toronto Film Festival, but David Ansen called it "an oppressively bad movie." But even while criticizing the movie, Ansen could not help but praise Roeg's technique: "Top-heavy with technique, overstuffed with cultural allusions, desperate to impress the audience with its multi-layered significance, *Bad Timing* is an oppressively bad movie although it is clearly the folly of a talented man."[6] The problem in evaluating *Bad Timing* is similar to the one which confronted critics with *Performance*. The subject matter is so distasteful that it can cloud our judgment of the final product. Feminist critics, in particular, were disturbed not just by the rape, but also by the manner in which it was presented. Susan Barber describes her objections to *Bad Timing*:

What is most frightening about the film is that its camerawork, associative editing and narrative structure relentlessly reinforce and participate in this sensual obsession with Milena from the opening images (as Alex hovers over her) to the closing moments of the film (silent confrontation with and farewell to Alex), compelling us in the audience to identify with this assault on the female victim. On the one hand, this strategy leads to the fast-paced, visually dazzling cinema full of intensity and excitement. Yet it also makes some of us very uncomfortable to be drawn into a complicity with these male predators.[7]

John Pyn's analysis in *Sight and Sound* offers a contrasting opinion:

He debates with himself what to do. She has led him such a dance that perhaps it would be kinder to let her die. In the end he cuts off her undergarments with the pocket knife with which he was nervously toying at the party when she had first propositioned him, lifts her carefully to the bed, contemplates the "lineaments" of her body, hesitates and then, in what may be interpreted as a definitive act of rejection, rapes her.[8]

The complaints against the film's content are similar to those made against *Psycho, Peeping Tom*, and many other thrillers, but for Roeg the focus of the film is not the rape. It is the events leading up to it (if it even occurred) and those that follow it. Is the rape really that much uglier, he would seem to ask, than the other ways in which Alex maltreats Milena? In fact, the entire film seems to be a condemnation of men. Both Stefan and Alex attempt to constrain Milena, while for Netusil she is something out of his fantasies. Other women portrayed are either sexual partners or sexual objects (the strippers). Roeg seems to be saying that men can only relate to woman through sex. Roeg has drawn us in, but we do not emerge unscathed.

What Roeg has done is to create a mystery which has no real solution. It is like the story of the tiger and the lady, except we are left wondering not which door to choose, but whose interpretation we are to believe. Alex never denies he has raped Milena, but there is nothing to prove he did. Where other mysteries often lose their impact once we are presented with a solution, *Bad Timing* only gains impact with each viewing. Words and gestures take on new meanings, as do entire scenes. The film may not be Roeg's masterpiece, but it is the closest approximation to his long-stated desires. It also foreshadows the film Roeg believed would indeed be his masterpiece, but instead would be his greatest failure, *Eureka*.

Notes

1. *Film Criticism*, Fall 1981, p. 46.
2. *American Film*, January 1980, p. 22.
3. Ibid., p. 25.
4. *Film Quarterly*, Fall 1981, p. 48.
5. *The Times*, April 10, 1980, p. 9.
6. *Newsweek*, October 6, 1980, p. 72.
7. *Film Quarterly*, Fall 1981, p. 46.
8. *Sight and Sound*, Spring 1980, p. 112.

SIX

Eureka

I wanted the gold, and I sought it;
I scrambled and mucked like a slave.
Was it famine or scurvy—I fought it;
I hurled my youth into a grave,
I wanted the gold, and I got it—
Came out with a fortune last fall,—
Yet somehow life's not what I thought it,
And somehow the gold isn't all.
                    —Robert W. Service, "The Spell of the Yukon"

When Roeg sat down to read James Leasor's book *Who Killed Sir Harry Oakes,* it was not with the intention of turning it into a film. With *Bad Timing* completed, he was simply reading up on one of England's most famous murder cases. Oakes was something of a legend even before his ghastly murder in 1943. He was a self-made millionaire who found one of the largest gold strikes of all time, after having spent 14 years looking for it. He was friends with the former Duke of Windsor and had ties to Jewish gangster Meyer Lansky, and even during World War II his murder was news. For Roeg, it was not the murder or even the discovery of gold which attracted him to the story, but the fact that Oakes had been a man who had reached his quest and then lived out the rest of his life without a purpose in mind.

> Something touched a chord. I found that the incident and the position of the character reflected some kind of truth in my head. I would hope that anyone who sees the film would feel something of Jack McCann's predicament. It's about a man who experiences the ecstasy of finding what he is searching for. But ecstasy is a dangerous emotion to reach. Where do you go after that? What can you reach for after ecstasy? In a way his story is over, but his life is not. He has to live on to wonder what his life means.[1]

Approached by MGM executive David Begelman about possible film projects, Roeg suggested the Oakes story. For two years Roeg and Paul Mayersburg worked on a script that ran up to 1800 pages at one point. In the beginning they had intended to keep the original names, but legal reasons prevented this. Time restraints also meant the deletion of much material, including that dealing with the character based on the Duke of Windsor. The working title for the project was *Murder Mystery,* a title which encapsulated the first word spoken in the film and the mystery surrounding the protagonist. This title seemed somewhat misleading, however, because it hinted at a typical mystery plot, something the film most definitely did not have. A more appropriate title was *Eureka,* taken from Edgar Allan Poe's essay on the mysteries of the universe. It was Poe's final work, and his words often seem a portent of Roeg's style in this film:

> I cannot accomplish my purpose without first counting and weighing all the atoms in the Universe, and defining the precise positions of all at one particular moment. If I venture to displace, by even the billionth part of an inch, the microscopical speck of dust which lies now on the point of my finger, what is the character of that act upon which I have adventured? I have done a deed which shakes the Sun to be no longer the Sun, and which alters forever the destiny of the multitudinous myriads of stars that roll and glow in the majestic presence of the creator.[2]

The actions of the protagonist will seem to alter not just his life, but also the ground from which he takes the gold. The discovery of the gold is the culmination of his life, but Roeg will take the story in directions that return to many of the themes of *Performance.* When he was discussing the work with Mayersburg, Roeg's attention was focused on a single scene, one that ironically would be cut from the film. Mayersburg relates their conversation:

> When Nic first proposed this story to me, he had one image in mind. Just one. And that was a scene where Jack McCann and his daughter are sitting in a car, many years after the gold strike. He had been showing her where it all happened. As the car drives off, he looks out of the window and sees the icy peaks of his earlier days. When she looks out of her window, she sees a shining blue sea, the Caribbean, which is where they live now. That image was the origin of the film. One looks back, the other looks forward. They are both in the same place at the same time.[3]

Despite the film's potential commercial risk, Roeg was given a budget of $11,000,000 and a cast that included Gene Hackman, Mickey Rourke, and Rutger Hauer. Russell was also on hand, her importance to Roeg's career already evident. Filming took five months and moved from the Canadian Rockies (where temperatures reached forty degrees below zero) to Jamaica (where the temperatures were much higher). Despite the technical challenges presented, the filming was relatively problem free. Expectations for the film were strong, particularly for Roeg, who believed it would be his masterpiece. Instead, events behind the scenes would again delay its release in America.

In the first image of the film, gold nuggets float in space like an alchemist's dream. Throughout the film there is the sense of an omniscient being looking down on events, often in the form of the moon, as in a shot of the earth bathed in the moon's shadow. The camera hurtles across a white landscape, creating a feeling of isolation. Later Jack McCann will talk of the abyss, of nothingness, and this is its visual equivalent. Periodically Roeg cuts to gold flowing like a river, as if it lurks beneath the surface. With the credits over, the camera moves down toward two men locked in a struggle, their belongings lying discarded in the snow. A woman tries to pull them apart, and as Jack McCann lifts a pick axe to strike the other man, the first word of the film is heard, "murder." The fight concerns Jack's unwillingness to have a partner because he has "never earned a nickel from another man's sweat." He forces the man to shout "that Jack McCann will find the gold so loud that the gods will hear," while the camera tracks toward the moon. Thus even before the gold has been found, it is the source of conflict.

McCann has made his way into a mining town but it is as deserted as the frontier. A house has been boarded shut with the words "No Trespassing" scrawled on the wood, foreshadowing McCann's sign at Eureka, and the few occupants seem on the verge of departure. Outside a claims office Jack comes across a man lying in the doorway. With a dazed look, the man stares silently at McCann, who asks him what he is smiling at. He repeats the question, but the man only looks down at his bare feet before pulling a gun from his shirt. As he puts it to his mouth, he finally speaks, saying, "The end." McCann can only stare at the man and whisper "it's not over till it's over," as the man pulls the trigger. The back of his head blows open, and Roeg cuts to sparks flying in the air, an image which will be repeated at Jack's death. McCann runs away, as if he considers the man's suicide to be a premonition of his own fate. He remembers the sight of the explosion and falls to the ground, the shot ringing out once again.

Jack cannot go on indefinitely, and he ends up lying frozen underneath a tree, only his eyes and breath revealing signs of life. The camera looks down on him, just as it had in the previous scenes, while his prone position resembles that of the miner. Three wolves circle Jack, waiting for him to die, three wolves who will later take on human form. As if resigned to his fate, Jack makes no effort to defend himself, but only looks up at the gnarled tree above him. Like the characters in Roeg's previous films, Jack is saved only through others. An explosion takes place at his feet which provides both warmth and protection from the wolves. From the moon a rock hurtles down toward Jack, and Roeg cuts to Frieda looking through a glass ball as if she were watching him. A fire burns inside the glass ball and Jack's hand falls to the side, holding the rock tightly. Inside Frieda's glass ball the figure of a miner appears, and she sets it down, smiling to herself. With Jack's acceptance of the rock, his life takes on a preordained course.

With renewed strength Jack begins again, while Frieda waits for him at the front window of her whorehouse. She is photographed through a curtain, a shot that will be repeated later with Jack's daughter. (This scene is also an indirect homage to *Dr. Zhivago*, whose opening sequence it stylistically resembles. Roeg had initially been director of photography for this film, but had been fired six weeks into production. Aesthetically, however, the opening of *Dr. Zhivago* presages *Eureka*, with its soft colors.) Jack arrives at the door just as Frieda opens it, so that he seems to fall in. Behind them the clock strikes midnight, and she shouts to the others that Jack has returned home. She stands over him as he lies on the couch, and he wonders if he's dead. His hand still clutches the philosopher's stone, and she is forced to pry his fingers loose to examine it. He tells her he found the rock, but she disputes this: "No, Johnny, this stone found you. It has your name on it. Not outside, but inside. It's your destiny. But everybody pays."

Thus Jack's fate will be tied to that of the stone, which he will retain even years later. If the stone acts as a metaphor for his soul, it is also an autobiographical touch by Roeg: "I wanted Jack to have something that I've got, that I've had since I was eighteen—it's unimportant why, I don't know why—it's just a metal washer. Whether it's a talisman or whatever, I feel less than that washer. And Jack finds himself with the rock—it's the only thing he's clinging to, linked in his mind to the philosopher stone or whatever—in similar circumstances to those in which I had my washer."[4]

Inside Frieda's crystal ball, the small figure is engulfed in fire, a scene that again announces Jack's fate. Having cleaned up, he sits alone in a bedroom mumbling that "gold smells stronger than a woman." Around the house, the women lie asleep with their customers, their energy spent. The house is quiet except for the sound of the clock as Jack and Frieda sit in the living room, a fire burning in front of them. As he holds onto his relic, she sits across from him remembering their past together: "We never did find the gold, but we did have something. Something between us that was better than gold. My Jack had all the nuggets we needed right between his legs. You interested in men and women? With you the gold is everything. You'll never give up." She remembers how they had loved one another before she woke one day to find him dead beside her. "It was when I started to smell bad," she says, echoing his earlier remarks as she splashes perfume across herself for effect.

"You'll find what you're looking for. But after?" Her question hangs in the air as she leans over and takes the talisman from him. Looking into it, Frieda can see the gold Jack is seeking: "It's right here. I can see it, the gold. It's run like a river to the shore of the lake. There it goes diving under the water." The camera has moved in on Jack as he takes in what she is saying. As she hands the stone back, she begins to cough, hinting at her own mortality. If the dialogue here is sometimes strident, it still manages to work, both through the acting and through the force of Roeg's direction. It is by now apparent that the film exists in its own plane, one of heightened melodrama. This atmosphere continues as Jack prepares to leave, with Frieda reminding him of what has occurred: "When you took the stone, you made your choice. You're alone now."

Jack walks off into the wilderness as the camera pulls back to show him dwarfed by the white landscape. In the background we hear the prelude from Wagner's *Das Rheingold,* an opera that represents another monumental quest. Jack trudges along in snow that reaches his knees, but he moves in a determined way, even trying to run at times. Climbing a hill, he begins to strike his pick into the surface, as Frieda staggers about her room coughing. The discovery of the gold is laden with images of death and sex. Losing his footing, Jack falls into a cavern whose very walls seem to sparkle. He moves purposely toward one wall, and as his axe strikes the rock, Frieda doubles up in pain. Later Jack's son-in-law will say he raped the earth to find the gold, and the imagery here confirms it. As gold begins to fall from the hole McCann has created, the earth seems to explode. An eruption sends rock up into the air, while water and gold rush out of the hole. Roeg photographs Jack face down, lost in the rush of the water, as if he has drowned. Thus when Jack emerges on the surface above the water, it is as if he has been reborn. His clothing covered in gold, he reaches back into the water to pull out a large gold nugget, the culmination of his search.

Jack's earlier words echo in the air ("I never earned a nickel from another man's sweat") as he stumbles about in joy. Jack looks around, but he is alone, with no one to share his ecstasy. The gold, however, comes at a price and returning to Frieda's whorehouse, he learns what it is. He finds the house empty except for Frieda, who lies dying on a couch. He tenderly touches her cheek, but he thinks of his needs, not hers, as he wonders about his future: "A mystery. The end, the beginning. There will be another after you. After the war." Behind her the fire seems to explode, sending sparks out. There is a quick cut to an older McCann brushing an ember off his lap. Twenty years after his discovery he is reliving the moment with a young woman. Behind him his limousine, a symbol of his success, is mired in the snow.

This flashback alerts us to what is to come, encapsulating not just the themes, but also all the characters. Each figure from this opening will return in an altered form in the rest of the film. As in *Don't Look Now*, the main character's fate is already determined, and the key images of the film have already been brought out: fire, the sparks from the miner's death, the glass ball, and, indirectly, the influence of the Cabala religion, which seems to infuse the film.

There is an ambiguity about the relationship between Jack and Tracy that will continue throughout the film. She is not immediately identified as his daughter, and their manner is like that of two lovers. When asking about the women in the Yukon, she wonders how he would have reacted to her. "My darling Tracy. I would never have taken my eyes off you," he says. She wants him to continue with his stories, but he grows curious about a flask she has taken out, wondering who gave it to her. "You think I'm jealous. I'm not jealous. I just know he'll never appreciate you," he says. She is not persuaded and argues that she is not a work of art, unconsciously verbalizing the central difference between the two of them. He brushes her cheek in a manner that is reminiscent of his gesture toward Frieda, while she thanks him for taking her to Paris, indicating he unwittingly led her to her husband, Claude. The past and present are contrasted as the young Jack walks through the snow while the limousine manages to make its way again.

The wealth Jack has made from the Yukon has allowed him to purchase his own island in the Caribbean, where he has built his home, Eureka. From his estate he looks out on Tracy, who cavorts with her husband, Claude Maillot Van Horn, on his yacht, the *Pandora*. Both names create immediate images; *Eureka* is an exclamation of discovery, while *Pandora* foretells a discovery leading to calamity. That Jack considers himself lord of his domain is brought out not just by his appearance (he wears a long white robe), but by his manner. He condemns his wife, Helen, for her drinking and dismisses the attempt of his friend Charlie Perkins to form a partnership. Perkins physically resembles the man Jack had fought with in the Yukon, while Helen's belief in the occult ties her to Frieda. She is laying out tarot cards, and as Jack passes by, she hands him the hang man card, which he will carry throughout the scene. Of the many cross-references spread throughout the film, this is one of the most important.

Many of Roeg's films contain an element which points to an understanding of the film; in *Performance* it is the works of Borges, in *Walkabout* it is the radio the children carry, and in *The Man Who Fell to Earth* it is the television Newton watches. Here the Cabala religion infuses the film, in small details which gradually accumulate. The hang man card is open to a variety of interpretations, many of which predict what is to happen. It foretells a choice that will end in parting (Jack choosing the gold over Frieda), the failure of a test (Claude losing Tracy), and ultimately a crisis

(Jack's death). The most important interpretation, however, is that the death it predicts will result in a rebirth. It also foreshadows the psychic communication between Tracy and Jack. There is a danger in attributing too much to an element lost on most viewers, but to understand *Eureka,* all pieces of the puzzle must be examined. In fact, the tarot card points to a larger influence on the film, the Cabala religion. The tarot cards Helen looks at, the shirt Claude will later wear, and the influence of the moon on many scenes are all taken directly from this religion. Even the dialogue alludes to the religion ("the abyss of nothingness"). Thus the actions of the characters seem more the work of a higher being than simple acts of happenstance.

The conflict between Jack and Claude is already evident. Jack believes Claude married Tracy because of his wealth, while Claude openly boasts to Tracy that he will triumph: "I'll always win. I won you, didn't I?" Claude is obviously Jack's rival, but if we assume that Tracy is the source of their conflict, this assumption will soon prove to be false. A French emigré count, Claude is Roeg's stranger in a strange land, an outsider who only relates to Tracy and to the black natives of the island. The war Frieda predicted is not just between Claude and Jack, however, but also between Jack and Mayakofsky, a gangster who wants to build a casino on the island. Despite his profession, Mayakofsky is tied to traditional American values — family, religion, the flag, and a capitalistic philosophy. He is first presented praying in a mosque in Miami before returning home to meet with his attorney, Aureilio D'Amato, to discuss the "war."

The Second World War serves as the backdrop for Mayakofsky's own private war against McCann. One of his men is a soldier on leave, and the radio constantly reports on the war in Europe. Roeg had intended to include more evidence of the war, including scenes on a battleship and a friendship between Jack and an admiral, but budgetary constraints prevented this. The smaller war is not just about control of an island, but also about Jack's determination to remain independent. Mayakofsky believes the way to get through to Jack is to find out his desires: "A man is made up of desires. Understand his desires you understand the man." Jack had desired the gold, but once he found it, what was left? "Who is he now? What does he desire?" wonders Mayakofsky.

What Jack desires is not just the gold, or even his island, but his daughter's affection. He invites Claude to Eureka, ostensibly to offer him financial assistance, but it is more likely that he wants to learn Claude's intentions. As Jack greets him, Claude is running the talisman along his forehead, perhaps aware of its significance. Jack calls it a relic from the past, like himself. His next words are eerily prophetic of the manner of his death, even to the mention of the book: "I'm an open book, cut me and I bleed." Claude turns down any offers of help, admitting that it is "often harder to receive than it is to give." As Helen walks up to the two men, she asks about her misplaced glasses and Claude produces them from his pocket. This small detail, along with others, will cloud our minds concerning Claude, making us wonder about his true motives. As this meeting ends, another is taking place thousands of miles away, a meeting that also has an element of distrust. Charlie Perkins has met with Mayakofsky to discuss the Luna Bay deal, but he is obviously apprehensive and even calls the deal un–American. Mayakofsky dismisses this comment, saying: "Everybody's an American now. The Germans, they're Americans. In Chicago there's many Germans. The Japanese, believe me, one day they'll be Americans also. Languages, that's all the difference. This war, what is it? It's a war between Americans who all speak different languages. So how can we lose? Mr. McCann is an American. He knows we're all on the same side."

Eureka physically resembles Kane's Xanadu and as in the film bearing that name, there is a distinct Gothic influence in its presentation. In the guest bedroom, Claude is warning Tracy that Jack will become sick (using a chart based on the Cabala religion), but she dismisses his prophecy, just as Jack shuns Helen's beliefs. She is preparing for the evening, but it is his opinion that determines her appearance. She crawls onto the bed beside him, saying "[You] can do what you like to my body, I don't care. For God's sake leave my mind alone. Stick to my spirit." The two begin to make love, and the camera moves in toward the moon, which is still an omniscient presence. Downstairs, Jack walks up to the talisman, while Charlie watches from the shadows. As Jack touches the relic, he pulls back as if burnt by it, while upstairs Tracy screams in the midst of lovemaking. Jack senses that something is wrong, but discovers nothing when he looks around. Going up to the talisman, Charlie cautiously touches it, but finds it cold; only for Jack does it contain any power.

The bond between father and daughter is brought out further in a dinner party held at Eureka, as both demonstrate an ability to work out complex mathematical equations in their head. With the exception of Mayakofsky (who will never meet Jack), the scene unites all of the major characters, including Charlie and D'Amato. The sequence is filled with portents of the future: the references to *Alice in Wonderland* ("Tracy in wonderland"), D'Amato's flirting with Tracy despite Claude's presence, and Jack's dismissing his wife's fear of bad luck. ("I don't believe in luck. Good or bad. Everybody believes in a little bit of gold. Even if it's just a wedding band," Jack concludes, looking directly at Claude.) The discord between Claude and Jack is also brought out into the open, as each seems to ridicule the other. The conflict comes to a head when Jack passes around a plate of gold nuggets for the others to take, and Claude swallows one. Jack is furious, but Claude tells him that like all things it will come to pass, and then he will send it back. When Jack orders Claude to leave, Tracy must finally choose a side, and she clings to Claude as she says to her father: "I don't want your gold. I want to touch human flesh. I want to kiss it. Hold it." With Claude and Tracy gone, McCann returns to the table, but he is no longer in control. His emotions are barely held in check as he says, "I won't rest until I see that man dead." The scene ends as it had begun, with the talisman in the foreground.

Away from Eureka, Jack seems more composed, as he meets with Charlie in the forest. The stress is evident on Charlie, who admits he is afraid in his own home, but Jack is unsympathetic, saying, "You're frightened someone's trying to break into your house. I'm frightened someone's trying to break into my life." Jack walks out into the water and sits on a rock, once again united with the landscape. "First, I don't believe in chance" he says. "Second, I don't have partners. Not for some time." Jack dismisses Mayakofsky's threat, saying, "I'm the most dangerous man I know." Although Jack seems to realize Charlie is hiding something, he still offers to let him stay at Eureka. Their friendship, however, has become strained. Even Mayakofsky seems to realize this and says, "These men are without faith." D'Amato suggests that McCann believes in himself, but to Mayakofsky this is the same as believing in nothing: "He dug up his fortune. We can not allow him to stand in the way of new men who want to build their fortunes."

Roeg is most identified with his visual style, but in Eureka the dialogue is as important as the mis-en-scène. This is evident in the next scene, which is filmed in one long take from medium range, a technique Roeg will later employ in *Insignificance* and *Sweet Bird of Youth*. Jack has allowed Helen to spend the night with him, which indicates just how distant their relationship has become. There is a sense of melancholy as he admits that he is "under siege by everybody and everything." Jack believes this is because he represents the man "who knew what he wanted and went out and got it." More than any other Roeg film, *Eureka* contains numerous monologues, which create visual images of their own. In one important monologue Jack sums up his life:

> Nobody can help me. Know what eternity looks like. It's white and yet very dark. It's like a desert of snow at night. Now I've reached the edge of eternity and beyond eternity. The abyss, nothing. Once upon a time I was Jack McCann, I had a name. I don't know how much longer I can hold on. I'm in the middle of my second world war. I still can't hear. What you said to me the other day about my not being able to see. You were so damn right. I can't see. I can't hear. I'm paralyzed. Once I had it all. Now I just have everything.

Claude's sense of isolation and his potential for violence are brought out at a dinner party Tracy is hosting. He sits in another room reading, while Tracy (dressed as a geisha, a visual reminder of Mayakofsky's speech that everyone is an American) moves among Navy men and their wives. Claude is brought a letter, and after silently reading it, he asks the others to leave. When they protest, he turns violent, even striking out at Tracy before pulling her close to him. After the guests have gone, Claude confesses to her that his mother has died in Paris (he had left her behind when he fled the Germans). "She knew I wanted to be free," he explains. As they hold one another, he promises never to leave her, but Tracy already senses that their relationship is a troubled one and says: "Sometimes I wonder whether I'm ready for you. It's too much of you and not enough of me. Do you understand? It's very simple. It makes me afraid for us." The background, a white sofa speckled with red, anticipates the white pillows that will be splattered with Jack's blood when he is murdered.

With Claude asleep beside her, Tracy writes to her parents. She admits to them that Claude "is not of our blood, but he has become the center of my life. My blood is his blood and his is mine." As she begins to kiss him tenderly, Roeg cuts to Helen reading the letter to Jack as they move out onto the patio. Tracy writes that all of their lives have become empty and she has found what she desires (her relationship with Claude is thus tied to Jack's discovery of the gold). Still loving them, she loves Claude even more than herself. "I would not exist without him," she writes. As Helen reads the letter, she replaces the word *war* with *way*, an unconscious but significant attempt on her part to avoid the conflict. Helen is confused by the letter because she thought Tracy understood the situation. Jack, however, reassures her by saying, "She does understand and so do I." The two go to the bedroom, where they make love a last time, the camera moving in on the letter as Jack tells Helen to "remember always that I love you." Afterward, Helen leaves the island to visit the mainland, and Roeg cuts to the talisman, which emits a sigh as its light fades. Beside it the clock stops ticking, both actions seeming to seal Jack's fate.

In a restless mood, Jack reads over the letter once again, then sits outside Claude's house waiting for dawn to break. Inside, Claude and Tracy lie nude in one another's arms as Jack kicks in the door. While the couple struggle to cover themselves, Jack calls Tracy the "flesh of his flesh," as he tries to understand Claude's motives. "The truth is you want me. You want my soul," he asserts. He roughly takes hold of Tracy and holds her in front of a mirror, shouting that nothing is hers. The fight between the two men echoes the one which opened the film, as Tracy tries to separate them and is cut in the process. Wielding a meat axe, Jack chases Claude outside as Tracy screams "murder." Having cornered Claude, Jack confronts him about the letter because he believes he has forced Tracy to write it. Standing over Claude, Jack seems to slip in and out of the past as he remembers the earlier fight, even shouting that he "never earned a nickel from another man's sweat." Holding the axe in one hand and the necklace he gave Tracy in the other, he seems to realize what is happening and quietly asks her to return with him. She again tells him that she desires flesh, not gold, and then asks if he has ever really loved someone. Tracy begins to kiss Claude as a dazed Jack walks off, the necklace falling from his hands.

With Jack gone, Claude whispers that "the triangle is broken." The reference is not to him, Jack, and Tracy, but to Jack, Tracy, and the gold. The dialogue constantly contrasts flesh with gold, and Roeg expresses the concept visually. On his yacht, Claude lays a bundle on a table and opens the blanket to reveal a nude Tracy decorated in gold. She calls him her Abel, and he refers to her as Cleopatra. After making love, the two go on deck, and Tracy confesses that the last day and night have been unlike anything she has ever experienced before, bringing both pain and happiness. She asks if Claude wants to kill her father, but he reminds her that it is Jack who threatened him. Picking up a spear gun, he acknowledges that "from now on it's war." The initiation of the war results in a separation of the lovers, with Tracy leaving to join her mother in Rhode Island. Both men are alone, even as Mayakofsky's men begin to move in on the island. While the gangster is paying off his men, the radio is broadcasting about Iwo Jima, another island under siege.

The emotions the characters feel are expressed not just through their words, but through the forces of nature. A storm begins as Jack goes off in search of Claude, even as he ignores Perkins's warning that Mayakofsky's men are coming. The montage that follows takes on the feel of a nightmare, with both the storm and a voodoo ceremony that Claude attends adding to the atmosphere. Some critics would condemn this scene as visually extravagant and inconsequential to the film, but it is both factual (Haitian witch doctors do act as advisors) and thematically critical to the story. The ceremony reintroduces the images of death and the occult which open the film. A woman seemingly bathed in blood, the snake which so often represents evil, the images of fire, and a beheaded chicken all act as footnotes to Jack's murder. The sequence also condemns Claude morally (he goes there with two married women and seems oblivious to their resulting plight). Claude moves easily among the participants, beginning an erotic dance with the male witch doctor which leaves both men spent and Claude hallucinating that Tracy is among the women in an orgy.

Jack's search for Claude at his house and through the town proves futile. Standing in an empty bar, he is reminded of his past. As he looks into a mirror, he remembers dancing with Frieda, an image that also occurred when he discovered the gold. In calling her name, he demonstrates his inability to function without Frieda's guidance. Outside, Jack begins to drive off on his motorcycle, only to be struck by a car racing up the street, which sends Jack and his gun sprawling. A concerned Charlie gets out, again arguing that Jack has to meet with Mayakofsky's men. Once again Charlie's alliance seems somewhere in the middle. He seems to have hit Jack with his car intentionally, but his concern seems genuine. Jack surprises him by saying he is ready to meet with Mayakofsky. Getting into Perkins's car, Jack remarks that the interior smells of perfume, and he recalls that "gold smells stronger than a woman." At Eureka, the talisman begins to crack as Jack tells Charlie that he has been "waiting for this a long time."

Arriving at the wharf where Mayakofsky's boat has docked, Jack continues to demonstrate he has no fear of death. He ridicules the men for their greed and shows no fear as the three killers attempt to intimidate him. "You know the problem with murder, it never lets go of you," he tells them. Claude arrives at the wharf, as if he were united to D'Amato and the three killers. He keeps to the shadows, while Jack tells the men that they can't touch him: "There is no last will and testament for Jack McCann. Where I come from you don't own a thing. The most you can do is stake your claim." Noticing Claude standing off to the side, Jack tells him that he was looking for him, but that it doesn't matter anymore. All that does matter is the end to his own story, a story which began with his discovery of the gold.

The storm has turned explosive, mirroring the violence that is about to take place. Entering the gates of Eureka, Jack is struck in the head by a rock and shouts back, "you can do better than that, partners." The first man enters through the window, carrying with him a blow torch which ignites not just the curtains, but his own clothing. As this man is letting D'Amato and his two companions in, Charlie arrives outside, soon to be followed by Claude. Claude's intentions seem particularly sinister, for he carries with him a club. As one of the men puts on a record, Jack shouts from above, "It's not over till it's over," throwing down first the deeds to the land, then gold dust. In his taunting of the men, Jack seems to be inviting his own death. Fire is a central image of the murder, beginning with the first killer's entrance and continuing as the same man runs the torch along the railing as he goes up the stairs.

Jack escapes to the bedroom, while the three killers move in and out of the other rooms looking for him, the only light coming from the storm outside and the torches they carry. Cornered in his bedroom, Jack strikes out at his attacker, but his clothes are set afire and he writhes about in pain. The fire motif continues as downstairs D'Amato pulls down the still burning curtains. The nightmarish quality of the sequence recalls *The Masque of the Red Death*, a film for which Roeg first received attention as a cinematographer. Another recurring motif is the chain, which Claude is picking up as Jack is first struck. This chain plays an important role in the murder, seeming to symbolize the passing of Jack's soul to Claude. The chain had first appeared in a scene in which Tracy had asked Claude if their relationship was incomplete. The chain had dropped to the floor, signifying it indeed was. Later Jack had found the chain in Claude's house and had thrown it around his neck, wearing it even as he met with the men at the wharf, only to discard it once he arrived at Eureka.

The murder is presented in graphic detail as Jack is carried unconscious to the bed and beaten, the blood splattering the pillow behind him. The murder, however, is filmed in such a way that the actions or even the placement of the characters are not immediately apparent. Claude, Charlie, and D'Amato all seem to be in the room where the murder is taking place, but none seems aware of the others' presence. Frieda's glass ball, through which she had watched over Jack, falls to the ground and shatters into pieces. One of the men picks up the figure from inside, another representation of Jack's death. Still Jack clings to life, even as the torch is run along his body. Looking out of the frame, Jack whispers that he "knew it would be you," but the subject of his words is not identified. Like John Baxter's death, Jack's is preceded by various images of his life, in particular the time he nearly died in the Yukon as the wolves circled him. One shot is particularly important: a woman looking through a curtain. Both Frieda and Tracy are photographed in this manner, and this image seems to combine both their likenesses.

It is not just Jack who is being eliminated; all reminders of his life are also being destroyed. The torch is run along the talisman, which, like Jack, seems impervious to the flame. Later the fire will strike a copy of *Alice in Wonderland,* a reference to Helen's earlier pun "Tracy in wonderland." The murder is obviously patterned after the suicide Jack had witnessed in the Yukon: the use of slow motion, Roeg cutting to the sparks flying in the air, and the feathers from the pillow falling through the air like snowflakes. The moment of the miner's death occurred as his head was blown off; Jack's occurs as his head is cut off. It is significant that the man who wields the axe which kills Jack is left unidentified, but it is Claude who first emerges from the room, feathers clinging to his clothes to implicate him in the crime.

The murder initiates Tracy's break with Claude. With the image of her father's decapitated body still fresh in her mind, Tracy visits Claude in prison a full week after his arrest. There is a distance between the two as she wonders what part he played in the murder. She tells him that she will do all she can for him, but her downturned eyes call her statement into question. It is only when he worries that he is alone in the world that she lets her guard down. She tells him that he still has her, and she embraces him, saying: "Claude, I saw him, it was horrible. I am a jinx." (She had earlier remarked that she brought her father bad luck.)

The murder trial is the centerpiece of the film; not only is Claude's guilt or innocence examined, but the legacy Jack leaves behind is also considered. Various individuals take the stand against Claude, but it is still

Jack who condemns him, because a large photograph of his body overlooks the proceedings. On the first day of the trial, Tracy sits next to D'Amato and that night the two end up in bed. The act is not just a way of getting back at Claude for his infidelities; it is also a means of saving him by making herself as morally suspect as he is and as morally corrupt as he is. But even as D'Amato dresses, Tracy is distressed by what she has done and pushes him away when he tries to kiss her. Alone, she begins to scream Claude's name. Helen testifies that Claude had a hold over Tracy, but Tracy's letter is read back to her. ("I will not tear myself apart because of your unrelenting hostility toward us. I don't want us to fight a war. I want us all to live together in peace. If that's not possible then I will find a place of peace in my heart for Claude.") Claude's lawyer characterizes the letter as a declaration of love, saying, "Aren't lovers necessarily under the spell of one another?"

Having learned of his wife's affair, Claude bars her from visiting him and fires his attorney. Now totally alone, he confronts Tracy in the only manner open to him, the courtroom. He questions her on her love for him, asking if he could have persuaded her to write the letter. She responds by talking of her father's love: "My father was a simple man. He loved me completely. I wanted to explain to him that my love for you is more important than anything." She grows impatient with his questions referring to violence, but he reminds her that he is on trial for his life, saying: "This isn't a time or place to be shy about violence. Please, Tracy, tell them who you think I am. When you look at me, what do you see?" When Tracy begins her speech, Claude seems genuinely surprised.

> I see a man unbuttoning a new frock for the first time and trying to get me tipsy, while staying sober himself. Because he's beginning to realize I can hold a hell of a lot of liquor. I see a man with other women. Secretive. Dissatisfied with me. Telling lies, small ones, but feeding me more than anything. I see a man who can't pass a mirror without looking into it. A man whose face hangs over mine at night, like a moon, a guide. I see a picture of love, only you can't put it into a picture. It's two people in league with each other, who want each other and are willing to kill or die for it.

While the two talk, Roeg photographs them in tight shots so that they are isolated. Behind Claude stands a guard, a reminder of what he is facing, while Tracy is dressed in black as if she were in mourning. She begins to describe their love, while the room gradually fades to black, with Claude and Tracy highlighted by a spotlight. For Roeg, the courtroom is an arena for Claude and Tracy:

> It's a dramatic setting for a confrontation between two characters. It's formalized. And when you see Claude cross-examining Tracy, it's he

who's being exposed. "I taught you everything you know," he says. And he still doesn't understand that he's talking to someone who has McCann's soul when he's talking to her, that they're the strong ones, she and McCann, the ones who understand, the ones with a capacity for life, knowledge, not him. She saves Claude's neck, but in doing so all things have to be said between them. And very few relationships can survive that moment of truth.[5]

Tracy understands what Jack's death meant and even argues that it occurred much earlier:

> I'm talking about what happened to Jack McCann on that day in the winter of 1925 when he found the gold. He'd been looking for fifteen years. Day after day. Week after week. Year after year. Then one day he found it. How could he ever recapture that moment of triumph? He couldn't share the gold. That was his and his alone. How he realized that his joy at having done what he'd set out to do all alone was gone. Poor Jack. He was like a man struck by lightning. One moment of rapture followed by decades of despair. Jack McCann wasn't murdered three weeks ago in his bedroom at Eureka. He died in 1925. What happened that night was just his physical end. He needed someone to finish him off and that night he found him, just as he had found the gold.

This monologue seems to encapsulate the entire film, returning to the images of death and fire (the lightning) that dominate the film and to the isolation Jack felt after discovering the gold. Tracy's assessment of her father's death, that he willed it, is in keeping with how screenwriter Mayersburg has characterized the murder: "The clues to who murdered this man lie in the man himself, rather than in the people around him at the time of his death. In a way they represent his state of mind. The point is that Jack McCann carries his own story with him. It is as if he is set on a course which he only recognizes bit by bit."[6]

The parallels between Jack's life and Claude's continue as Tracy talks of having picked Claude up after he had stumbled, just as Frieda had done for Jack. Both men were driven by desires, but Tracy argues that Claude is still searching: "You don't know who you were when you married me. You don't know who I am. You were born under the sign of innocence." She tells him that he is despised for having married her, that she is despised for being Jack's daughter, and that Jack is still hated for having "found what they're all still looking for. I found you, but you still haven't found what you're looking for." The confessions continue even as Claude tries to stop her. She shouts that on the first night they made love he told her he had reached the limit of his passion. This aligns him with Jack, who reached the limit of his passion on finding the gold.

Roeg was particularly interested in the way Tracy resembled her father:

> One reason that the film isn't a murder thriller is that McCann doesn't die. That's to say, what he is, what he represents is absolutely continued in Tracy. There are children—I've seen it in friends of mine and their families—who are quite literally soul-clones of their parents, their father or mother. In surface things they can be quite different, but the essence is passed on.[7]

Like Jack's discovery of gold, Tracy's love for Claude is only an illusionary experience. Even before the trial has ended, Roeg informs us that the conflict is over. The war in Europe ends, and the celebrants spill into the courtroom, interrupting Tracy's testimony. Claude is found innocent, but the judge, believing him to be of a violent nature, orders him to be deported. The central question of who murdered Jack is thus left unanswered. Listening to a radio account of the dropping of the atomic bomb, Mayakofsky tells his daughter that "now there will have to be some changes." Claude and Tracy sit down to a meal she has cooked as Claude admits, "I suppose I can say I nearly died in the war." He expresses his gratitude for what she has said in the courtroom, saying, "It's more important to me than anything." With the war over, the two can go anywhere, and Claude wants to return to France. When he asks Tracy what she wants, she tells him she "wants to do unto others as they would do to me," a phrase that echoes her father. She seems genuinely happy as she announces they will have "a damn good time," but her words seem to have little meaning. Saying he is cold, Claude leaves the room to get something warm, but both seem to know his true intentions.

Standing in the hallway, dressed in clothes that make him resemble Jack, Claude has become him, even to the point of repeating his last words, "I knew it would be you." He leans his head against the mirror, just as Jack had done when remembering Frieda. Tracy may have inherited Jack's soul, but Claude has become his double. He walks outside, as Tracy looks from the window in an image that duplicates exactly an earlier shot of Frieda. That a transfer of souls has taken place is evident; it is Jack who narrates as Claude rows away, and the scene changes to one of Jack walking through the Yukon: "There's gold and its haunting and haunting. It's luring me on as of old. Yet it isn't the gold that I'm wanting as much as just finding the gold. It's the great, big, beautiful land way up yonder. It's the forest where silence has lease. It's the beauty that thrills me with wonder, it's the stillness that fills me with peace."

Eureka is Roeg's most audacious work, one in which everything is larger than life, including the themes. The visuals are stunning, but Roeg also demonstrates a new sensitivity, as in the scene where Jack and his wife escape to the bedroom. The film is flawed, however, particularly in the presentation of the story line. If the film involves the transfer of souls, who in fact is the beneficiary? Both Tracy and Claude seem to inherit Jack's traits and failings. Roeg's chief drawback may be his own talent. The opening is so visually stunning that everything that follows seems aesthetically anticlimatic, with the obvious exception of the murder. The critics would savage the film when it was released, as did the reviewer in *Variety*: "Even by his own standards, Nicolas Roeg's *Eureka* is an indulgent melodrama about the anti-climatic life of a greedy old prospector after he has struck it rich. Pic reeks of pretentious Art, not just visually but also in a strained, confusing and overstretched plot on the theme of (what else) obsession."[8]

Not all of the reviews were negative, and some of the most insightful were those that praised the film. Harlan Kennedy wrote: "*Eureka* is a treasure-trail of optic clues, mythic psychedelia and eyeblink rags of illusion and allusion, which leads into one of the richest movie labyrinths since *Citizen Kane*."[9] Still these critics were in the minority. The mainstream critics seemed united against the film. Not only did the disparaging reviews resemble the treatment *Performance* received, but the studio once again did not handle the release of the film well. *Eureka* would be completed in 1992 and be released in England the following year, but at MGM events were going in a different direction. Begleman was gone, after having become involved in a financial scandal, and the new executives seemed confused about how to market the film, despite the presence of Hackman. They decided to sit on the film, just as the executives at Warner Brothers had done with *Performance* nearly fourteen years earlier. Finally, after two years, the film received a limited release through the MGM/UA Classics division and then quickly moved to videocassette.

The failure of *Eureka* perhaps hurt Roeg more than that of any other of his films. He thought he had created his masterpiece, but instead it was his greatest disappointment. The years will most likely prove Roeg right, but for now the film is virtually ignored. Roeg did not allow his disappointment to carry over into his work, however. Instead he began another film, which was far removed from *Eureka*.

Notes

1. *Film Comment*, April 1983, p. 22.
2. Edgar Allan Poe, "Eureka," pp. 47–48.
3. *Sight and Sound*, Autumn 1982, p. 283.
4. *British Film Institute Monthly Bulletin*, May 1983, p. 119.
5. *Film Comment*, April 1983, p. 22.
6. *Sight and Sound*, Autumn 1982, p. 281.
7. *Film Comment*, April 1983, p. 23.
8. *Variety*, June 8, 1983, p. 20.
9. *Film Comment*, April 1983, p. 20.

SEVEN

Insignificance

In an ironic twist of fate, *Eureka* would be released in the United States just as Roeg's next film was also going into theaters, so that it would often be reviewed in conjunction with *Insignificance*. For the first time Roeg was adapting a work from another medium, the theater, as he recalls:

> I went to the play initially without much in mind about it. Then things began to turn in my head afterwards, about what it meant for me and how it might be a tool to use. It always has to do with one's own predicament. An incident came up in my own life, and I thought, good God, nobody knows a damn thing about anyone. That was the very first premise that started me thinking about the piece again.[1]

The author of the play, Terry Johnson, was retained as screenwriter. His first task was to pare the play down, but at the same time open it up, both spatially and temporally. Then he began to incorporate material that seemed more in keeping with Roeg's primary interests: allusions to the past and future, as well as constant references to time. The new material would not only flesh out the characters, but would provide them with motivations and condition their responses. Johnson soon discovered that there were many differences between approaching a film and writing a play. To his credit, Roeg helped him adapt to the new medium, while still allowing him freedom, as Johnson recounts: "Roeg's work on it was in the nature of suggestion and inspiration. As he felt his way into it, he sent signals from the other side, and then we started making those feelings specific in the choice of image and character development. We tended to develop the characters backward into their own histories."[2]

The film also parallels Roeg's own cinematic career. If thoughts the characters carry with them influence their actions, so do motifs and themes in Roeg's work, as he explains: "Things that haven't been finally resolved in the head keep growing. There's always a vehicle that you come across that reflects your thoughts. It's such a delicate whimsy that once they get put into words maybe I wouldn't have anything to do with them. But that's the way I work; one continuing thought that hasn't been resolved."[3]

The film opens with Will Jennings singing as the credits roll on a black screen, the perforations of the film visible along the edges. Like the music in *Bad Timing* and *Track 29*, Jennings's words create an immediate mood ("I can help you dream again in a world you'd like to know"). The first two images of the film are not just central to the film, but to Roeg's entire oeuvre. A watch falls through space, followed by an explosion of sparks. In *Bad Timing*, Roeg distorted time and events to create a mystery, but here he does it to take us into the thoughts of the characters. Roeg describes his intentions by saying:

> It is a film which should take the audience out of their present lives into the re-creation of an event. It is part history. It is not actually important that the events shown took place in a particular era. They are imaginary. But what they represent is still with us. We relive everything we have ever done, every day. It's there, and continues to be, since it has happened.[4]

The montage that follows is as kinetic as any in Roeg film. We witness a film crew preparing to shoot a scene resembling the famous shot of Monroe's skirt blowing up in *The Seven Year Itch*. Among the crew is Roeg himself, making a Hitchcock-like cameo. The technicians are busy about their work as a crowd looks on in anticipation, while up the street a professor is going over his notes in his hotel room. Hearing the noise below, he goes to the window to look out. In another area of town, a senator sits at a bar, oblivious to the baseball game on television. At the film site, two technicians have set up a fan underneath the grating. As the one works to get the antiquated fan started, the other positions himself to look up at the actress. Asked what he sees, the man tells his companion that he sees the stars, saying, "I like the stars. You look at the stars and you feel like tomorrow you feel you can do anything. Kiss that girl, walk on the grass. Stars won't think the worst of you. Stars won't even notice you."

The scene is set as the actress prepares to stand on the grate, but all we see of her are her famous legs. Down below, the men start the fan, which sends out a shower of sparks. The skirt blows up, but as the people strain to see her, the professor is imagining something darker: a white sheet falling onto a charred body. Lost among the spectators is the ballplayer, who grows uncomfortable as the skirt continues to billow, revealing not just her legs, but also her panties. That she functions as an object is apparent because her face is kept from view. The shot over, the fan is shut down and her skirt falls back. Stunned, the man below tells his companion that he "saw the face of god."

In the bar a patron is about to finish his drink when the senator asks if he is aware of what he is drinking. According to the laws of probability, it probably contains part of Napoleon's feces, "maybe even Mussolini's, but more like Napoleon because he's been dead longer." It is not just the senator's manner which is crude, but also his look. At all times, he seems bathed in sweat, even when the others appear cool. He continues espousing his philosophy, arguing that Attila the Hun died too early to be still part of the canal system: "So don't you see, all of us, we're all part of that great fucking elementary canal." The man doesn't respond, only shakes his head and drinks from his glass as the senator gets up. Her scene finished, the actress is hurried to her limousine, not just to escape her enthusiastic fans, but also her husband, the ballplayer. He vainly chases after the limousine as she watches through the back window. He is left looking after her as a fan asks for his autograph.

From the beginning there is an elegiac quality to the actress, not just in her quest to escape everyone, or even in the slow jazz music which accompanies her, but in her childlike manner. She says to the driver, "Wherever it is you're taking me, I don't wanna go." Russell's imitation of Monroe is obvious in her appearance and even her voice. Despite Roeg's disclaimer that the characters are not based on the real characters, we react to them at first as historical figures. Only gradually do we lose this association and become aware just how stunning Russell's performance is. The Monroe mannerisms are just that, something the character of the actress has created for her persona. When she lets down her guard and does away with these mannerisms, her character is fully dimensional. It is significantly different from the character Johnson originally wrote in his play. The actress is more confrontational and more calculating, and thus she is less sympathetic to the audience.

Just as the actress is identified with specific music, so too is the senator: throbbing music plays as he walks down the hall to the professor's room.

The movements of the characters define their personalities: the senator strides about making the place his own, while the professor constantly fidgets, eventually retreating to the bathroom. The senator pats the professor's papers, the symbol of his life's work, while trying to convince him to attend the next day's hearings. He admits he is not an educated man, but says that he would love to know what the professor knows: "I guess I'm just a man that likes to know things." The professor searches for knowledge for its own sake, but the senator searches for knowledge to control others. As the two men talk, the actress goes into a five and dime, seemingly on a whim, but with an ultimate purpose in mind. The link between the actress and the professor begins as her voice is overlapped with his turning his head, as if he heard her speak.

Tony Curtis bears no physical resemblance to Senator Joseph McCarthy, but his look and attitude prejudice our perceptions of him. The hat he wears, the way he holds his hands in his pocket, and his use of physical intimidation align him more to a gangster than to a political figure. He will also be associated with various vices: the alcohol he carries in his pocket, the prostitute he later hires, and the violence he is capable of. The senator is curious what the professor's response would be to the hearings' most famous question, "Are you or have you ever been?" He compares him to a movie star, the "kind that mud sticks to." The hearings that are his platform must soon come to an end, and the senator knows that the professor could be their last big witness. Musing on the professor's role in history, he calls him the father and mother of the atom bomb and thus inadvertently touches upon the professor's fear.

The professor fulfills our perception of Einstein, an eccentric in both appearance and manner. His hair is dishevelled and he wears a college sweatshirt. Despite his seeming naïveté, the professor is well aware of what is being asked of him. The professor begins to recount how various organizations have labeled him different things, all contradictory. "I didn't choose America. I was escaping Dachau," he says. The senator considers it strange that all Jews make references to Dachau and states that these hearings are designed to prevent such a thing. When the senator calls World War II a Soviet plot, the professor loses his temper, saying, "I think you should see a psychiatrist."

The professor starts to walk away, but the senator continues to speak, worrying that what he stands for could get "muddied up haggling over constitutional realities." He tells the senator he intends to ignore the subpoena and instead plans to make a speech to a conference on world peace. Despite this statement, the senator tells him he will pick him up in the morning and makes a veiled threat to his papers. "I'm afraid you'll have to let the peace conference slug it out for themselves," he insists. The senator gone, the professor takes out his watch and looks at it, seeing an image of fire.

If the actress cannot escape her fame, her husband cannot escape what she represents. Sitting in a bar, he can see an art work of his wife's nude body. (Created by David Hockney, the work seems a two-dimensional representation of the film itself, a mosaic composite of a character.) When asked about the film, the actress admits she is a fantasy figure who spends her time either in the kitchen, the bath tub, or with her skirt being blown up. It is obvious that she is selling herself, but the point is underlined when she looks out at a prostitute walking the street. There is a silent bond between the two women, as the prostitute is whistled at in the same manner as has been the actress. The latter nervously bites her nails as she watches the woman.

As the senator gets on the elevator, a group of Japanese businessmen get off. They are the only vestige of a peace conference that was to be included in the film, the conference to which the professor alluded. The senator throws them a quick look of disdain as he takes his place beside a Native American elevator operator, a giant of a man who looks down at him. There is a brief insert of a Japanese woman tending a garden, and we are unsure who is imagining this until we see the professor standing in front of a mirror and again seeing the woman. This woman, who seems to have no connection to any of the characters, will recur at various intervals of the film, along with the white cloth falling onto the charred body. These subliminal shots are just two of many vignettes which take us into the minds of the characters. It was this idea, that people bring with them various memories that influence their personality, which attracted Roeg to the play, as he explains:

> We're all very complex, every one of us, desperately complex. And I want to get closer in a visual way, to how human beings actually behave in front of each other. When I talk about boyhood, I need to get a reference of how I felt. So I see it: I take myself back there. When we're talking, we're all the time going back like that.[5]

The past the actress remembers is perhaps most familiar to us, as it draws so much on Monroe's life, in particular, her incarceration in an orphanage. The other girls in the orphanage take her watch from her, a watch which was a gift from her mother, and they toss it out the window (this image opens the film). It passes through a grate, while in the present the actress asks the chauffeur for his watch. For both the actress and the professor, watches have a meaning beyond their function as objects that measure time. As the professor settles down to sleep, the actress spots his hotel and convinces the driver to pull over. The professor dreams he is fishing, but then sees his boat being torn apart by Nazi soldiers. He watches gleefully from the shore, even sticking his tongue out at them in childish retaliation. His dream ends when he is awakened by someone knocking at the door. Having untangled his legs, the professor goes to the door and finds the actress, who tells him she is being pursued. Opening the door, he is less surprised by who she is than by what she carries: the three balloons. Realizing he has failed to recognize her, the actress is both surprised and hurt and identifies herself by pointing to the flashing marquee outside. He asks if she is any good, and her answer is both brief and poignant: "She tries hard."

If the professor has not heard of her, the senator has and makes her the subject of his fantasies. Having contacted a prostitute, the senator waits for her while reading a *Life* magazine with Monroe's picture on the cover (the only direct reference to Monroe in the film). In his hotel room, the professor is comparing himself to an old clown. He sits by the window with the actress, but she seems to overwhelm him in her form-fitting white dress. She glances at his papers, then looks out at the street where she had earlier been filming. She tells him she spent the last four hours having her skirt blown up, but her next line is similar to one spoken by Newton in *The Man Who Fell to Earth*: "ever get the feeling it might be later than you think?" She tells the professor the only way she thought she could meet him was by waking him up in the middle of the night. When she asks him what he has done that night, the professor tells her he washed out his socks and worked out a problem.

When the professor admits he would have liked to watch the filming, the actress confesses it would have made her uncomfortable, saying, "I don't think a girl should go through something like that without feeling embarrassed, it doesn't seem natural somehow." In a flashback she remembers standing as a young girl in front of a group of leering boys and beginning to undo her top. The professor wonders why his presence would bother her, but instead she asks if she can explain the theory of relativity to him, "only the specifics, it's too late for anything more." At first he tells her he thinks she understands it, but when she asks him to swear to his god, he has a change of heart. He hands her some blank paper, but she turns to the material she bought in the store. As she dumps out her supplies onto the floor, he sees the burning image again.

The actress's explanation of the theory of relativity is a brilliant set piece incorporating balloons, toy trucks, *The Brothers Karamazov*, and flashlights. She begins by hurling the professor's book against the wall to demonstrate the effect of movement on gravity. Holding onto a flashlight, she mentions the speed of light, but he corrects her figures. "You mean it got faster," she says. "We got more accurate," he replies. Like a child she runs across the floor, clearing everything away to make room for her trains, and he joins in, pushing one train toward her as she pushes a second. Passing one another, the two end up on opposite sides of the room, a balloon swaying back and forth as they shine flashlights. When she asks him the time, he tells her it is 8:15 P.M., and there is a flashback to the professor as a child, involved even then in an experiment, one which causes his watch to stop.

The actress runs across the room and flashes her light back across the room, where it seems to refract. As she stands in front of the professor holding her flashlight, a group of boys shine their flashlights on the young girl's skirt as she stands on a stool. The next image shows the actress as a young brunette attracting the attention of two agents. She has made her career because of her body; thus she wants desperately to show the professor she also has a mind. Her explanation of relativity completed, she tells

Michael Emil and Theresa Russell in *Insignificance*.

him he must show her his legs and begins to pull up his pant legs. Laughing, he promises not to show his legs if she will not espouse his theory. Then he is stunned to hear that she has learned about the theory of relativity without really understanding it. She compares it to riding on a subway car: she knows when to get on and off, but not how the car moves. Shocked, he tells her that her belief in something does not make it a fact, remarking that: "Knowledge isn't truth. It's just mutual agreement."

The professor admonishes the actress that a person who says he or she knows all about a subject stops learning. "As long as I keep thinking, I come to understand. That way I might approach some truth," he explains. She tells him it is the best conversation she has ever had, but he tells her he must go to bed. Like Mary Lou in *The Man Who Fell to Earth*, the actress has developed a bond to the professor that is tinged with sadness and does not want to go. She begins to gather her belongings, as she tells him she once put him third on a list of men she would like to sleep with. When she learned how old he was, however, she made him number one. Deciding that he cannot throw her out on the street at this hour, he finally relents and says she can stay, but only if he is allowed to sleep in the bathtub; Cary Grant had done a similar thing in the only movie he has ever seen. The professor encourages her to visit him at his home, but her argument is like his: she has no time. "I'm sorry I have none to offer you beyond tonight," she says.

The prostitute who has meanwhile arrived in the senator's room is notable for her likeness to the actress. The senator's sexual encounter will be contrasted with the relationship between the professor and the actress. Back at the hotel, they are looking out the window at the stars, as her name still flashes on the marquee. The scene of them innocently preparing for bed duplicates a similar scene in *The Man Who Fell to Earth* and shows just how long Roeg can extend time. Their motions are slowed down, while the actions of the other participants continue at a normal pace, as if some bizarre theory of relativity were in effect. He picks up an alarm clock and wonders if it is late or early. "It's relative," she tells him, smiling. She holds up the watch the chauffeur gave her, while she remembers the time the ballplayer presented her wih a diamond watch, when times had been happier between them. The ballplayer takes down his wife's portrait and tears it into small pieces, while he recalls her face as she watched him through the window of the limousine. The senator's encounter with the prostitute proves fruitless, and he ends up in tears as she tries to comfort him; meanwhile the ballplayer goes off in search of his wife. Seeing the limousine parked outside the Roosevelt Hotel, he seems to know instinctively where to go. In this same period of time, the professor and actress have done little more than remove their accessories. They stand across from one another as she begins to undo her dress, but just as she is about to reveal her famous body, her husband knocks at the door.

The ballplayer's arrival turns the film into a bedroom farce, and the dialogue is properly absurd. ("You've finally slept with a delicatessen," he shouts through the door on hearing the professor speak in Yiddish.) She tells the professor that the ballplayer is one of her fans, but when he wonders about the man's persistence she admits that he is her husband. The professor and the actress rush about the room, while the ballplayer continues to bang on the door, shouting he will go to the manager. Although the actress is in a panic, she realizes the ballplayer is only angry, not livid ("he's not using his head"). When she talks to the ballplayer through the door, she first obtains his promise not to get violent. He remains hostile, however, saying: "If I want to see my wife, I just go to the movies. If I want to see her in her underwear, I just go to the corner like all the guys."

The professor opens the door, not realizing what a strange sight he makes wearing only his sweatshirt and underpants. They tell the ballplayer that they have only been talking, which he might believe if the professor were dressed. He assumes the professor is a psychiatrist and that his wife has come to be analyzed before being bedded, a practice she has often repeated. The ballplayer demonstrates his intellectual limitations by constantly referring to Freud as Floyd. Learning his wife has come to find out the shape of the universe, he cajoles the professor into telling her the answer, as he sits to one side. The professor nervously starts to explain as the actress licks her lips in anticipation. He compares it to a solid object turned inside out indefinitely, but the ballplayer takes exception to this. He believes the universe is round, like all things in nature, something Columbus proved. He also credits Columbus with having taken the country from the Native Americans.

The discussion is forgotten as the actress openly derides the ballplayer, calling him stupid. The two have moved away from the professor as the ballplayer quietly asks if she wants a divorce. There is a flashback to an earlier time when the two were genuinely in love, but now he tells her he has contacted a lawyer friend about a divorce. Her response, however, is not what we expect. She takes the news as a sign of his love and falls into his arms. Having seemingly renewed their marriage, she goes to the bathroom to clean up. Surrounded by mirrors, the actress begins to hallucinate, finding herself confronted by images of the past and the future. She sees her hand strike one of the mirrors, smearing blood on the glass, and remembers her head covered in shampoo when she first dyed her hair blonde, the initial step in creating her image.

Left uncomfortably alone with the professor, the ballplayer opens a package of baseball cards, a habit he engages in throughout the film. He is searching for reminders of his own past, but instead finds only the card of some unknown player. In one of the funnier monologues of the film, the ballplayer lists all the series he has appeared in while the professor nods his head in bewildered understanding. He tells the ballplayer that he once appeared on Chewy Fruit's "Great Scientific Achievements," and the ballplayer grudgingly admits that at least someone has heard of him. The ballplayer tells of having heard of explorers handing out baseball cards within isolated civilizations, which means that even in the Amazon he would be recognized. The ballplayer calls to his wife, and although she tells him she is all right, she is actually drawing on the mirror with lipstick. For both the actress and the professor, the bathroom is their attempt to escape, but it only puts off the inevitable.

The two men sit on the bed together as the ballplayer admits his wife is smart, but says that her intelligence is nothing compared to his hands. He talks about the men he has found his wife with, saying he could kill them if it came down to just one man. Even his old teammates cannot seem to take their eyes off her and do not even want to talk about the old times. "Don't ever put a woman on a pedestal. It'll just give her the chance to kick your teeth right down your throat. She either needs thousands of people touching her or she needs to be alone all the time," says the ballplayer. He cracks his knuckles as he tells the professor how he gets tightened up around her, like he used to before a game. The ballplayer looks into a mirror, just as his wife is doing. To both of them, image is everything. The film is as much as anything an examination of fame: all four figures are celebrities of some type. The ballplayer sees the reflection of the painting in the mirror, and there is a swish pan as he looks first one direction, then the next, and is transported to a baseball stadium, swinging the bat for the crowd. He goes to the bathroom door once more, asking his wife if she is bleeding again, and he confides to the professor that a child could kill her. ("All bright lights on the outside, inside she tore up, she fell down and hit the street.") The past continues to assault the actress, and she falls to the ground in slow motion as the screen turns black.

Having carried the actress to the bed, the ballplayer admits she has a habit of fainting in strange bathrooms. The professor tells him he will get a new room and walks toward the door, as the ballplayer follows. He asks the professor whether he asked the actress up or she came on her own, and the professor's response tells us that he already knows the actress better than the ballplayer does: "I think she was feeling lonely, with all those people." The professor escapes to the elevator, his shoes in hand, and the operator looks down at him with bemused pleasure. He asks the professor if he is a Cherokee, which causes the professor to laugh. He says instead that the other man is obviously a Cherokee, but the man says he is only an elevator operator. The professor asks if it is true that Cherokees believe that they are the center of the universe, but the Cherokee finds this hard to believe in an elevator. "I watch TV. I'm no longer a Cherokee, but I watch TV. And I see your face and I hear your thoughts. And so I know you're a Cherokee." The professor says he does not want to be the center of the universe, but the Cherokee tries to comfort him, saying, "The thoughts in your head will lead you there."

This idea, which is one of the central themes of the film and pertains to the title, seemed to Roeg to be perfect for the film:

> We must have a sense of something greater than ourselves, we must have a sense of wonder and awe about ourselves. We must have another kind of belief, not a belief in our own practicality and what we know. That's what I like about the title of the piece: the idea that the world, society, has very little sense of a mystical movement of things. What it means is not that "it's all insignificant," but that nothing has more significance than anything else.[6]

In a scene which recalls Jack McCann's reconciliation with his wife, the ballplayer and the actress discuss their feelings for one another, while an acoustic version of the title song overlays their conversation. The actress awakens and starts to speak, but he is tired of her stories. She tries to tell him how she loves him; not how much, but how. To the ballplayer there is no difference; to the actress there is a world of difference. She wants to have a child, but he tells her he wants the child she aborted. When she suggests that a new child might be a son, he tells her it will only be a mess. He says she is broken and bruised inside, a comment which applies not just to her internal organs, but also her psyche. He is not even sure if he loves her, but as he falls asleep the actress whispers that she thinks she is pregnant. She shuts off the light, while outside her name continues to flash.

In the lobby, workers go about their business as the professor sleeps on some chairs. With his breakfast in his hand, the Cherokee goes to the roof. As he watches the floor numbers light up, Stuart Albright sings "America," which combines a dialogue on America with bizarre music. The Cherokee steps out onto the roof, the wind howling past him. Looking out at the city as morning arrives, he begins to chant, while in a room below, the senator is awakened by the departure of the prostitute, her blond wig in hand. He quickly checks his wallet, while the Cherokee starts to laugh, as if he can see what is happening.

The senator starts down the hall, accompanied by two associates who also seem out of a gangster film. He bursts into the professor's room, but only finds the actress naked and alone in the bed. His two associates remove their hats in silence before they go off to look for the professor. The senator is startled by the actress's resemblance to the famous movie star, and she takes it in stride, saying, "I know, if I was eight years younger and took better care of myself." He automatically assumes she is a prostitute and is surprised that her hair is real.

Of the four characters, the senator's character is the least drawn out. The past he does recall concerns his Catholic upbringing, when he served as an altar boy and was commended by the priest. The script contains more references to his past, his being ridiculed for being overweight and his experience on an island in World War II, when he shot down Japanese soldiers in a blind panic. With this background material omitted from the film, we are left with few clues to his motivation, and his character seems out of balance with the others.

The senator goes about the room collecting the professor's papers. He tells the actress her customer from the night before was not what it seemed, something that could easily be said about all four of the characters. Realizing the papers are in danger, she gets up from the bed, holding a sheet around her. She threatens to call the police, but the senator points out that her presence puts the professor in an awkward position. Starting to grow angry, he says he is not interested in "playing games." He insists that his concern "happens to be the survival of the free world." Realizing bribery and intimidation will not work, the actress decides to entice the senator by using her screen persona as bait. "You've really studied the lady," she remarks. He asks if she is exchanging sex for the papers. "What the hell. It's not me you want. It's her, "she replies. The burlesque music starts up, as the actress equates her offer to the senator with being ogled in the casting agency. After feigning interest in her, the senator brutally punches her in the stomach and begins a tirade against her screen persona, not knowing she is in fact the one he just struck: "She only got where she was going by doing just what you were doing." He makes a weak apology to the actress, unaware that the blow has resulted in the death of her fetus.

With the professor's arrival, the senator explains the real reason that his testimony is needed. The president must show that the professor backs him if he is going to give support to the Atomic Energy Commission. The professor argues that all of this is not important, even if "mc^2 equals one big bang." The shot of the watch is followed by the image of fire, and the actress writhes in pain on the bed. Believing the professor's papers are his life blood, the senator tells him that if he makes any speeches, he will destroy them. "Comes a time in every man's life when he has to figure out what's more important—what he thinks or what he does," he tells the professor. Taking the senator's advice to heart, the professor goes to the window and casually throws the papers out. The papers seem to explode in the air, cascading slowly to the street below. Some fall through the bedroom window, landing on the bed where the actress is still fighting the pain. When the senator calls this his life's work, the professor laughs, saying, "Not only that, I've seemed to have lost my shoes."

Sitting up the actress sees blood on the sheets and as she gets out of bed, she throws the blanket over the stains. Returning to the bathroom, she runs her hand along the mirror, as she did in the shot she had earlier imagined. With the papers no longer a possible threat, the senator prepares to leave, only to run into the ballplayer. Believing the senator is another of his wife's lovers, he pushes him back into the room. The professor is gleefully throwing a few more papers out the window as the ballplayer demands to know why the senator was there. Saying he wishes no violence against anyone, the professor admits the senator has come to visit him.

The ballplayer goes into the bedroom and attempts to talk to the actress through the bathroom door, which serves as a metaphor for the wall that exists between them. Still carrying his bag of baseball cards, he tells her he now wants to have a kid. The ballplayer boasts that he is not as stupid as he appears, that it is only an act: "From an early age, I've reveled in the appearance of stupidity, which has given me a great deal of time to think. I've been thinking. I've got it figured out. You want me to smarten up, well I figure you're worth it. So you go do your movies and I'll sit at home and read a few good books and you can come home and quiz me." As he is outlining his plan, the actress is continuing to clean up. Quietly she tells him it is over, that he should call his lawyer friend. At first the ballplayer seems to take the news calmly, then he crashes in the door to confront her in person. The two are framed in a tight close-up as she tells him she no longer wants him. She is crying while she tells him to go, and he walks out, not noticing the blood on the mirror.

Standing outside the elevator, the ballplayer opens a package of cards, finally finding his own. As the professor gets off, the ballplayer hands him his card, believing it will impress him. In the room, the actress has already dressed and applied her makeup when the professor enters. As he begins to gather his clothes, he laughingly tells her he threw his papers out the window. He admits he has destroyed the four previous drafts, but says that each time he rewrites his research he comes up with new ideas. He tells her he would like to go to a quiet place and slip off the earth, "the way Columbus never did, unfortunately." He remembers the ballplayer's comment that they all could have been Indians, Cherokees. He argues that each person is different, that some are smarter or more beautiful, while the ballplayer is visible on the street being asked for an autograph. "They will not take responsibility for their world," the professor says. "They want to put it on the shoulders of a few."

The actress is no longer content to hear theories, but needs to know what the professor is hiding from. There is a flashback to the professor hearing of the dropping of the atomic bomb, and he admits to the actress that it is his part in creating this weapon which has haunted him. As he speaks, he looks at the clock and then recalls that it was 8:15 A.M. when the bomb dropped, the time his watch is forever frozen at. He tells the actress he has burnt children, but that "there's something even worse." When she asks what it is, he admits he does not know, but that he must not think about it. She begins to leave, then stops, the curtain blowing in behind her. She tries to cheer him up by acting out a scene from her movie (with the sound effects from the scene overlaying her actions), only to realize she has no dialogue in it, that she is only an object. She tells him they will never use the bomb unless they can learn how to blowup the people and leave the buildings standing. The actress puts on her sunglasses, and he stares at the watch in his hand.

When he hears a plane flying overhead, the professor shuts his eyes, but this is not enough to block out his nightmare. The papers he threw out are shown once again, containing the seeds for destruction as they land on a Japanese courtyard. The hotel window seems to implode in a rush of flames and wind. Instead of the actual sounds, Stanley Myers created a music which seems to combine a Japanese motif with the roar of the explosion. The actress is caught in the destruction, her billowing skirt having caught on fire. Her body and face become disfigured as other objects catch fire. Included are scenes following the destruction: the black remains of the buildings and the actress's burnt form lying on the ground. This apocalyptic scene has been hinted at throughout the film, and Roeg allows it to continue for nearly four minutes. A clock burns, then everything goes in reverse, like the aborigine's hallucination in *Walkabout*. In the end the actress, once again herself, leaves. Her hand waves good-bye from around the corner and the film ends.

Insignificance is a work in which Roeg's love of film is genuinely apparent, a textbook example of how to adapt a play for film. Instead of opening the play out, Roeg takes it inside, into the minds of its participants. It is his most perfectly realized film, where every detail seems flawless, from the acting to the cinematography. If his ambitions are slighter than they were in *Eureka*, they are not to be dismissed in the way some critics have done. In one particularly critical review, John Coleman, writes:

> The invitation, as in all his films except the excellent *Walkabout*, is to suspend normal expectations of logic, continuity, even sense in favour of some greater, supremely cinematic "experience." Gnomic utterances are broadcast like revealed truths, if we could only connect. What continues to defeat me is the banality (where it is not crassness) of what is verbally communicated, coupled with the facile and open-ended cross references — a kind of aspiring paranomasia for the eyes only.[7]

Richard Combs offers a much more positive view of the film:

> The "message" of the play has also been respected: that the responsibility for the forces that rule the universe is too great for those who would take or be given responsibility for them; that fame is a religion in which the famous are guiltily burdened with being a replacement for rather than an avenue to God. The film incorporates this, but its critique of fame is not so much the end of an argument as the beginning of a puzzle. Fame is a mask, both a key and a baffle to reality; it is a spiritual state difficult to substantiate. Like the ecstasy of the man who finds gold in *Eureka*, its rewards confer a strange state of non- (or suspended) being.[8]

In the space of five years, Roeg had created three of his finest films, any one of which could have established him either critically or commercially. Of the three, *Insignificance* received the most critical attention and even opened the Cannes Film Festival, where it would eventually receive the French Technical Commission Prize for Technical Excellence. Its eventual fate would be no different from that of any other Roeg film, however: a limited commercial release followed by a quick disappearance. The promise of Roeg's career had long been met, but he remained mired in seeming obscurity. Thus it seemed as if Roeg would either have to adapt his style or disappear from the scene completely.

Notes

1. *British Film Institute Monthly Bulletin*, August 1985, p. 237.
2. Ibid.

3. *Millimeter,* March 1981, p. 175.
4. *Films and Filming,* August 1985, p. 16.
5. *Cinema Papers,* September 1985, p. 43.
6. *British Film Institute Monthly Bulletin,* p. 238.
7. *New Statesman,* August 9, 1985, p. 28.
8. *Monthly Film Bulletin,* August 1985, p. 235.

EIGHT

Castaway

Since the early seventies, Roeg had dreamed of filming the story of Donald Crowhurst, a man who set out to sail around the world by himself. His trip seemed to be going well, at least according to the optimistic radio reports he was sending out, but in fact it was predestined for failure. The reports were actually the product of his imagination, for his ship was not only off course, but his supplies were nearly out. Crowhurst would die while still trying to make his fantasy a reality. The film would have been based on his journal, but Roeg was never able to get financial backing for it. Years later Roeg was to film a movie based on another journal, Lucy Irvine's *Castaway.* She had accepted a man's offer to spend a year on a deserted island, during which time her feelings for her companion changed, as well as her attitude toward herself. The adventure was arduous, with both participants becoming sick and weak from a lack of food an water. By the year's end, they found themselves depending on another island for supplies, with nothing uniting them but their island itself. Once the year was up, they went their separate ways.

Allan Scott wrote the script for the film. He had last worked with Roeg on *Don't Look Now,* but was to become one of his closest collaborators, writing the scripts for two more of his films. Scott read the book several times and spent nearly six months on the script before the premise of the film was established. The difficulty in adapting the project resembled that Roeg had faced with the Crowhurst project: how much was fantasy and how much truth? Irvine's companion, Gerald Kingsland had also written an account of their exile, *The Islander,* which differs significantly from Irvine's version in many details. Thus the problem became not just how to present the material, but what material to present. This dichotomy only added to the filmmakers' frustration as they attempted to create a cohesive story, a frustration that Scott explains:

> I read Lucy's book and I was drawn to the concept, but I couldn't figure it out. When I'm approached about a film I ask myself, "can I drag my life into this piece of work or not?" I get a surge of adrenaline. I go for it. With *Castaway*, it was nine months before I felt I could do something with it, though I knew I should be able to because it's such a classic form, so attractive to so many people.[1]

The central idea of the film would be the examination of a couple's relationship as it progressed through the period of a year. For Roeg, the central theme was not a struggle against nature, but the relationship between two people:

> What is it—the lonely girl or the lonely heart—I didn't want that; or dropouts, no, and then suddenly one morning I thought, this is an extraordinary metaphor—a marriage of 20 years reduced to a year. It goes on everywhere, but generally it's expanded to 20 years because in the modern day marriage, you hardly see each other and you're not under scrutiny. But on a pretty little island, every hour becomes a month, every day, a year. Actually looking at each other the whole time.[2]

The events of the story take place on Tuin, an island off the coast of Australia, but the actual filming would take place on the island of Seychelles, an island cinematographer Harvey Harrison was intensely familiar with, having lived there for 18 months. Harrison had worked with Roeg on many of his commercials, but *Castaway* would be his first film as director of photography. The filming would prove difficult: the island was intensely humid, and the underwater photography was sometimes dangerous because sharks were often in the vicinity. For the climatic storm sequence, nine and a half tons of water were dropped onto the nude leads, while wind machines and a tethered airplane helped to blow apart the hut. To add to the complications in the filming, much of the underwater photography had never before been attempted. Roeg was also directing a cast he had never worked with before. Oliver Reed had been contemplating retirement when he read Scott's script and accepted the role of Gerald Kingsland. For Amanda Donohoe, this was her first featured role in a film, and the nudity required for most of the filming only added to the pressure.

Castaway opens with a lithograph of a figure on a desert island; the man is presumably Robinson Crusoe, the traditional romantic image of a desert exile. Kate Bush's music, however, informs us that the focus will not be on adventure, but on relationships. ("I don't know you and you don't know me. It is this that brings us together.") Even its title ("Be Kind to My Mistakes") will be echoed by one of the characters at the end of the film. Lucy Irvine's book opens on the island, but Roeg introduces the characters before they have even met. Gerald fills out a classified ad for *Time Out* magazine, requesting a woman to spend a year with him on a desert island. He changes his age from 45 to 35, already building the adventure on a falsehood, albeit a minor one. His life seems based on illusion, from the fish he watches in aquariums to the magic tricks he performs to entertain others. He looks at a window display of a hut on an island, but hurries off when the shopkeeper glares at him through the window. Because he is divorced from his wife and his relations with his children are apparently strained, the island will seem to be Gerald's chance to escape. Few details will be given of his life, and these omissions serve a purpose. In real life, Kingsland had already spent two sojourns on other islands, including one with his sons.

Lucy Irvine's motivation is different; it is more a need to challenge herself than to escape. As he had done with the characters in *Walkabout*, Roeg sketches out the routine in her life, which includes a job where people are huddled silently over computers and relationships that are based on confrontation (her roommate tries to bore Lucy's boyfriend with culture). The society Roeg depicts is one of violence and moral corruption, evidenced by reports in the media of rapists and attempted assassinations. One of Gerald's companions ridicules a blind beggar, while the wall by the phone from which Gerald makes a call contains the phone numbers of prostitutes. Lucy seems to sense her susceptibility to violence, as she runs a red marker along her stomach while watching a news report on a serial killer.

When Gerald first calls Lucy, both are watching a broadcast of the *Pumpkin Eater,* Harold Pinter's examination of a woman's search for her identity. The style of the film predates Roeg in its use of flashback to show what is going through the female protagonist's mind. The excerpt Roeg includes concerns the breakup of the woman's marriage: Anne Baxter shouts that she has never been unfaithful, presaging Lucy's later protestations. There can be no missing the connection between this story and the relationship Roeg is portraying, just as the announcement of Princess Diana's wedding later foretells that of Gerald and Lucy. All of these references do not help to take us deeper into what is happening, but only serve as shortcuts to tell us why. In his best works, Roeg uses the opening to delineate the themes of the film, but in *Castaway* the opening disappoints us, offering little more than simple exposition.

Although the opening does not come from Irvine's work, one can see Roeg's impetus for including the world Lucy and Gerald are leaving. Traditionally his protagonists are fleeing an unhealthy environment. In *Performance* Chas is escaping his criminal life-style; in *Don't Look Now* the Baxters leave the place of their daughter's death, in *The Man Who Fell to Earth* Newton leaves a barren planet, and later, in *The Witches,* Luke will leave the site of his parents' deaths. Here, however, the approach seems almost satirical and sometimes pedestrian.

From the beginning it is obvious that Gerald is seeking a lover more than a companion. Lucy seems to anticipate this when she calls their first encounter the "ultimate blind date." In his first meeting with Lucy, Gerald expresses relief that she is not the short, dowdy woman he had mistaken her for. "You are the first woman, I mean girl, that's made me feel that way," he says. At their second meeting, he seems to repeat this sentiment, admitting she is "definitely on his short list." When she innocently places her hand on his knee, he immediately covers it with his own, only to have her quickly pull it away. The difference in their ages also means a difference in role expectations, and Gerald seems to have built up various preconceptions about women. First he asks if Lucy is either a nurse or a secretary, then he states what he wants in a woman: "Give me a woman who can cook, sew, put up a tent, mind you, those could be useful."

The specter of Robinson Crusoe haunts Gerald. He confidently tells Lucy it is the "preparation which is important," and he ridicules Crusoe because he relied on the ship's stores for survival. The statement is ironic, considering Gerald's later dependence on a neighboring island for supplies. (It is noteworthy that Lucy mentions Friday, who was at his beck and call.) Crusoe, however, demonstrates a resolve that Gerald lacks; his insistence on careful preparation will not translate into action. Gerald and Lucy seem to fall easily into the role of lovers, as he spends the night with her. As he sleeps, she kisses him, an act of tenderness she will not later demonstrate toward him. The next morning he is cleaning up when Lucy's roommate, Laura, comes in, not noticing that Lucy is gesturing to her to leave. When Gerald comes out clad in a robe, both he and Laura are obviously embarrassed, and he falls back on his magic tricks to relieve the awkwardness. As the sequence ends, the camera pans toward a map of Tuin, but it becomes apparent that the island will not be an idyll.

The relationship quickly breaks down when Gerald and Lucy learn that to live on the island they have chosen they must be married. Lucy is furious, insisting that she will not be forced into marriage by an outdated law. It is the first indication of how unprepared the two are for their journey. (The publisher reminds them that they have already spent their advance, which they had decided not to insure.) Lucy lies alone in her bedroom crying while Puccini's "Nessun Dorma" is playing on the stereo, but the record begins to skip, diminishing the recuperative power of the music. The couple marry in a ceremony devoid of any romance (the publisher acts as best man and the music is piped in). Gerald vainly apologizes to Lucy, but she will have none of it. In the background a cell door inexplicably bangs shut as if a sentence has been carried out. That night Lucy cries to herself as Gerald sleeps beside her.

The voyage to the island seems to bring the couple together, as both are overwhelmed by the natural environment. There are still reminders of the society they are retreating from, primarily the photographer who accompanies them and tries to position them in artificial poses. They are still viewing the island of Tuin from a distance, but Roeg inserts a montage of the island that shows the natural landmarks which make it up and the life which lives on the island and in its waters. On their arrival Lucy races up the shore, as Gerald shakes his fists in triumph behind her. If they view the island as a paradise, the boatman's response is less romantic: he urinates into the bushes as Gerald looks on. Gerald escapes into the woods to find a small pond, from which he fills a cup with water. He returns to Lucy to have her drink from it, a symbolic act, but also a hopelessly romantic one.

From the beginning Lucy demonstrates a willingness to accept anything, saying, "This is mine, I'm going to do it. And it's Gerald's too." In contrast, the photographer, Janice, is ill at ease in the milieu; she wants to wait to use a public restroom, but she is forced to go in the woods. She offers to send a helicopter back in a week, but Lucy declines her suggestion. Gerald continues to look on the adventure as a sexual fantasy, encouraging Janice to photograph his penis as he says that this is what the island will be about. With Janice's departure, Lucy seems free at last and strips off her clothes to walk naked along the beach. His first reaction is a sexual one, but as he races up to her, she instead offers him tea, the first intimation that their relationship has undergone a change.

After they stack their crates on the beach, Lucy fans the fire and Gerald finishes setting up the tent, which he brags is impervious to anything because it is constructed of man-made fibers. He climbs in behind her, beginning to take off his shorts, as she reminds him that the tent is only temporary. He kisses her thigh, but when she learns he has forgotten the iodine and the extra flour, she grows angry and storms from the tent as he tries to apologize. She walks along the surf, running her hands through the water, but the sounds of the jungle frighten her and she returns to the tent. If she at first seems fearful in this environment, she will eventually become at one with the island, as the visuals will emphasize. When she returns to the tent, Gerald is still aroused, but once again she turns down his overtures.

The underwater photography of *Castaway* contains some of the most beautiful scenes that have appeared in any film; the camera often glides along the sea bottom among schools of fish and natural vegetation. The perspective here is Lucy's, for it is in the water that she seems most relaxed. When she emerges from the ocean, Gerald is sitting on the rocks along the shore, seeming more a spectator than a participant in the experience. He is fishing, but he admits he not only hates the smell of fish, but also its taste (he will soon prove allergic to fish). Lucy lounges naked in the water as she recalls having once read a book on fishing, which she had found extremely boring. When he asks why she finished it, her response is telling: "I've never given up once I've started." She dives under the water once more, and he calls her a bitch, the strain of their relationship having already manifested itself. Later, when they fight their way through the forest, he seems more in control as he warns her of alligators and stands firm when she is frightened by something.

Lucy constantly analyzes Gerald; on one occasion she asks him what he thinks or feels when he performs boring tasks. He starts to answer the question, but grows confused and finally grumbles that it is a stupid question. She wants to talk about what goes on inside his head, but he returns to his magic tricks. When he does speak, he compares his head to his penis, saying it goes up and down and sometimes explodes. "When you see it lying there just doing nothing at all, you'd be surprised what it's capable of thinking," he tells her. She laughs at his answer, and he points down the beach, asking if they should build their shelter there. Gerald will come across as a man of incongruity, one who assumes the manner of a slob, but actually craves knowledge. When they met, he had been reading Buddhist scriptures, and while safely secluded in the woods, he reads *Teach Yourself to Express Yourself.* For him the island will be a retreat where he can admire the scenery and educate himself; Lucy will quickly grow weary of this view and even call him lazy. On the beach, Gerald begins to teach himself to dance, but she shouts that they need food and shelter, causing him to wonder if their retreat is becoming Devil's Island. Thinking she is alone, she too begins to dance, but it is her own routine, not one dictated by a book. Seeing that he is watching her, she throws down her knife in defiance and continues.

Lucy keeps pressing Gerald to teach her to fish, arguing that their supplies are running low. Instead, he begins to tend his garden, saying they need the vitamins for their diet. He tells her they must pray that they will survive. As she is wondering if he does pray, he breaks into a limerick. She reminds him not to break the skin on his legs, her warnings echoing the ones the girl gives her brother in *Walkabout.* These too will prove prophetic. One of the few scenes of intimacy between Lucy and Gerald occurs when he accidently knocks down a hornet's nest and the angry bees go after him. As she runs through the jungle in panic, she chases after him and the two fall to the ground. She lies on top of him as she brushes off the bees, and she remains there stroking his hair. That night she tends to his legs as he asks if this is what she expected when she answered the ad. He takes her hand and begins to move it toward his groin, but she quietly tells him no, pulling it back. The island is what neither of them expected, and this interests Roeg: "I liked the idea of two actors naked on the empty stage of a desert island with no place to hide from each other—a generically attractive place, but in fact really poisonous and dangerous."[3]

The estrangement between the two continues, and it becomes apparent that Lucy is more at peace when she is alone with the landscape. When they are together, the sexual tension is evident, reaching its apogee as the two are fishing from a rock. She lies underneath a wet blue cloth, but instead of covering up her sexuality, the cloth seems to accentuate it. (Ironically, the scene recalls one from *Walkabout* in which the boy is covered by a white cloth.) Gerald throws aside his fishing pole, even as Lucy complains that she is becoming weak from lack of protein. Gerald's anger seems reflected by the landscape: at one point he makes a fist that duplicates a rock formation in the distance. He begins to apply makeup to his eyes while they discuss their lack of sexual contact. She admits she is sometimes frightened by him and says she cannot make love to him. His potential for violence seems to reach its peak as he tears off the cloth and throws himself on her, saying, "Nothing has changed with me. You've changed." He tells her she has lied and whored, and then he wonders if they can actually make it on the island together. He forcibly kisses her, then rolls off her in frustration.

The central mystery in Gerald and Lucy's story is her decision not to have sex with him once they reach the island. According to Kingsland, Lucy had informed him even before they had left for the island that they would not have sexual relations, but she gave him no reason for the change in her attitude. Kingsland thought this was a betrayal of her agreement with him, and most of his account is openly hostile toward her. In her account, Lucy seems unsure about what predicated the change, but says that it was gradual, occurring after they arrived on the island. Roeg and Scott provide their own hypothesis on Lucy's change in attitude: the island becomes Lucy's obsession, eliminating her need for Gerald.

As the tension is diffused, Lucy suddenly feels a yank on the fishing line that she has tied to her finger. In another example of Roeg's motif that all is not what it seems, the fish they struggle to bring in looks like a giant shark. After both become united in the task, they finally bring the fish onto land, only to find that it is a small shark, barely enough to feed one person. The preceding events seem to have disheartened Gerald, and he loses himself in the forest. For the first night since their arrival, the two are physically separated, and the next day Lucy goes looking for him. She shouts that it is not fair, that she cannot go searching for him, but in fact she does. When Lucy finally finds Gerald, he is lying in the mud beside a pond, his legs bleeding and covered with sores. Again he apologizes to her, saying he had not intended to be gone for so long, while she starts to cry. He begins to kiss her, and Lucy holds him tightly as he runs his hand along his infected legs.

Without iodine, Gerald's legs gradually grow worse; he can barely move about the garden to water it. Lucy takes over the work as he reads an old newspaper, and she muses about how words have lost their meaning:

"Weird isn't it, I mean the changes. You can say the words pub, copper, bus, friend, and they just don't mean anything anymore . . . . They've seemed to lost their images. They're just sounds." Gerald has little interest in the topic and instead points out areas she is to water. She seems in danger of becoming his man Friday, serving all his needs but his sexual ones. Later he tells her that a "screw and cold beer is the summit of my whole life's ambition. You know something, you could found a whole new religion on this island, with a screw and a cold beer." She hands him some soup, and he reminds her he said screw, not stew.

Lucy tells Gerald that his whole character is a lie, that he pretends not to read or think, but that his manner is a camouflage. He is defensive, arguing that "everybody needs their secret life, where even their secrets have secrets." He mocks the way women think they understand men, but in the end know nothing. As he continues, the image fades to black, one of the few methods that Roeg uses to indicate time passage. Another indicator is a pair of panties Lucy discards on a small sapling; Gerald later comes across them when the sapling has become a tree. Joseph Lanza has noticed the difference in how time is treated in *Castaway*, in contrast to Roeg's previous work:

> While *Insignificance* converts the subject of time into a parlor chat between "knowing" parties, *Castaway* reduced it further to an ongoing marital squabble. Gerald and Lucy arrive on the Isle of Tuin and immediately retreat into separate mental worlds. Gerald, dejected and sexually famished, constantly refers to clocks and moon variations to keep track of the passing days; while Lucy, enamored with her tropical surroundings, loses all awareness of time and has to be informed when their one-year experiment finally terminates. The time conflict in *Walkabout* is absent here because Lucy has no desire to return to the old life. Even Gerald's preoccupation with clocks is more out of boredom than concern.[4]

When Gerald and Lucy's worlds do intersect, it is often with abysmal results. Gerald returns to the camp while Lucy is cooking and comes across a page from her journal. He starts to laugh at her description of her concave navel that allows her to make love to the sun. She angrily pulls the page away, showing that she too has secrets she wishes to protect. The page is a direct passage from Irvine's journal, and much of Lucy's dialogue is also taken from it.

Gerald eventually grows more comfortable with Lucy and even opens up to her about his past. He begins to reminisce about his mother, but his memories soon turn to other women and his first feelings of arousal. By now, however, Lucy has little interest in such matters and demands to know when a shelter will be built. This in turn leads to a discussion of food, and as they speak, their words are overlayed with the sounds of their stomachs growling. Each mention of a different food seems to excite them even more. He seems to realize how involved they have become in the imagery and tells her it is better than sex. Her embarrassed look seems to confirm this, but her sexual desires become even more aligned to the landscape. One night she dreams of languishing in the sea, unaware that she is lying on a very awake and very aroused Gerald. Seeming near the point of climax, he tries to waken her, but she continues to dream, moaning of secrets. When she does awake, his attention is on the pain of his legs, which keeps him from sleeping.

In many of Roeg's films the relationship of a couple is often strained by the arrival of third parties (the gangsters in *Performance*, the boy in *Walkabout*, the sisters in *Don't Look Now*). Here the dissolution is accentuated by the arrival of two Australians on a catamaran. The men have brought with them a census form which the couple is to fill out and they ask to come ashore. Gerald is mistrustful of the men and is only willing to invite them to shore when they mention they have food to spare. When Rod introduces himself and asks how things are going, Lucy's response is noticeably sparse: "We like the island." The two men cannot help but notice the couple's shriveled stomachs, but Gerald remains defensive. The men not only supply them with food, but treat their wounds, while Lucy shows them photographs of their stay. Gerald muses that it is the first time they have entertained anyone as a married couple, and Rod comments on the intimacy of their situation, asking them what they talk about. "Practical things of course and about our lives, memories, ideas. It's all a bit beyond talking," Lucy replies. Rod, who is sitting against a tree playing the guitar, remarks, "Yeah, that's what happens when people know too much about one another. Nothing to hide behind." Jason says that at least they are married or else they would have something to hold over the other when they leave. Rod admits he would have to kill someone who had information like that. Gerald confesses that they only married because the government worried about "hanky panky" on the island, but comments ironically that it could be worse, there could be no hanky panky.

Lucy and the two men begin to climb among the rocks, and she can be heard talking, either to the men or in voice-over. She admits their problems are not all Gerald's fault, but says that he "just lies there doing nothing. No imagination." She believes it is because he is older and has the leg infection, which has hindered his mobility. The crucial omission Scott and Roeg made in adapting Irvine's work was to leave out Lucy's true feelings toward Gerald. In her book, she confesses to the two men how repulsive Gerald has become to her. This explains her refusal to have sex wtih him, but also makes us wonder what it was in him that attracted her in the first place. By leaving this out, Roeg and Scott change her motives to a need to confront the ordeal on an equal footing with Gerald.

In the woods Lucy makes a feeble attempt to play the flute, and Rod offers to give her lessons, as Jason walks off. "I love this place. Everything I dreamed for it to be," Lucy says. The two kiss, but Lucy's attraction to Rod disturbs her, ironically because of her responsibility toward Gerald as his wife. She also worries about what she has become and wonders if she still has a sexual identity. When she examines her misshapen body in the mirror, she can see that her hair is ragged and her body painfully thin. That night Gerald calls her a "randy little bitch" and says that if she acts the same way the next day he will beat her. She pulls a knife close to her body as she imagines swimming in the water and striking out at something with the blade. When the men do leave the island, Jason admits he liked Gerald, then asks Rod if he slept with Lucy. Rod does not answer, but looks wistfully toward the shore. With their departure, Lucy angrily tells Gerald she had been forced to defend him: "The way you just lie there useless, hopeless." He goes to the corrugated tin that has been made into a shelter, banging it as if it were a sign of accomplishment. He returns to the subject of the men: "No sex on Tuin, no. Not until Jason and Rod arrive anyway." She shouts that she wanted to show that they had survived on their own, but she could not even say that. She throws down her ration of food and runs off.

In another dreamlike sequence, Lucy wrestles with vegetation which has seemingly grown about her waist. She rolls around on the ground, as if she were having intercourse with the plants. Next she walks along the beach, running her hand along her body, confused as to who she is. She is also fearful that she is pregnant, and at one point she holds a clay formation that resembles a fetus, but her shriveled stomach seems to contain no possibility of life. In their garden, Lucy and Gerald find the bones of other inhabitants, a discovery that points to their possible fate. Like their bodies, the plants have also shriveled up; Gerald carefully spoons out what little water they have. He falls onto the ground and looks up at the sky in frustration, saying, "I can't grow these without water." In her desperation, Lucy eats from a poisonous plant and becomes violently ill. Once again a crisis brings them together. Gerald discovers that the plant is safe if eaten cooked but is poisonous in the raw state. He carries her lifeless body to the ocean and begins to caress her face with the water, as if he were trying to restore her life. Beverle Houston and Marsha Kinder have pointed out that in Roeg's first four films "water is used as a means of subjugation or restriction," and this use seems to reach its apex here.

Although Lucy recovers, the lack of food and water continues to drain them and the situation begins to resemble the children's plight in *Walkabout*. Insects attack the remains of the fish they have caught, while they lie in their tent too weak to move. When a plane flies overhead, Gerald remembers how he explored aircraft parts in a junkyard, while he was searching for their supplies and Lucy recalls riding on a subway. These memories seem insignificant, however. The screen fades to black, as if their fate is sealed, but once more outside forces arrive to save them. They are cared for by a pair of nuns, one of whom admonishes Gerald for not bringing the proper supplies. In real life, the pair were tended by nurses, but the nuns serve as symbols of celibacy and divine intervention. When the nuns are about to leave, they find their boat motor is out of order. Gerald manages to repair it, impressing the boatman, who promises to return with more appliances that need to be fixed.

The island no longer seems as isolated when Gerald and Lucy journey to a nearby island, Bandu; this trip makes their plight seem more masochistic than unavoidable. It is night when they return, and Gerald drunkenly sings the praises of the locals. With their connection to the neighboring island cemented, they seem to be overloaded with materials. Even the rain becomes more a hindrance than a salvation. Their camp is cluttered with debris and Gerald is trapped on the island by the rain. He no longer requires a branch to knock down coconuts, but can shoot them down, and the two quickly regain their weight. While he is busy repairing a motor, she comes up to him, offering him food, but he no longer needs it. She playfully feels his full arms, and he confesses to her that she is good company. He tells Lucy that he knows "what this last year has meant to her," but in fact, he has little awareness of her feelings. When she starts to answer, Ronny, the boatman, arrives and Gerald hurries off with him, not waiting for her to finish.

Lucy returns to the shelter and listens to a record, while narrating her feelings about how they have changed and how nothing she has is hers to hold onto. She admits she "never really knew him when he wasn't down," but realizes that now his confidence has returned. They have almost forgotten that they do not make love. Lucy walks along the water and then lies naked on the beach, her loneliness apparent. Only when Gerald returns to their island does she once again throw on her clothing. He apologizes for being a day late and invites her to come with him the next time. They walk into the shelter, and Gerald pulls out a piece of frozen meat from his pouch. He throws it to Lucy, and she holds it with a bewildered look, confused about what has happened to their original goal. "Who am I?" she asks him, but he is in little mood for such self-reflection. She begins to list a variety of labels that could be applied to her, culminating with "survivor," but admits to having no love for the title of "mechanic's wife" and wonders what happened to the adventure the island had promised them. He replies that if he did not have to go off the island for sex, he would not have to leave.

Lucy's determination to remain on the island and to complete their original plan takes precedence over everything, including her conflicting feelings toward Gerald. He is lying on the cot as she stands in front of a mirror, wearing a nightgown. Using a cockney accent, she tells him to call her Rosy, as if she is assuming another identity to make love to him, something Irvine did indeed do. In her journal Irvine talks of herself as if she were a third person. Lucy comes up to Gerald and begins to lift her gown, revealing a pair of black panties, a bra, and a garter. Gerald is both aroused and disturbed, worried that Lucy is taunting him. The two begin to kiss, and Lucy asks him not to go to Badu because she thinks they should stay on the island till the year is over. Gerald understands that her actions are selfish and says that she is selling herself, even as they begin to have sex. The covering over the bed falls on to them as they roll around, and she seems to agree with what he has said: "You want what I want. So what's new in the world. O.K." With Gerald asleep, Lucy takes out a book she has hidden, just as Gerald hides books; her book is the *Criminal History of Mankind*, another reminder of Robinson Crusoe.

In *Eureka*, the emotions of the characters seem to influence nature; a violent storm occurs as Jack's conflict reaches its climax and he is murdered. Here Roeg uses a similar storm to show Gerald's passion, his desire for Lucy having finally been met. The winds tear at the hut as he races about trying to start the generator, while she tries to gather up the papers of her journal. He comes upon her and begins to grope at her, causing her to shout he would make love to a statue if given a chance. The two fall to the ground as he reminds her of their deal and says that they have only a few days left. Their sexual encounter is nearly lost in the rain, wind, and falling debris. As he did in *Insignificance* and *Track 29*, and as he will do in *The Witches*, Roeg turns the scene into a catastrophic event, the walls giving way to explosions of water which engulf the participants.

Their passion spent, as well as nature's passion, Gerald and Lucy lie asleep among the debris that had once been their home. Only the sound of boats coming to the island awakens them, and they hurriedly dress as Ronny comes up to meet them. He and his men have already hauled away most of their belongings, but as Lucy absentmindedly holds onto a small clock, she argues that they must wait for their year to be over. Gerald quietly tells her that the year has been over for nearly a month. Thus the adventure ends with another deception: he has kept from her how much time has passed, presumably to continue their sexual encounters. Sadly, she looks out over the island, remembering various images of her stay, but it is significant that the images are of her alone, naked and united with nature. Returning to the present, she turns to Gerald and hugs him, her relationship with him and the island over.

The trip to Badu is in sharp contrast to their arrival; the two are quiet, elegiac, as they dress. Gerald will live on in Badu, where a repair shop has been set up for him. As they part, he asks her to be "kind to my mistakes" and hands her a small package. After Lucy has left, Gerald takes off his

Amanda Donohoe and Oliver Reed in *Castaway*.

jacket to settle into the work at hand, only pausing to watch as her plane flies overhead. She looks down at the island, both sad and happy, and turns her attention to the gift. Inside is an egg, a reminder, and a message from Gerald saying he loves her. She smiles through her tears and a smile comes to his face, as if he is aware of her feelings. From the perspective of the plane, the island of Tuin gradually fades into the distance. Despite the problems with the film's presentation, the ending is surprisingly effective, conveying a sense of loss in the separation of the two characters.

Castaway is among Roeg's most beautifully photographed films, but thematically it is among his weakest. At times it seems that Roeg is responding to the criticism that his films are too complex for the general audience. With the exception of two flashbacks, the film is told in a linear format, with few allusions to other materials. Only in a brief flashback as they lie near death, do we learn a little more about the past lives of Lucy and Gerald, and there are few allusions to other materials to draw us further into their conflict. The film is not a failure by any means, however; the portrait of Gerald Kingsland is one of Roeg's most detailed characterizations.

Jonathan Hacker and David Price have hypothesized that "Roeg's heart was not in the film," citing an interview with Amanda Donohoe in which she admitted that she felt he had "lost a lot of direction, while we were making that story."[5] Perhaps Roeg had not lost interest in the project, but had never fully come to terms with how to approach it. If *The Man Who Fell to Earth* contains too many ideas (as some critics have suggested), *Castaway* does not contain enough. Pam Cook was correct when she argued that the "film compounds rather than clarifies the confusion in Lucy Irvine's rambling, impressionistic novel."[6]

With *Castaway*, Roeg's career seemed to run into a new hurdle: indifference. *Castaway* had begun preproduction with United British Artists, then was continued under Thorn EMI, and finally came under the aegis of Cannon Films. The financially troubled Cannon seemed intent on marketing the film on its sexual aspects, emphasizing the nudity over the content. In Britain the film was favorably reviewed, but in the United States it was barely noticed by critics. It was a trend that would continue with the next films as well. Roeg was no longer the subject of debate, he had become simply another director making interesting films. When he was discussed, it was as a director whose prime was either past or whose promise had never been met. Neither assessment would be accurate or fair.

Notes

1. *Sunday Times*, Feb. 15, 1987, p. 3.
2. *Lighting Dimensions*, October 1987, p. 74.
3. Jonathan Hacker and David Price, *Take 10*, p. 369.
4. Ibid., p. 362.
5. Joseph Lanza, *Fragile Geometry*, 107–8.
6. *Monthly Film Bulletin*, October 1987, p. 43.

NINE

Aria

Roeg's next project seemed ill-advised from the start. The idea was ambitious enough: to combine some of the top directors of the world with some of the most famous opera arias. Producer Don Boyd had first come up with the idea soon after he completed a short film based on Vivaldi's "Four Seasons." During the next ten years he worked to interest not only financial backers, but also some of the world's most prominent directors. The first he was able to interest was Federico Fellini, and it was his marquee value which finally convinced a company to back the project. The talent Boyd would gather was indeed impressive—Robert Altman, Jean Luc Godard, and Ken Russell among others. Ironically, Fellini would later back out of the film due to prior commitments, but by then preproduction had already begun. Roeg was one of the last to hire on, having just completed his work on *Castaway*. The original title for the film was *Imaginaria*, as if in homage to the thirties cult film, *Imagine*.

For his story Roeg took an episode from history. In 1931 assassins had attempted to kill King Zog of Albania just as he was leaving an opera house. Roeg gives the story a peculiar slant by having the incident appear to be a woman's fantasy as she looks out at modern day Vienna. Theresa Russell plays the woman, and she will also portray the king in what is easily the most bizarre casting move of Roeg's career. Ironically, the idea had been Boyd's, but both Roeg and Russell quickly embraced it. Roeg would use neither a hot list nor a script. The film opens with a beautiful woman standing in front of a mirror and then going to the window to look out at the city. What follows is her fantasy, even her assumption of the role of the king. The film will be shot in the manner of a silent film and will include titles. "It was rumored that King Zog of Albania was on a secret visit . . . and in love. A group of exiles took this as an opportunity to attempt an assassination."

Theresa Russell as King Zog in *Aria*.

The camera pans slowly over the city, then stops at the statue of a man on a horse and another title follows ("but"). On a park bench three men are reading of the king's romance, one glancing in the direction of the palace. Inside, the king's advisors have also read the newspaper, but say nothing as the king walks by. At the bench one of the men rolls up a gun inside the newspaper, then hands it to his companion. As the three men go their separate ways, the king is photographed alone in his room. His silence indicates his isolation from those around him, even from his mistress, whom he can only admire from a distance.

The mistress is introduced sitting with her family and playing with a baby. If she is associated with innocence, the assassins are associated with the tools of war. One of the men stops at a shop to look at a variety of armaments. Zog seems to anticipate the assassins; after noticing one of the men looking up at the palace, Zog puts a gun into his pocket as he goes out for the night. One alteration Roeg makes in history is to change the opera Zog attends: he substitutes excerpts from Giuseppe Verdi's *Un Ballo in Maschera* for *I Pagliacci*. The Verdi opera is appropriate for the assasssination theme because it concerns the murder of a king by his best friend after the king has an affair with the man's wife. In fact, Verdi's opera would seem ideal material for Roeg because it contains many of the same ingredients as *Eureka*: betrayal, adultery, murder, and an extravagant dance sequence.

While the singers on stage dance around in costumes, wearing masks, the king's mistress looks from her balcony to see the king arrive to take the box opposite her. Outside the opera house, the king's car is waiting for him, and from the shadows one of the assassins emerges and walks toward the car. In the auditorium Zog lights a cigarette and admires his mistress from a distance as her companion whispers something to her. From the woman, the camera seems to pan across to the three assassins standing outside. One separates from the others, and a female dancer moves around the stage in costume. The mistress's eyes seem riveted on Zog, and the camera first closes in on his eyes, then hers, and finally onto the eyes of the singers in masks, thus uniting everyone in the action. The opera is not yet over as the king and his men make their departure. They are soon followed by the mistress and her companion.

On stage a murder occurs, as a knife is struck into a woman's breast. Zog moves toward the entrance as the assassins position themselves, while one of the characters in the opera hands another a gun. Outside, one of the assassins shoots, wounding one of Zog's soldiers, and the king quickly moves to cover, even as his other companion is shot. King Zog fires back, and the gunfight is juxtaposed with the performance on the stage. The assassins are eventually shot, their blood dripping into the snow as they die, while on the stage the participants seem to be circling the camera. The mistress, who has looked on in horror, runs to the king, and the camera pulls back to show the couple embracing. The action returns to the present, where the woman imagining the scene turns from the window to look directly into the camera. The final title is flashed ("King Zog Shot Back") and the sequence ends.

Roeg's contribution lasts nearly 12 minutes. It is one of the longest of the film and one of the few that is true to its source, dealing with murder and deceit, as well as romance, all of which are the subjects of the opera. It also includes a performance of Verdi's work on the stage, but the final product seems of little consequence. Although the sequence confirms that Roeg could have easily survived in the silent era, it is simply a reenactment with none of the cross-referencing or themes that one usually finds in his work. A further difficulty arises from Roeg's treatment of the music. If the viewer is not familiar with the opera, Verdi's work is simply background music. This complaint applies not just to Roeg's segment, but to the picture as a whole. Roeg's work is still infinitely more interesting than most of what follows.

Verdi is also the source of the next vignette ("Le Vergine degli Angeli"), which was directed by Charles Stutteridge and is among the most pretentious of the group. Having found solace in neither their education nor their religion, a trio of children try to escape their existence by stealing a car. The police give chase and the children are killed in an explosion. The film is filled with religious imagery and shot in black-and-white to enhance the austerity of the milieu.

Godard's piece also incorporates the music; it is a modern reworking of Jean-Baptiste Lully's *Rinaldo*. Lully's opera concerns a sorceress who finds one man she cannot entice and then debates whether to kill him or to allow him to live. "Rinaldo Asleep" is the aria announcing her confusion. Godard reworks the story by setting it in a weightroom, where the female attendants are unable to entice the athletes, even when they have stripped naked. If Godard remains faithful to his source, the vignette points to a crucial omission of the film. If the purpose was to make opera accessible to a larger audience, then subtitles would have been very important. Without knowing what the music means, it simply becomes carefully composed muzak. Even without the subtitles, however, this piece is obviously an exercise on narcissism.

More imaginative is Julian Temple's sketch, which takes a satirical approach to the material. Buck Henry portrays a film producer who goes off to a retreat for a dalliance with his mistress, unaware that his wife is next door to him involved in her own affair. The farce builds as the participants narrowly miss one another, only to learn the truth when they return home and find a videotape exposing their sexual escapades. If the humor is sometimes strained, it does offer the unique sight of an Elvis impersonator mouthing the famous aria from *Rigoletto*.

Bruce Beresford's piece, by far the shortest one, also has the participants lip-synching to the music. A woman strips as she acknowledges her love for her suitor, and after a series of shots of the city, the couple disappears. Beresford's choice for his music would be "Gluck, das mir Verbleib" by Korngold.

Like Roeg's story, Robert Altman's piece has a basis in fact. In the sixteenth century the inhabitants of insane asylums were allowed to attend opera performances. Altman's camera simply pans across the collage of bizarrely costumed individuals, while "Les Boréades" by Rameau is performed unseen on the stage.

Franc Roddam's vignette closely resembles Beresford's, but his story is set in Las Vegas. A young couple check into a hotel, only to kill themselves in the bathtub after having made love. Although Roeg's films often contain a large amount of nudity, it seldom seems gratuitous. *Aria*, however, seems to consist entirely of a large number of nubile women who strip for no real purpose.

Ken Russell's episode is also a woman's fantasy, although this is not immediately apparent. A beautiful woman stands in a stylized setting as a group of black shamans apply jewels to her body. One of the men moves toward her with what seems like a branding iron studded with jewels, which he places over her mouth. This image changes to that of a man attempting to give a woman mouth-to-mouth resuscitation following a bloody car accident. The earlier sequence was her hallucinations, and the pattern of the jewels was actually the cuts and bruises that resulted from her being thrown through the window. She is treated by paramedics and then taken to the hospital, where she is ultimately saved. Among the startling images in the sequence are a group of mannequin parts which are contrasted with the human form. Ironically, the music Russell chose, "Nessun Dorma" by Puccini, would be used in Roeg's *Castaway*.

Derek Jarman had the unenviable task of following Russell, but even if his sequence had followed Altman's it would have seemed incidental. An old woman recalls her youth, in particular a romance with a former lover.

All compilation films seem to have the need for an encapsulating story which serves to unite all the pieces. *Aria* opens with John Hurt walking the streets of Cremona. As the film progresses, he exchanges his suit for a clown costume, leading up to the film's conclusion. He sings an aria from *I Pagliacci* to a beautiful woman on a balcony, only to die on the stage at its conclusion. While the credits roll at the end, there is a montage of still photographs of the making of the film that are easily its most interesting feature.

If it were not for the music, the film would be of little interest, but because of its use of famous arias and because of the participants involved, the film received a surprising amount of attention. Little of it was positive, however. "A concept whose time had come and gone even before the cameras rolled," said critic Amy Taubin.[1] Roeg's piece was often singled out as one of the more successful, but this seems faint praise at best.

Another critic, Janet Maslin, at least found the concept of the film interesting: "The best of *Aria* isn't any more than cheerful kitsch and a lot of it is junk. But the underlying idea, that of unleashing these film makers and encouraging them to set their flakiest daydreams to beautiful music, is at least as amusing as it is profane."[2]

Aria would receive limited theatrical release, but seemed destined for a video release from the beginning.

Notes

1. *Village Voice,* May 31, 1988, p. 69.
2. *New York Times,* May 21, 1988, p. 18.

TEN

Track 29

When John Baxter says "nothing is what it seems," he is speaking of the illusions that exist not just in the world, but also in Roeg's films. In *Don't Look Now* Baxter has premonitions but misinterprets them; in *Bad Timing* a rape might or might not have occurred, and in *Aria* the attempted assassination of the king of Albania is actually a woman's fantasy. *Track 29* does not just contain illusions, it may be one itself. Although we eventually learn that one of the characters is actually the creation of another's mind, we are left wondering if another character has died and how much of the story was real.

Much of the hallucinatory quality of the film is the result of Dennis Potter's script. For the first time since *Performance*, Roeg was working with a collaborator who was as well known as he and had an equally distinctive style. A writer for television since 1964, Potter had quietly gathered a successful body of work, winning awards and praise along the way. It was the broadcast of his *Pennies from Heaven* in 1978, however, which made Potter as well known as any director. He later adapted the work for the cinema, but the film did not equal the success of the initial work. Eight years later, Potter wrote what many believe to be his masterpiece, *The Singing Detective*. This six-part miniseries enthralled viewers with its mixture of past, present, and illusion, along with musical set pieces that sprang from nowhere. Potter's success in television carried over into film (*Gorky Park*, *Dreamchild*), novel (*Ticket to Ride*), and theater (*Insufficient Carbohydrates*). Thus when *Track 29* was reviewed, it was considered a work by both Roeg and Potter.

In another ironic tie to *Performance*, *Track 29* was the first Roeg film that was not based on another source, although Potter's script was loosely connected to some of his television works from the seventies, in particular *Schmoedipus*. The film would also closely parallel the story elements of *The*

Man Who Fell to Earth: a màn who arrives from nowhere claiming to be an Englishman, a lonely woman who lives in a small southern town, and a doctor who is caught in his sexual infidelities. This time, however, Roeg's attention was not focused on the isolation of individuals, but on how relationships are all built on the same maxim: "In every relationship—a man and woman, man and man, man and dog, man and woman and dog—there is always the victim and victimizer, though the roles might change, as they do by the end of *Track 29*. It's just a belief of mine: I like the thought that a relationship, however good it is, always has a victim in it."[1]

The hallucinatory quality of the film begins with the very first frames. The first image is of a bridge along a country highway, where Martin magically appears. His back to the camera, with no signs of movement, he seems more like a statue then a man. His hand is out for a ride, but there are no vehicles in sight. As he appears, John Lennon's "Mother" begins, the words of the song announcing the film's theme ("Mother you had me, but I never had you"). A dog moves cautiously toward Martin, but when he does not move, the dog loses interest. Roeg cuts to the home of Dr. Henry Henry and his wife Linda, a house that is an urban equivalent of the house in *Psycho*. It sits on the edge of town, with a water tower on one side and a satellite dish on the front lawn. Inside the house, Linda Henry takes a break from her exercises to watch a television documentary on mysteries and reality. ("Even time itself can be bent and twisted and, unbelievable as it may seem, two or more things can inhabit the same area at the same time, coexisting in parallel dimension.") The camera closes in on the screen as the narrator speaks over an image of Earth. He tells the viewer that the population is "always seeking and always solving the mysteries of the cosmos, but at this very moment, one of those mysteries is about to become a menacing reality."

Back on the road, Martin's position has not changed, but his face is finally revealed. His appearance is as odd as his manner: he wears a cowboy hat on top of another hat, a pair of sunglasses, and a dress suit. The central image of *The Man Who Fell to Earth* is Newton seated in front of a group of television sets. Television sets are also used in *Castaway* to comment on the relationship between Gerald and Lucy. In *Track 29* the television becomes a character in the film, one with an ironic tone. For the first time Martin shows signs of life as he screams, "Mommy" and the next words could easily be our response: "He's gone all to pieces and lost his head." The words are spoken by a character in "Danger Mouse," another program Linda is watching. If she is distracted by her television, Henry is obsessed with his gigantic train set, which fills the room with track, plastic villages, and artificial landscape. To enhance his illusion he plays a tape containing the sounds of a train.

Our confusion over Martin's manner continues as a truck approaches him. The driver seems to ignore Martin's outstretched thumb, even as Martin runs beside him sticking his arm through the window. From the radio, railroad music emanates, and as the truck goes off into the distance, Martin yells at the driver, who still seems oblivious to his presence. Linda continues to yell for Henry, who methodically shuts off his train as he heads downstairs. As they sit on the patio for breakfast, it quickly becomes evident how strained their marriage is. Even as they eat, they are involved in their own separate activities; Henry is engrossed in a train catalog, while Linda watches a small television. When her attempts at conversation fail, she begins to mimic a train. He asks what is wrong, but she is quick to remind him that he is already late for work. Further proof of how routine their marriage has become lies in her ability to predict what he will say on his way out the door.

Linda is the culmination of the characters played by Russell: barren women who have lost themselves in alcohol. In the case of the female characters in *Insignificance* and *Eureka*, their inability to have children makes them feel incomplete (Milena has had an abortion as does Heavenly Finley in *Sweet Bird of Youth*). In *Track 29* the heroine has given birth, only to see the child taken from her and given away. Linda is also a return to Mary Lou with her preference for gin, her southern accent, and her lonely existence in a small town. Her connection to the girl in *Walkabout*, however, is more subtle. Left alone, Linda looks into the mirror, wishing for some salvation. "Come home soon. Today," she says, her words recalling the girl's plea in *Walkabout*.

Having managed to get a ride with a truck driver, Martin cannot help but notice the man's tattoo, "Mom." Admitting he normally disapproves of such disfigurements, he says that he finds this one touching. Despite the driver's warnings that it is not a good idea to "jump up into a man's truck and start talking about this tattoo," Martin continues. He interprets the tattoo as a sign of the driver's love for his mother and confesses that he was taken from his mother when he was only two days old. The man jokes that it was probably to a funny farm, but his grin fades as Martin admits that this is exactly what happened. Looking at the scenery, he tells the driver he was born in the United States, saying, "I should have had my childhood here, but they took me away." In the meantime, having finished her exercise class, Linda and her friend Arlanda sit in a roadside café, where Linda complains about Henry's toys. While looking wistfully out the window, she asks, "Did you ever wish you were someplace else?" Outside the semi-truck Martin is riding in goes by.

Growing impatient with Martin's constant talk, the driver pulls over to the side of the road and orders him to get out. He tells Martin that a small town such as this one should be glad to get someone like him. As he speaks, he takes off his shirt to reveal a second tattoo, "Mother." The sight of the

Martin (Gary Oldham) and Linda (Theresa Russell) in the café in *Track 29*.

tattoo triggers a flashback of a young Linda making love to a man with a similar tattoo. The intimation is that this is Martin's father, but a larger question arises. Martin possesses a memory he could not possibly have or even have learned of. Thus there is already evidence that all this is taking place in Linda's mind. Having seemingly been dropped off at random, Martin finds himself at the same café as Linda. Even before he has entered, she notices him through the window as he fumbles with the door.

Martin's difficulties in adapting to his environment continue as he tries to order breakfast, and his inability to understand American terminology draws the attention of Linda and Arlanda. When Linda asks if he is English, Martin goes to their table. His attention focused totally on her, he says, "There is something about your face that reassures me." He takes her hand as he introduces himself, saying he has come from England in search of his mother. After he introduces himself to Arlanda, he turns back to Linda, who continues to scrutinize him. He begins to panic, believing there is something on his face, but then realizes it is something more. "I remind you of someone, don't I?" he says to Linda. Nervous, she gets up to leave as he continues to question her, asking, "I will see you again, won't I?" Even as she and Arlanda make a hasty retreat, Martin shouts that he will see her again. The women gone, the waiter brings Martin his food, and he viciously slices the egg.

That night the semi-truck passes the Henry home, as if the driver is caught in the pull of the town. Kept awake by Henry's snoring, Linda calls him "piggy," much like a child would, and gets up from the bed. Even with her hair in curlers, she comes across more as a child pretending to be grown up than as an actual adult. As Linda looks out the window, Martin magically appears on the lawn below. Frightened, she returns to the bed, crawling onto Henry in an attempt to arouse him. It is significant that she calls him "Daddy," but he feigns sleep to ignore her. Finally getting out of bed to turn out the light, Henry passes the window, but Martin is no longer visible, and their conversation indicates that Linda has had such visions before. "It's outside you know. It's come back. He's outside and he's waiting," she tells Henry. "No, he isn't," Henry insists. Later scenes will indicate that Linda spent time in a clinic. Like Heavenly Finley, Linda has gone from her parents' care to that of her lover and found no freedom for herself. Heavenly Finley accepted the change from one restricting influence (her father) to another (Scudder), but Linda is trying to break free.

Roeg finds the interplay between childhood and adulthood very interesting: "I suppose it's about how we become the person others want us to be, although we stay the child that we originally were. You can become a great brain surgeon or politician—which are intervening titles given to us by others—but immediately the door shuts, out come the model aeroplanes."[2]

The camera pulls back from a house, which is actually part of Henry's train display, as someone calls for Linda. Linda's world is an imaginary one, but Henry's is only a little more real. He has created a miniature world through his meticulously detailed train, a world which Roeg's camera lovingly films. A train passes a plastic ferris wheel which fades into a ferris wheel that a much younger Linda rides. Looking down, she sees a carny watching her, even as another girl puts her arm on him. As Linda rides in a bumper car, the man comes up from behind and stands on the back of her car. The sparks from the car seem to cascade over Linda as she lies in her bed. Sparks recur throughout Roeg's films, most often at moments of high emotion (*Insignificance*) or in death scenes (*Eureka* and *The Witches*). Here the sparks represent Linda's feelings at the time of her sexual encounter.

The breakfast scene the next morning does not differ from that of the previous day. Henry examines one of his railroad cars through a magnifying glass while Linda glares at him, a swimming cap pulled tightly over her hair. Noticing her disparaging looks, Henry begins to speak to her as if he were a child, just as she did to him the night before. Having sliced an orange, Linda holds the knife menacingly as he takes exception to her saying he plays with his train. When she asks him why he has never used a railroad car she has given him, he tells her it is because it is a different style. "There you see, we know absolutely nothing about one another," she replies.

He gets up to leave, but this time she follows him into the living room, pleading: "I need that child. I want that baby. I'm suffocating. I'll just die without that baby." Handing her a prescription, he reminds her that it is not possible, but she goes on, saying, "There is no shape, no purpose." When he reminds her that her background makes it impossible to adopt, she runs outside, threatening to drown herself in the pool.

Having thrown herself into the pool, Linda struggles to stay at the bottom as she remembers the moment her baby was taken from her (the sounds are distorted by the water). Through the water, Martin can be seen coming to the edge of the pool, and he watches in fascination her struggle to hold herself down. When she does emerge, she screams "bastard," drawing the attention of a neighbor (another of the many "watchers" in Roeg's oeuvre). Because Linda is still ignorant of his presence, Martin throws an object into the pool to get her attention. In a frenzy she turns, asking what he wants as she escapes from the pool. He ignores her query, but instead criticizes her for her choice of words: he finds "bastard" too personal. He admits that he should have brought flowers, "a bunch of forget-me-nots." Looking into the water, he seems to understand her motives, but says: "You almost overdid it. No air left in your lungs." From the beginning, he represents both a physical and a sexual threat. "You're so much younger and so much more beautiful than I ever imagined," he says. She quietly asks who he is, and he replies: "We were very close once upon a time." She has climbed the stairs, and he stands just below her, his face near her chest as he asks if she remembers the "tug of his lips on her tender breasts." Shocked, she races into the house as he follows her up the stairs.

Martin's clothing, background, and even his name recall the antagonist in Potter's *Brimstone and Treacle*. In that film a very real Martin integrates himself into the family of an English house, where his actions inadvertently have a cathartic effect on one family member, but ultimately lead to the estrangement of the couple who own the house. In *Track 29* it seems as if Martin's spiritual cousin has come across the ocean, still possessing aspects of rebellion, but this time having a specific purpose in mind. Both films involve leading couples who are still together, but are obviously no longer able to relate to one another.

With their marriage in seeming dissolution, Linda and Henry have turned to others. He is in the midst of an affair with a nurse at the geriatric hospital, and the surroundings give their romance an immoral tone. They speak of their plans for the night while leaning over the naked buttocks of an elderly patient. Back at the house, Martin is already taking Henry's position, even eating breakfast in his seat at the patio table, while Linda watches nervously from the safety of the house. He tries to take her "back to the summer of rockin' free love," and she holds her robe shut, remembering the sound of a baby crying. Martin begins to break down, saying he has looked all his life for her. When he finally tells her that he is her son, she relaxes and a smile comes to her lip. As she goes into the living room, her doubts return even as he grows angry at having been abandoned. She argues that she had no choice, and he mocks her just as she does Henry. She blames the decision on her parents, saying there has not "been a day since I haven't thought about what happened or what should have happened."

The tension escalates as Martin pounces on Linda, telling her he wants to play a game in a voice that again mimics a child. Many of Potter's works concern adults who assume the posture of a child; two examples are *Blues Remembered Hills* and *Stand Up, Nigel Barton*. Although Martin is the most persistent example in *Track 29*, Linda and Henry seem just as arrested in their emotions. He is associated with his trains, and she with her collection of dolls, which she and Martin continuously pick up. Linda is constantly watching children's programs, and Henry and she use childish voices as part of foreplay. It is not just a means of escape for these characters, but more a shield they can put up to block out reality. Linda has even created an imaginary companion who comes to her at moments of anxiety. Although the character assumes the role of her son, this does not mitigate her fear of him. She is confused by his behavior and tries to deny her relationship with him, accepting it only when he tells her that he was taken away when he was two days old and given to the housekeeper. In the background, Wonderdog is heard to exclaim, "My son, my child." In the meantime, Henry locks himself in a supply with Stein, the nurse with whom he is involved; he drops his pants as she puts on a pair of rubber gloves. With train sounds playing to heighten his excitement, Henry yells out in ecstasy as she spanks him. His sounds carry into the hall, where patients and hospital attendants look about in confusion.

Linda has gone out to the garage, and even though Martin's voice can be heard, he is concealed from both us and Linda. Only when she is backing the car out does he jump out from the back seat to cover her eyes, scaring her in the process. He falls back into the character of a child who wants to play, but she remains serious. She asks if he is out of his mind, and he admits he has been "ill"; his words also serve as her own admission. She backs out the car, and they drive along, as Martin happily views his surroundings. "I'm not a bit like you'd thought I'd be," he says. An ironic statement, considering he is a product of her mind, and she admits the shock is just hitting her. When she tells him she is going to the clinic to talk to Henry, Martin grows violent, saying, "No doctors, no clinic. Nothing medical whatsoever." He was in a clinic once and believes Linda intends to take him back. As they drive, they are passed by the truck driver who had earlier given Martin a ride and could possibly be his father.

Martin and Linda escape to a lounge, where his potential for violence continues. He roughly grabs her wrist, saying she owes him. ("Most definitely you owe me. Or am I just a dirty secret?") He gives her permission to kiss him, but as they move closer together, she suddenly pulls back, saying she must not get drunk. As they talk, the waiter comes up to Linda, asking if she is speaking to him. She brushes him off, and as the man returns to the bar, he laughs to the bartender about the lady sitting alone, talking to herself. In the background Linda is indeed alone. This moment disturbs our identification with her and our involvement with her fantasy, but this may have been Roeg's intention. With few exceptions (primarily *The Witches* and *Don't Look Now*, both the work of writer Allan Scott), Roeg intends viewers to remain disassociated from the protagonists, so that they remain in the character of the audience. Although this scene is meant to validate something the audience has already guessed, this blunt confirmation detracts from the film. For a moment we are taken outside of Linda's mind and view her as the disturbed woman she really is. As he kisses her arm, Linda begins to tell Martin a story, presumably of the moment he was conceived. The two become lost in their masturbatory fantasy, as he pleads with her to continue, while she holds her hand between her legs. In both the past (the rape) and the present (her fantasy), Linda's partner comes to a climax, while she breaks down in tears, once again remembering the birth. The hospital door closes shut (a "No Entry" sign appears on the door), and the young Linda lies shattered in her bedroom.

Having returned to the house, Linda again takes on the role of parent, ordering Martin to wash his hands. She is in a constant state of confusion, unsure of who Martin is and what her reaction to him should be. She is uncomfortable with the role of a parent and even more uncomfortable with her sexual attraction to Martin. He starts to have a tantrum, and as she tries to stop him, he takes her up in his arms. The two embrace as Martin asks if they are going to make love. "Are you going to make Martin go bye, bye? Are you going to put Martin to bed?" he says, but Roeg cuts away before she answers. In another homage to *The Man Who Fell to Earth*, Henry is called into his director's office because of his sexual improprieties. His work level is down, and although he tries to laugh off the matter, his superior is well aware of what the problem is. After asking how Linda is, he tells Henry that Stein will be let go. As Henry stammers, he is asked about his special "therapy."

More than anything else, *Track 29* is a bleak portrait of a suburban wife with a life and a husband she considers boring. With no career, she has lost her life in exercise, alcohol, and television. Through Martin, Linda can act out her frustrations, whether it be something as slight as his drawing a mustache on Henry's portrait or his later destruction of the train set. He continues to ask for his American childhood, mimicking the children dancing on the television before he begins to explore the room. With no toys available, he makes do with Linda's dolls and the various items around the room. He takes a diaphragm out of a drawer and puts it to his mouth as if it were lips, then places it on a doll. As he does this, his shirt falls open to reveal a "Mother" tattoo that is identical to that of the truck driver. He pulls a tube from the drawer and talks of "old geezer's with prostate problems," before putting it into the doll's mouth like a bottle. To Martin, being a child is a "good career."

As Linda works out the demons of her past, Henry's personal and professional lives are coming to a head. That night Henry and Stein attend the Trainorama, a national gathering of model railroad collectors, where he is to be the guest speaker. It was to be his proudest moment, but now he and Stein are unemployed and he also learns that Stein did not call Linda to say he would be late ("It's time we stopped pretending," she says. He reminds her that the matter is to be handled his way, but she responds that she will not lay another finger on him as long as he is married.)

Linda wistfully looks out at the town, her image reflected on the window, while Martin shouts "Mommy," and amuses himself with Henry's trains. Linda does not seem to hear him as she lies quietly on her bed, surrounded by her dolls. As Martin continues to yell, two trains crash into one of her dolls, signaling the pandemonium that is to ensue.

The Trainorama foreshadows the political rally in *Sweet Bird of Youth,* but utilizes a satirical form. Standing in front of a large American flag like General Patton, Henry gradually works his audience into a frenzy. He speaks of the ignorant and uninformed who ask him why a grown man plays with trains, while they sit in front of a television set watching soap operas and football games. (This is a direct reference to his wife.) He shouts at his audience, asking if they know how he feels. "I feel damned sorry for them," he says. He tells his listeners that the precise detail of his work represents American history in miniature: "There in the layout is a record writ small of what built this great nation." People reach out toward him, and he kisses babies, while Stein wipes her eyes. As he speaks of the old values the train represents, a locomotive begins to move through the crowd and he then sings "Chattanooga Choo Choo" (a song containing the phrase "track 29"). Female dancers run up on stage, and he is carried on people's shoulders to the train.

Perhaps the central difference between Potter's and Roeg's philosophies can be seen in the handling of this scene. The first half of the sequence is filmed as written, but as the song "Chattanooga Choo Choo" begins, Roeg takes the material over as his own. Potter had the original song played with Stein lip-synching for the male voices and Henry for the female ones. This is in keeping with similar scenes in *The Singing Detective* and *Pennies from Heaven.* Roeg, however, uses the scene for his own trademark of contrasting events. The music serves as background music not just for the scenes of the Trainorama, but also for Martin's destruction of the very trains Henry is speaking of. The family values that the song seems to conjure up are contrasted with the dancers, who unveil their panties to the audience. The destruction builds as trains collide and Martin walks about the plastic houses and hills, smashing them as he goes. Martin appears to be rebelling not just against Henry, but also against the social standards he represents. The cataclysm is a peculiarly beautiful sequence, with blood and large explosions thrown in for effect. Roeg takes the destruction even further as the scene begins to resemble the apocalyptic vision that ends *Insignificance*. Lying on her bed, Linda imagines that the semi-truck crashes through the bedroom wall and the ceiling falls in on her.

With both the destruction and the rally complete, Linda and Martin race down the stairs, falling onto one another at the bottom. As the two begin to kiss, Linda finally realizes what is happening. This Oedipal scene is typical of Potter's work, but also has its precedents in Roeg's work, particularly *The Man Who Fell to Earth* and *Walkabout*, where hints of incestuous attraction also exist. Linda breaks down, which causes Martin to ask if he really is her baby boy. When she says she does not know, he disappears, even as he continues to ask to play.

Stein and Henry sit outside her home, and his pleasure is obvious as he tells her his life has turned a corner. One of the men in the audience has offered him a job, provided he can relocate. Stein gives little response to the news until he asks her to accompany him. If both his name and his hobby evoke images of immaturity, so too does his speech. He seems unaware of what Stein is asking (if he is going to divorce Linda) and instead wonders what word is correct, *who* or *whom*. Infuriated, she shouts at him, and he then pins a ribbon on her, calling her his little caboose. As she goes down on him in the car, one of his patients watches their sexual encounter from the window.

Linda stumbles to the kitchen to pour herself a drink, while the piano in the living room begins to play. As she moves into the room, Martin begins to sing "M.O.T.H.E.R.," a sentimental ballad describing the perfect mother. When he finishes, Linda says it is "beautiful and so true," and he starts another song espousing the qualities of traditional motherhood. Sitting beside him, she strokes her cheek as she imagines a chorus and an orchestra joining in with Martin. The song finished, he holds her hands and asks if she liked it, before he gets up to leave. His next words seem out-of-place here, as if they were to precede the earlier destruction: "I'm coming to smash up the trains. Good-bye, Mommy." Faintly, she tells him good-bye and says that she loves him; she then passes out on the couch. There is a dreamlike quality to the entire film that is imparted by the way Martin appears and disappears and by the destruction which is shown, but does not actually take place. When Linda awakens from her sleep, the house is still, and we indeed wonder if everything was a dream. In a panic she calls Arlanda, who agrees to come right over. The sound of a baby crying is again heard.

With Arlanda's arrival, Martin's importance will diminish, as Linda faces her real fears. She mentions the man they met the day before, but Arlanda's silence makes us wonder if he existed even at that point. While Arlanda attempts to find out what has happened, Roeg cuts to the television set, which shows a man looking through binoculars, as if he were watching the proceedings. This is a scene form *Cape Fear*, and Roeg will cut to it here much as he used *The Third Man* in *The Man Who Fell to Earth*. Arlanda and Linda sit on the couch as she tries to discuss her rape. "When you've kept something inside you for so long, so very long, it isn't easy to bring it all out into the open. I don't really know how to tell you," Linda says. She begins to recount what happened to her when she was fifteen and met with the man who ran the bumper cars. As her mind returns to the event, Arlanda settles back to listen, but Linda's words are often incoherent as she becomes lost in the event. As Linda tells about the two of them making love, Arlanda cannot help but be distracted by the television, where Robert Mitchum and Polly Bergen seem to be acting out Linda's memories. Finally Arlanda gets up to shut off the television, saying, "It sounds like true confessions with a soundtrack."

Lost in her memory, Linda begins to sing "the Red Red Robin," the music which played at the time of her rape; here the words take on a sexual connotation. It is Arlanda's turn to be disconcerted, particularly when Linda begins to worry about Henry's trains and asks her to check on them. "This is giving me the creeps," Arlanda remarks, as the music builds. With some trepidation, she starts for the stairs, as Henry arrives home. Seeing Linda's state, he tells Arlanda that she has gone crazy; his patience has obviously worn thin. Arlanda tries to tell him what happened, but only her confusion comes through. Sending Arlanda to the kitchen to make some tea, Henry slaps Linda, calling her a drunken fool. He is about to do it again, when Arlanda runs in and stops him. Henry paces about the room, while Linda remembers her child being taken away and wonders if it cried at the time. All she can remember is her parents' threat that God would punish her.

Henry storms upstairs, and with his departure Linda seems more composed. She shows Arlanda to the door, asking her to remember what has happened. Upstairs, Henry finds his train set intact and begins to turn on the controls; then he shouts for Linda to come up to talk. As Henry sits among his trains, Martin looks out from a nearby closet, and the tension begins to build. Linda starts up the stairs, a knife in her hand, and a naked Martin emerges from the closet to pounce on Henry. There is little sound except for the sound of the knife going into Henry and the blood splattering onto his train set. As Henry falls to the ground under Martin's weight, Linda goes to the bedroom, the knife no longer in her hand. "I didn't do it. It wasn't me," she insists. She picks up a doll, saying, "I told you he would come back for me." She throws the doll to one side, while Henry shouts out her name and then calls, "All aboard." She changes into a white outfit, as if she has been reborn, and Henry continues to call for her, even as she goes downstairs. Glancing at the piano where she had once imagined Martin playing to her, she adjusts her hat and leaves the home for the last time. There is a shot of the living room ceiling, where a bloody stain suddenly appears. Linda drives off, now seemingly free of both her husband and her lost son. When the credits are completed, the first close-up of Martin is repeated, with him yelling, "Mommy."

Much of what was specific in the script has become obscure in the film. In Potter's original work, the secret that Linda hides is not that she lost her child to adoption, but that she murdered it when it was two days old. The deletion makes Linda more sympathetic, and Martin has also been made into a more attractive character. Potter envisioned him as more violent (there are intimations he murdered his parents) and more sexual (he grabs at Linda's breast at one point as if to suckle it). One of the most significant changes, however, is in Henry's final fate. The script has Henry's murderer alternate between Linda and Martin, and there is no question he has died in the end. Roeg, however, keeps Linda out of the grisly murder (although she does start up the stairs with a knife) and instead has Martin emerge nude from the closet. As a result, we wonder if this too has been a fantasy, and the blood which seems to appear magically on the ceiling is properly dreamlike. The final disconcerting detail is that Henry calls out to Linda even as she leaves the house.

Roeg explains his view of Linda by saying: "She's freed herself from the guilt imposed upon her as the result of an act that was not her fault. She became pregnant from her first fuck, at a time when people were very strict and blamed the woman. She lived with that terrible guilt until she realized that others were using her humiliation as a license to be wicked themselves."[3]

There can be no denying that *Track 29* is a disappointing film, but it is not easy to say why this is true. On a technical level, the film is flawless, particularly with regard to Alex Thomson's photography, which equals his work on *Eureka*. It is in the characters that the film falters. Gary Oldman manages to convey a character who is both dangerous and childlike, but Russell's performance is more problematic. Many writers criticized her for seeming to fall in and out of her southern accent. This remains one of her best performances, however, a study in confusion and paranoia in a woman who is mentally unbalanced. The main difficulty may lie in our own expectations. The thought of Roeg and Potter working together conjured up dreams of a truly bizarre film, not the rather routine fantasy that emerges. One critic who shares this view is Suzanna Moore, who writes in the *New Statesman*:

> While *Track 29* documents the shared obsession of its makers, one suspects that it is in fact the differences between them that would have produced something more disturbing. For although Roeg's self-consciously "modern" approach to film spatialises time into a series of visual images and fragments a single incident by multiple viewpoints—rather like a cubist painting—Potter's scripts demand a single dramatic moment in which everything comes together and is somehow resolved. Likewise, there is a tension between Potter's use of sexuality as revelatory and Roeg's own repeated forays into the innately self-destructive power of sex.[4]

The change in Roeg's style was apparent to many critics, not just in his mechanics, but also in his choice of material, as Richard Combs has noted:

> The films of Nicolas Roeg, which once seemed cosmically too restless to be contained by the normal parameters of movie space and time, are beginning to look at home within those of the stage or TV play. Which suggests that the problem with the normal narrative is not that it restricts Roeg's cross-cutting aesthetics, the exploration of mental states worlds apart, but diffuses them. A real movie "yarn" like *Don't Look Now* duplicates and confuses his leap-frogging philosophies with its own metaphors and associations when what he needs is a dramatic situation that cabins and confines, the better to allow the philosophy to develop its own space and time. Of the recent films, *Castaway* was derived from a book and real life rather than a play, but was still a one-set, two-character drama structured round some Pinteresque lacunae in its couple's understanding and expectations of each other. Even *The Man Who Fell to Earth*, Roeg's most gigantic curate of cinematic effects and time-bending propensities, was essentially a two-hander about a problem of adjustment (an acclimation problem), about negotiating the void not between Earth and Out There but between men and women.[5]

Notes

1. Interview, July 1988, p. 63.
2. *Listener*, May 26, 1988.
3. Interview, July 1988, p. 64.
4. *New Statesman*, August 12, 1988, p. 40.
5. *Monthly Film Bulletin*, July 1988, p. 191.

ELEVEN

Sweet Bird of Youth (Television)

In addition to his film work, Roeg has also found a creative outlet in television. For twenty years he has worked in advertising, making commercials for products as diverse as Coca-Cola and J&B Scotch Whiskey and filming a public service announcement dealing with AIDS. He has also directed a music video, Roger Water's *The Pros and Cons of Hitchhiking.* But none of this work necessarily prepared him for directing his first feature film for television. In fact, some television executives were hesitant about using Roeg because they were concerned about his propensity for violence and sexuality and knew that his films were often labeled inaccessible. Producer Fred Whitehead, however, was convinced that Roeg was the right choice to direct a new version of Tennessee Williams's *The Sweet Bird of Youth.* The film was to have an all-star cast that included Elizabeth Taylor, Mark Harmon, and Rip Torn.

The screenplay was already completed when Roeg came onto the project, but this was not a cause for concern. Gavin Lambert had won an Emmy award and had already adapted one of Williams's plays for the 1961 film *The Roman Spring of Mrs. Stone.* For Lambert the similarities between the works even extend to Williams's motives for creating them: "They were written at about the same time, at a time when Tennessee himself was approaching the age of the actresses in the stories. He was asking personal questions about whether he was loved for himself or because he was a famous person. He wondered if he had sacrificed something in the search to be famous. And he was also writing about the price we pay for open, passionate love."[1]

Elizabeth Taylor seemed born to play the part of legendary actress Alexandra Del Lago, and she admitted that Williams had first written the part with her in mind: "We didn't sit down and discuss it. We discussed life more than work. I thought it was a great idea and we both agreed that

159

it was something that I had to wait to do, to grow into."[2] She and Roeg had a good working relationship, with each respecting the other's talent. "Nic was a brilliant choice because he has just that wonderful dark side in his work, just like Tennessee," Taylor later remarked.[3] Filming would take place in a variety of California locations, including Mike's Banquet Room in Glendale and a Catholic girls school in Pasadena which doubled as the Royal Palms Hotel.

Williams's play concerns Chance Wayne, a small town gigolo who leaves town to become a star, but returns as the paid companion of film actress Alexandra Del Lago. Her comeback having seemingly failed, Del Lago has lost herself in pills, booze, and sex. In fact, it will be Wayne's comeback which will fail, as he learns the lover he has left behind, Heavenly Finley, contracted venereal disease from him and went through a hysterectomy. Her father, Boss Finley, is the local political boss, who threatens him with physical violence if he does not leave. The advice is unheeded and soon Chance is left all alone because the actress learns her film has in fact been a success. With the couple unable to work out their love, Chance waits in his room, knowing Finley's men are coming to castrate him. The play concludes with one of the worst lines in theater, as Chance Wayne looks directly into the audience and says, "I don't ask for your pity, but just for your understanding — not even that — no. Just for your recognition of me in you."

As the film opens, the camera pans along the outside of a movie theater where Alexandra Del Lago's film *Imitation of Love* is premiering. Searchlights scan the exterior, while inside theater attendants wait for the audience to leave; the sound of the film is barely audible in the background. The set recalls not only an earlier era, but an earlier style of filmmaking. Gone is the rapid montage that opens most of Roeg's films; instead, the camera casually films the employees of the theater as they go about their work, sweeping the floor or wiping clean the glass doors. The tranquility of the scene is shattered as Del Lago races from the cinema, with gossip columnist Sally Powers following close behind. Alexandra looks the part of an aging star, her hair disguised by a wig and her overweight body wrapped in a purple fur. Alexandra shouts for a taxi as Powers pleads with her to return, telling her that anyone away from film for seven years would look older. Alexandra glares at her from the interior of the cab before it drives off, as Roeg's credits appear in its exhaust.

Roeg's style of filmmaking in this picture differs significantly from that of his cinematic releases. Censors restricted how Roeg approached his material, and the obvious differences in the screen caused him to shoot most of the film in either close-ups or medium shots. Ironically, both these restrictions work to Roeg's advantage, as they force him to focus more on the characters than on his customary references to other mediums. The

Elizabeth Taylor and Mark Harmon in *Sweet Bird of Youth*.

closer proximity of the characters also heightens their flaws; this occurs in a close-up of Alexandra as the action shifts to Palm Beach. She holds a drink to her face as she remembers a similar close-up in *Imitation of Love:* "That first close-up. I heard them whisper, is that her?" Her attention is drawn to Chance Wayne, who is giving another woman a massage in the distance. His words have an obvious sexual connotation ("Oh yeah, that's the spot"), and as his attention is focused on Alexandra, they seem addressed to her. With the massage completed, Chance gathers up his folding table, while Alexandra tosses her *Life* magazine to the side and heads to her room.

The relationship between Chance and Alexandra is quickly made apparent: he lets himself into her room with his own key while she pulls down the shades. Their relationship is infused with an air of decadence as he locks the door behind him and she holds out to him a container of hashish. His attention is already drawn to her wealth: he asks if she always wears her emeralds to the beach. She replies that it depends on the beach, that in Acapulco and southern France she would wear her diamonds. He also asks her if she is a real princess, which she grudgingly admits is true. Starting her massage, he casually undoes her dress to let it fall to the side, while he rubs his hands across her back.

A central theme in Williams's work concerns characters trying to recapture their pasts; here it applies to both Chance and Alexandra. She believes she has failed with her screen comeback, while he unknowingly clings to a past that is gone forever. Basking in what remains of Alexandra's fame and finances, he returns to his hometown of St. Cloud, but finds immediate proof that the town has changed. He is shocked to discover that the Sazarac Arms Hotel has been torn down, and as he looks at the site, he muses that it was there that he first made love. Looking around, Alexandra ridicules his memory ("I hope your experience wasn't as empty as the hotel"), but Chance is quick to reassure her: "Oh no, that experience is something that I'll never forget." Looking up, he thinks back to that time, while the images of the past are superimposed over the clouds. (In one of the few technical flaws of a Roeg film, the clouds are obviously a still photograph.) Chance's remembrance of the past has a romantic look similar to that of Newton's memories in *The Man Who Fell to Earth*. A much younger Chance races into a room, pulling Heavenly Finley behind him. While they undress, she reminds him that they only have three hours, but he throws aside the clock, promising to love her forever. In a film in which the past is so crucial to the present, Roeg deviates from his usual pattern by only including this one flashback. Instead the past will be recalled through the dialogue. Roeg explains the importance of time in this film:

> Time has been the central theme of a lot of my films. Chance and Heavenly, like most of us, think they have plenty of time. We always think it's never too late. But sometimes it is too late. I also like what Tennessee was saying about the violence of passion. He felt that to love and be loved is the only thing we can put our finger on to answer that eternal child's question, "Why am I here, Mommy?"[4]

In the present, Chance tells Alexandra that he left town seven years ago with the band playing and everyone expecting him to hit the big time, but she is still lost in her own worries. She is musing about her possible retirement, when she overhears him boast that he was the "golden boy of St. Cloud." Alexandra laughs, saying that his town has now become sleepy, and his reply is prophetically accurate: "When news gets around that I've come back, it'll wake up." In driving through town, Chance fails to see Heavenly emerging from a building, but he makes sure his arrival at the hotel does not go unnoticed. He lays on the horn as they pull up in front of the Royal Palms Hotel, a Spanish-style structure that seems as deserted as the hotel in *Don't Look Now*. When they check in, there is little indication of the animosity Chance's arrival will generate. The hotel manager, Hatcher, seems impressed when Chance introduces Alexandra as a princess, and the bartender, Fly, is quick to greet Chance, reminding him that he used to wait on him and Heavenly. Looking as if she were in a drunken stupor, Alexandra wonders about the bells she is hearing and is told they are for Easter. Mercifully, this is all that remains of Williams's reference to Christ's death and salvation, which he had associated with Chance's fate.

Having checked in, Alexandra goes to bed, but her troubles follow her even in her sleep. As she tosses about, mumbling about her film, Chance is taking a document from his suitcase. Going into the next room, he carefully reads over the paper, which will later be revealed to be a film contract. When there is a knock at the door, he sets the paper to one side and closes the door to the bedroom where Alexandra is sleeping. Opening the door to the suite, he finds Dr. George Scudder, who wastes no time with amenities, but walks in wanting to know why Chance has returned. When Chance tells him he has returned because of Heavenly, Scudder asks if he received the letters he sent concerning her tragedy. Chance admits he has not, but Scudder will not discuss with him what happened, particularly because he considers Chance to be a "criminal degenerate." He warns Chance that he should leave town, but Alexandra's scream from the next room takes Chance away. After looking in on her, Chance brags that she is a princess who is traveling incognito; George is not surprised at this, considering her present company. The tension between the men increases as Scudder warns Chance about Heavenly's father, Boss Finley. "If you're not out of town by tomorrow morning, he's gonna make sure you lose the only thing you got to get by on." Angered, Chance backs Scudder up against the wall, demanding to know what he is keeping from him. With visible pleasure Scudder tells Chance he himself is going to marry Heavenly; then he makes a quick exit.

Chance is shaken from his lethargy by Alexandra's screams for oxygen. Opening the sliding door, he finds her in a panic and quickly takes out an oxygen mask from a suitcase. He hands it to her, asking if she has had another nightmare, but she orders him to get her one of her pills, while the phone begins to ring. It is the desk clerk, and Chance tells him that they have no plans to leave. Despite Alexandra's requests, he identifies her as Alexandra Del Lago and says that she is suffering from exhaustion. After he hangs up, Alexandra tells him that she always gets out of breath when she dreams. She worries that she looks hideous, but he calls her exotic, "like a princess from Mars." When she does not recognize Chance or the place, he confesses he is her traveling companion. Her temporary amnesia stretches our credibility, particularly as she seems unsure about what duties he performs for her. This minor criticism is quickly forgotten when Chance takes off his robe to climb onto the bed beside her. The room is bathed in a soft glow, while the red canopy of the bed serves as a background. Chance holds Alexandra against his chest as she tries to gather her emotions, saying, "It's a terrible, trapped feeling, this memory block. I feel as if someone I've loved has died."

When Alexandra asks where she is, Chance replies that they are in the Royal Palm Hotel in his hometown. She seems to relax in his arms, and he asks if she feels secure with him. "I feel sleepy. I want to forget, forget who I am. I just wasn't young. I just wasn't young anymore," Alexandra replies. When she learns Chance is 31, she realizes that she was already a legend at that age (something made even more realistic by our knowledge that Taylor was indeed a legend at this age). She retired an artist, but what do artists do once they have stopped practicing their craft? "When you retire from art, where do you retire to? We tried the moon, but the atmosphere of the moon, there isn't any oxygen. I became empty," she laments. Now looking closely at Chance, she asks, "Will you explain why I feel secure with you? I don't even know who you are." This scene has a tenderness which is lost in their other scenes.

Despite Scudder's warnings, Chance contacts Heavenly, calling her on her private line. In one of many references to time, Heavenly tells him it is too late. When he mentions his meeting with Scudder, she advises him to ignore anything he has said. Although she knows that a meeting with Chance can only end in pain, she agrees to see him at the old El Dorado Gardens. As he hangs up, Alexandra emerges from the bedroom, waking from her stupor. She asks about her drugs, and when she learns he hid them under the mattress, she calls him a stupid young man as if she were treating him like a possession. Her memory having returned, she holds up the hashish, saying that this is what brought them together. Then she asks if Chance is a criminal. He replies that she is the one who broke the law, and she remembers that they had some sort of an arrangement. She had signed him to a movie contract, but even then he was not sure if she was for real and had held out, saying: "You're not like any phony I've ever met before. But then phonies come in all shapes and sizes. And they run the world."

Alexandra escapes into the bedroom, locking the door as she checks through her belongings. As Chance pounds on the door, she worries about the events of the past two days, remembering a "sort of intimacy between them." He says it was only minimal, and she asks if he has any talent for acting. "I've had lots of chances, and I almost made the grade every time. Then every time I always lost out. I don't really know why," he answers. She wonders if he was able to deliver in the love scenes, and this angers him even more. Alexandra remains in control, telling him she will let him know when she is ready for breakfast. When the two finally emerge in the hotel lobby, Chance is dressed in clothes that Alexandra has purchased for him. Everyone greets her as "Princess," but the hotel manager, Hatcher, is now unimpressed with either her title or her money and tells her she must check out. Alexandra dismisses his claim that the room has already been booked, telling him she will leave on her own terms. As they walk off, Chance is obviously pleased with her handling of the situation, but also wants her to sign over some traveler's checks to him.

Alexandra and Chance walk out onto the patio, but they remain isolated; only the waiters are present as she hands over the money. He is concerned neither that she is paying him off in public nor that he is unwelcome in St. Cloud, which he sarcastically calls a "moral town." When Alexandra asks if he has no feelings for her, he tells her that she should plug the last hole in her memory. She takes his statement philosophically, admitting she could have done worse, but wonders if there was not a certain amount of intimacy between them. "I wanted to hold your interest," Chance replies. He is eating his food ravenously, feeling himself the victor, but Alexandra is not through and says, "Well then, you miscalculated. My interest always increases with satisfaction."

Upstairs, Chance emerges from the shower and goes to his belongings to pull out a tape recorder, while Alexandra languishes on the bed. Smiling, he begins to play back a recording in which the two of them discuss the drugs. Shutting off the recorder, he reminds her that she was the one who purchased it for him, so that he could practice his diction. Chance turns it back on, and he is heard saying that she introduced him to the drugs, that he learned all his vices "from other people." When he wonders what would happen if the recording ended up with either the scandal sheets or the vice squad, his threat sounds much like that of the senator in *Insignificance*. Alexandra is perfectly aware of what his intentions are and says, "The language of the gutter is understood by anyone who's ever fallen in it." When Chance tells her he expects her to honor the contract, she begins to laugh and his smile fades. He bitterly tells her that if this reaction is her attempt at levity, it is obvious why her comeback failed. She retorts that his blackmail attempt is an even greater failure and that his naïveté makes her feel closer to him.

With the threat of blackmail having failed, Alexandra wonders how desperate Chance must be "to even try and play it." He has gone to the window, his back to her as she tells him that he too must honor his contract. She wants him to forget she is a legend because she herself wants to forget it through the distraction of lovemaking. Looking at his bare back, she tells him that "when monster meets monster one of them has to give way." She reminds him that she is the one who signs the checks and that delivery must come first, that he cannot increase his value by "turning away or looking out a window when someone wants you." Defeated, Chance turns back toward Alexandra and slowly walks to the bed. As he lies down beside her, he wonders if she does not feel ashamed, and she asks the same of him, saying, "While you have more than a little innocence left, put on some sweet music." Chance turns on the radio, first to a broadcast of Boss Finley's upcoming rally, then to the song "Oh, What a Night." The sound track will include many rock standards of the era, whose sentimental lyrics help to evoke the time period and offer a contrast to the moral corruption of the characters. Alexandra starts to rub her hand across Chance's bare chest, saying, "Now make me believe we're a pair of young lovers without any shame." She takes the towel he has wrapped around himself and gently wipes his face with it before they begin to make love. Although Roeg is best known for the sexual frankness of his love scenes, this scene is one of his strongest, capturing the sordidness and desperation of the two characters.

Outside his home, Boss Finley meets with Hatcher and Scudder, telling them that Chance must leave. Hatcher argues that Chance is with a former movie star and that he cannot force her out. Finley tells him to use any means, while upstairs Heavenly listens from the window. The men move inside, where they find Aunt Nonny sitting in the living room. She remembers Chance fondly, but Finley bitterly reminds her that she helped Chance ruin his daughter. He wonders how a man on a sacred mission can be dragged down by "every soul that he harbors under his roof." Even his son is not immune from criticism, as Finley remembers how he was forced to bail him out after a stag party. Tom counters by saying that it is his father who is keeping Miss Lucy and having her escorted by policemen. "Why don't you get rid of her?" he asks. Tom then recounts that he has heard that Miss Lucy wrote on the bathroom mirror of the Royal Palms Hotel "Boss Finley is too old to cut the mustard." Finley promises to look into the story, but thinks that it is obviously a false statement. Boss Finley is a politician in the same mold as the senator in *Insignificance*; both men even have a sexual dysfunction.

Heavenly makes her way down the stairs, and when Finley compliments her on her appearance she tells him that the "embalmer must have done a good job." She reminds him that he drove away the only man she has loved: "When Chance went to New York, the right doors wouldn't open, so he went in the wrong ones." She cannot forget that her father married for love, but now will not allow her to do the same. "I remember you cut the life out of my body, and turned me into an old sterile woman," she complains. He reminds her that she is to appear with him and Tom Jr. at the "Youth for Boss Finley" gathering and tells her that it is important for his crusade. When she starts up the stairs, saying she will not be part of the rally, he tells her that Chance has returned. She feigns surprise, and he asks her how she wants Chance to leave, "in that fancy convertible he's driving around in or in the barge that dumps garbage in the gulf." She tells him she will think about it and walks away. The relationship between Heavenly and her father resembles that between Tracy and Jack in *Eureka*, even to the way each father disapproves of his daughter's suitor.

At the hotel lounge, Chance and his companion are the topic of discussion when he walks in. He greets the two couples at the bar, one of whom remembers hearing that he had been working at a hotel in Palm Beach. Chance laughs this off, then mistakenly remarks that "time doesn't pass in St. Cloud." They are discussing Tom Finley's upcoming talk on desegregation and the recent emasculation of a black youth, an act the men seem to approve of, unconcerned that Fly, the black bartender, is only a few feet away from them. Chance says it was done out of envy, as he already aligns himself with the victim. Scottie pretends not to have heard of Alexandra and then asks what duties Chance has to perform. Chance shrugs him off, saying she is a major movie star and the head of a film company which has put him under contract. Chance concludes by ridiculing Scottie's appearance, to Fly's silent satisfaction.

Chance takes Alexandra to the El Dorado Gardens, but they too have changed; Tom Finley has turned them into an oil field. Chance throws rocks at the faded sign as Alexandra asks about his past. She tells him to think of his account as an audition, an idea that seems to please him. He begins by speaking of his mother's death, but she tells him to avoid subjects of death and sickness, saying she needs no reminder of her mortality. He talks of his friends who came from wealthy families, but Alexandra points out that he had beauty, just as she did. Chance recounts that he was in the chorus of Oklahoma and even made the cover of *Life* magazine as part of its cast. She smiles at his exuberance, but her smile fades as he speaks of his other vocation, lovemaking. "I gave people more than I took," he says. When Chance tells Alexandra that he lifted his lovers up, she remarks that he helped them forget. Each time he had the opportunity to leave, he tells her, "the memory of my girl held me back." Korea interrupted both of his careers, but once the novelty of the uniform wore off, the realization set in that his life was passing him by. He suffered a breakdown and received a medical discharge, but the nightmares stayed with him. Alexandra seems to sympathize with him, saying he probably got drunk and woke up in strange places. He wanted to return to Heavenly, he recounts, but something stopped him. When Alexandra asks him what it was, he only throws a rock at the sign in anger.

Miss Lucy had first been introduced as she received a police escort on her return from a shopping trip at the time Chance came back to St. Cloud. Here she is sitting at the bar of a nightclub, talking to a man who claims to be on a mission ("I just ask questions"), as Chance and Alexandra enter. Miss Lucy is one of the few people who are genuinely excited to see Chance, and she is also taken with Alexandra, although she cannot remember her name. Alexandra is brusque with Miss Lucy, but as Chance walks them to a table, he tells Miss Lucy that Alexandra was the first to recognize his talent. "It's been a long hard time to find someone who truly believed in my talent," he says. Miss Lucy jokes that his talent has always been well known, but she has noticed a change in him. Alexandra's response is typically pessimistic: "To live is to change, and not to change is to die." Chance wanders off, and Alexandra's attitude toward Miss Lucy turns openly hostile, particularly as the latter continually refers to her as "honey."

Chance continues to live in the past, coaxing the piano player to play "Big Wide Wonderful World," a song from Oklahoma, but if the song encapsulates his feelings, the reaction it draws points to the reality. He meets a couple from his past, but when he tries to get them to join in, the woman rebuffs him, saying he has been away too long. The pianist plays on until a disappointed Chance takes back his sheet music. Chance returns to the table, where Miss Lucy is attempting to talk Alexandra into getting him to leave town, telling her that a dangerous man wants him out. Overhearing the remark, Chance tells her that he will only leave when he can take his girl with him. He says Heavenly is to star opposite him in a movie financed by Alexandra's company, which is news to Alexandra, who says, "You expect me to bring both of you back with me to Hollywood?" She begins to laugh and takes a slow sip from her drink before telling him "not on your life." She thanks him for the distraction and promises to do the same for him. Announcing that she only needs him to help her pack, she exits as he weakly calls after her.

Alexandra's hostility cannot mask her genuine love for Chance. In packing she comes across his pajamas and holds them close to her chest, fondly recalling their lovemaking. When Chance comes in, she runs to him expectantly, saying she knows the real reason he is not wanted here. She knows it is not a moral town and not safe for either of them. "Your comeback is a failure Chance, like mine. I started to have feelings in my heart for you, which is a kind of miracle. It means my heart is still alive. I'm not angry anymore. I'm not even jealous. There is a true kindness in you, Chance, that you've almost destroyed by clinging onto that awful stiff-necked pride. The lost and defeated that I know so well." Still angered by Alexandra's earlier rebuff, Chance moves about the room, trying to find the car keys. He tells her the difference in people is not who has money and who does not, but who has experienced love and who has only watched with envy. It is not the kind of pleasure you can buy, and she seems to understand. When she asks if his girl was pretty, he takes a photo from his wallet. Taylor's performance is one of the finest of her career, much of it coming across simply through the emotions on her face. As she asks if he too was nude, her pain is obvious in the simple way she hesitates before asking the question. Finding the keys, he starts out the door, telling her to call Sally Powers about his film project, but she remains adamant, saying, "Your girl's not in your contract."

Chance returns to the El Dorado Gardens just as Heavenly drives up, but the two are separated by the fence, a vivid image of the barrier between them. She is hesitant at first, afraid even to walk up to the fence. Although she admits to Chance that she does not love George, she explains that things have changed. She tells Chance that after he left she found out she was pregnant, but could not find him to let him know. Stumbling, she falls to the ground, where she will remain as she tells him about getting an illegal abortion. After the abortion, she returned home, but became sick and was rushed to the hospital by her father. "When I woke up I felt better, till they explained I couldn't have a child. And I'm still bleeding," she says. Chance begins to cry as he tells her he will love her forever; only now does she come to him. He tells her they can have a future together, and the two begin to kiss through the fence. The moment is broken, however, when he mentions his movie contract, which she considers to be another of his pipe dreams. "I hoped against hope you would come back down to earth," she tells him. Her attitude changes as she shouts that her father saved her life and that he can do the same by leaving town forever. She even seems to accept her marriage to George, saying that a "sterile woman is damn lucky to find a husband." Her car pulls out in a cloud of dust as Chance clings to the fence, still calling her name and saying, "You have to believe in me."

When Miss Lucy comes across Alexandra sitting in the hotel lounge, she is relieved to see that she has not run out on Chance. She remembers Chance as someone so attractive she could not stand it. "Now I can almost stand it," she says. She admits that the two never made love, but that it was not for lack of interest on her part. Alexandra seems lost in her drunken haze, reminding herself that she too once had beauty. The film often involves scenes like this, with two people talking to one another, but each on a different subject. Miss Lucy is telling Alexandra of how Boss Finley presented her with a jewelry clip, only to have the clasp shut on her hand. Alexandra is mumbling that she is dead, "dead as old Egypt, but my heart's still alive." Miss Lucy continues with her story, saying that Boss Finley had told her to write a description of the clip on the mirror of the Royal Palms Hotel. Not only has she lost Boss Finley, but "maybe a fingernail as well."

That night Chance is confronted by Tom Jr. who cannot even bear to hear Chance speak his sister's name. They argue and Tom tells Chance it was George Scudder who performed the operation on Heavenly. "You left her carrying your bastard," he charges. When Chance says he should have been called, Tom tells him that there is no address or phone in the gutter. Tom threatens Chance that if he remains in town until after his father's rally, he will get the knife, a statement underlined by a gesture to his pocket. Tom departs in his car, with Chance left to his thoughts.

At the rally, police cars escort Boss Finley's car, wherein Heavenly is flanked by her father and brother. The images alternate with a black and white television broadcast of the rally, which Alexandra and the others are watching. Chance stands at the bar looking on as Heavenly is shown taking the stage with her father, with Scudder at her side. After Boss Finley accepts the flowers and cheers of the crowd, he begins his speech by saying he heard the voice of God when he was younger and that he was given a mission. As he talks, Miss Lucy sees the man she had earlier talked to in the bar, who now says he too is on a mission. As Boss Finley talks of pure blood, the man begins to shout at him, asking him about his daughter's operation. Chance looks away from the screen, but Miss Lucy cheers the man on. Security guards take the man down from the tree as Finley attempts to evade his question. The man is then savagely beaten off-camera.

Although Alexandra cannot see the violence that is taking place, she seems to sense the danger Chance faces and begs him to leave. A drunken Chance begins to ridicule Alexandra as she says she cannot leave alone. He tells her to go to the moon or to the edge of the gulf, where she will have a better view. "I have a fine view of the gulf right now. The gulf of misunderstanding between you and me," she retorts. He tells her she should go upstairs and begins to shout for someone to bring her a wheelchair. Fly tries to calm him down as a stunned Alexandra walks off. At the rally, Finley begins to introduce Heavenly, but she runs off through the crowd. If Chance seems pleased by the turn of events, Alexandra is more philosophical: "After failure comes flight. That's something, Chance, I know about. Nothing ever comes after failure, but flight." Chance has already left, and Heavenly runs down the street from the rally.

Tom Jr. and his men are let into Alexandra's room, but find Chance is not there. Instead he is at the site of the rally, which is now deserted and covered in the debris of Finley's campaign. Chance is much like Claude in *Eureka*, a man who has gotten through life on his looks, but has little to show for it. He will also seem more at ease with blacks than with the bigoted whites who make up the town. Walking aimlessly down the streets, he comes to a black nightclub, which he enters without hesitation. The crowd grows silent as he walks to the bar, but when he orders drinks for everyone, they quickly accept him. The singer comes up to him, and the two begin to dance together as she sings "It's a Big Wide Wonderful World." As Chance dances with a woman of another race, we are reminded of the earlier remarks on the "purity" of the white race and the punishment which the local black man has received.

Returning to her hotel room, Alexandra finds Chance sitting in a chair; he has evaded the men downstairs by coming in through a window. She tells him she has called for a driver, but he stands up, stating that he is still her driver. Alexandra turns sympathetic toward him, saying, "Ever since you told me of your life I've been remembering all those hopeful young men, the young men that I chose to play bit parts in pictures I made years ago. They believed they were on their way up, but they never quite made it." He tells her he will make it and asks for her address book. In the lobby Hatcher contacts Tom Jr. to tell him Chance has returned.

As Chance calls Sally Powers, the gossip columnist, Alexandra begins to panic, going to the oxygen tank for support. Pulling herself together, she takes the phone, trying to seem confident as she talks to Powers. She is shocked to hear Powers say that her film is a success and wonders about the gasp she heard at her first close-up. She paces about as Powers tells her of a film producer who is interested in her for a role, while Chance continues to shout for her to mention him. Covering the receiver, she tells Chance that "legends don't die easily. They hang on long, awfully long. And their vanity is infinite." She is reflected in the mirror behind her as the producer comes on the phone and tells her she could win an Oscar, but her excitement is tainted when he admits she would play a mother in his film. As Powers urges him on, the producer tries to assuage her by saying that the part depicts a woman of great courage. Chance lights up a cigarette, the smoke flowing up around his face as he looks at the lighter, which is a gift from Heavenly. Alexandra hangs up the phone knowing that her career is no longer a failure.

Chance tells Alexandra to call Powers back, but she reminds him of his wheelchair remark and says "I have comeback all by myself and you have gone past the one thing you couldn't afford to go past. Youth is the only thing you've ever had and you've had it." Once again the mirror is a primary motif for Roeg's film, as the two examine their images and their reality. Alexandra sees herself as a star, but she sees Chance as the ghost of a golden boy. She offers to save him, but he does not want any part of it and she goes on with her plans for her comeback. Stunned to hear that he plans to stay, she argues that he is still young, but he is unconvinced. "The age of some people can only be calculated by the level of wrought in them and by that measure I am ancient."

Sitting beside Alexandra on the bed, Chance for the first time notices the clock on the mantel and seems to become transfixed by it, remarking, "Quieter than your heartbeat, but slow dynamite. Time, who can beat it." Once again she tries to persuade him to leave, but he replies, "Whatever happens to me has already happened." She looks in his eyes and says, "You're trying to ask me something. I can see it in your face. Won't you tell me or do you want me to tell you? Let me try. You're asking me to recognize myself in you. To recognize the enemy time in all of us. I do." She tells him they must move on, past their youth. Forlornly, she walks away from him to gather up her stuff, as the bellman arrives. She leaves the room just as Chance looks up and quietly calls out her name.

As Alexandra's car pulls away, another car pulls up and Tom Jr. and his companions get out. Upstairs, Chance is pacing about, becoming frantic as he tries to find the meaning of what is happening. Looking in the mirror for guidance, he says, "Something's got to mean something, don't it? Even though your life means nothing." As he talks to himself, the reflection of Tom Jr. becomes visible in the mirror. He closes the cabinet to the mirror, saying Chance will not want to see this. There is a shot of operating knives, and the screen fades as Chance lets out a scream. Heavenly is shown crying while Alexandra's limousine leaves town.

Sweet Bird of Youth is Roeg's most pessimistic work, a harrowing account that leaves its principals not only defeated but sexually impotent. Yet, Roeg always maintained his films ended with a sense of hope and so too does this film. In fact, the film contains more humanity than Williams's original work. Despite her frequent tirades Alexandra genuinely loves Chance. Likewise Heavenly loves Chance, but she is aware that his world is only partially real, that he will be forever chasing his dream. Thus, both women are forced to abandon him to his fate. Alexandra, however, at least leaves on a note of optimism; not only her career, but also her ability to love has been resurrected.

Although Roeg's presentation of sex and drugs has been muted in this work, an air of decadence and immorality still surrounds the film. It is a surprisingly mature work despite the constraints Roeg experienced because of the medium. This work was a change of pace; his next film would represent a sharp departure from his previous career.

Notes

1. *New York Times*, July 20, 1989, p. 28.
2. *T.V. Guide*, September 30, 1989.
3. *New York Times*, July 20, 1989, p. 28.
4. Ibid.

TWELVE

The Witches

The thought of Roeg and Jim Henson collaborating on a film was likely to send a shudder through either man's admirers. Henson was forever identified with the Muppets, while the closest Roeg had ever come to filming a children's story was *Walkabout,* a film that included nudity and violence. Henson, however, had tried to create more adult products with films such as *Labyrinth* (a title appropriate to almost any of Roeg's films) and *Dark Crystal.* Roeg, on the other hand, had always expressed a wish to create a film that would be more accessible to audiences and thus lay to rest the argument that he was unable to make a film that was not too difficult for the average viewer. *The Witches* seemed the perfect vehicle, because it was based on a popular children's film, had Henson's name on the credits, and featured extensive special effects.

Roeg was in the midst of completing *Track 29* when he was approached by Duncan Kenworthy. He hoped to interest Roeg in directing an episode of Henson's television series "The Storyteller," but the story which appealed to Roeg had already been taken. Roeg then expressed an interest in another project the company was preparing, which was based on Roald Dahl's children's story *The Witches.* Allan Scott had already begun work on the script, which was a further incentive for Roeg. Filming began in the spring of 1988 with location work in Norway and Newquay, as well as studio work at Bray Studios. The live action work was completed in seven weeks, with the special effects taking another five. Henson's Creature Shop created three separate models for the mice: one was life-size, another was much larger, and a third rodent which was used for the facial movements, was more of a hand puppet. The budget was over $10,000,000, Roeg's largest since *Eureka.*

Although Roald Dahl is best known for his short stories with twist endings, he was equally successful with children's stories (*Chitty Chitty Bang*

Bang and *Willie Wonka's Chocolate Factory*). Many of his stories involve the transformation of the protagonist into an animal or insect as does *The Witches*. His parents having died in a car accident, Luke goes to live with his grand-mother, who regales him with stories of her encounters with witches. When the two go to an old English hotel, Luke finds himself in the midst of a witches' convention. When he is discovered at their meeting, the witches give him a potion which transforms him into a mouse. Undaunted, he teams up with his grandmother and another boy who has been similarly altered to try to save the other children of England. They manage to get the witches to drink their own potions and thus transform them into mice, which are quickly disposed of by the hotel staff. Luke and his grandmother return to their home, comfortable with the fact that he will always be a mouse.

Roeg has explained what attracted him to this story:

> *The Witches* was a strong adventure dealing with basic emotions. You tend to think you lose those emotions as you get older, but you don't. That's why the film can be appreciated by adults on higher levels. *The Witches* didn't strike me as simple comic book stuff, but a really great story about facing up to life and how we can all triumph over adversity. I was intrigued by the challenge of how exactly I would put that message across in the guise of a fairy story."[1]

The first step in making a children's story successful is to transport the readers, so that they allow their imaginations to take over. Roeg does this visually by having the camera hurtle across a snowy mountain range (much as he does in the opening of *Eureka*), as if the viewer is being taken to the top of the world. Stanley Myers's music heightens this effect, and even the credits seem somehow magical: green letters are thrown at the viewer. The credits completed, the frame seems to tear away to reveal a small village which has no place in time or geography. A woman's voice is talking of witches as the camera pans along a row of houses and a brick street where a man and woman walk with a bicycle. The camera moves in through a win-dow to a room where Helga is making candles as she tells her grandson, Luke, of her encounters with witches. She warns him of the Grand High Witch, who rules over all witches, and to emphasize the threat witches represent, Helga holds out her hand. One finger is partially missing, and Luke rubs at the stub in awe.

Roeg's ability to create a quiet menace through simple visuals resur-faces in a story Helga recounts of a childhood friend, Erica. A gnarled hand stirs a pot, and a woman goes to the window to look down at Erica. Erica's pigtails and costume recall an earlier time, as does the horse-drawn wagon which passes in front of her. The woman's eyes are purple and near her are a black cat and a toad, all indicators of her true nature. In her home Erica's father puts a painting into place and then sends her out to purchase some milk. The camera moves in toward the painting, a scene of a farm with some ducks behind a fence; the attention of the camera alerts us to the painting's significance. With her milk container in hand, Erica walks alone along the cobblestone streets while the witch waits for her in an alley. Just before her abduction, the black cat crosses her path, and as she is pulled into the shadows as the milk container crashes to the ground. The cat wanders off and Helga bemoans Erica's fate ("Oh, my poor Erica").

Children run through an alley to come out in front of Erica's home, which is crowded with spectators and the police. The action is photographed at an angle, so that the viewer is as disoriented as are the participants. A policeman is questioning Erica's father, but Helga informs Luke that she will not be found. Weeks later, Helga goes to visit Erica's family, and as she is consoling them the father becomes transfixed by something on the wall. "It was as though he'd seen a ghost," she says. He moves toward the painting he had earlier put up, which now contains a representation of Erica looking out a window. As the years pass, Erica's image changes position and seems to age, finally becoming an image of Erica as an old woman hunched over her cane. The figure fades away, but Helga warns that even then Erica was not necessarily free.

Helga is putting Luke to bed when his parents come in to kiss him goodnight. Wearing formal wear, they are preparing for a night out. The mother wears a scarf around her shoulders, which Luke seems to cling to as she leaves. She makes the grandmother promise not to tell any more stories of witches, but after they leave Luke convinces her to continue. Thus the parents' authority has already been diminished. As the camera photographs them driving off, there is a sense of finality to their departure. Helga warns Luke that witches can smell children from a great distance. Luke feels secure in the fact that he is clean, but Helga reasons that a witch then would have an even better chance of smelling him. With a dirty child it would be the dirt they would smell, but with a clean child it would be the child. Helga shocks him even further by saying that to a witch he would smell like dog droppings, "fresh dog droppings." She leaves him surrounded by the candles she has lit, objects Roeg always associates with innocence.

The next morning Luke goes to his parents' room to present them with drawings he has made, but finds it empty. Outside a police car pulls up, its light silently turning, and as the police leave the vehicle a plane can be heard flying overhead, predicting their departure. Helga opens the door to find one of the policemen holding the mother's scarf. The deaths of the parents are never directly mentioned, but the aftermath is apparent as Helga sits in the living room crying quietly. When Luke comes in, she wraps him in his mother's scarf. The separation of a child from its parents is a common theme in children's stories, but Roeg minimizes the pain by keeping the deaths off-camera and by having the parents make only a cameo appearance. This is in marked contrast to *Walkabout,* where the children are not only separated from their parents, but must witness their father's suicide. In fact, many of the changes from Dahl's story are the result of a conscious attempt not just to soften scenes, but to make them more accessible to the viewers, particularly the younger ones. Under Helga's care Luke returns to England to attend school, another scene echoing *Walkabout* (Luke wears a school uniform). She acts as narrator, but is unable to verbalize the accident which befell the parents, and Luke's manner tells us he is over the shock. He is carefully telling a classmate about witches.

Through Helga, Roeg has told the viewer and Luke what to look for to identify witches: their purple eyes, the wearing of gloves to cover their misshapen hands, their clubbed feet, and the manner in which they constantly itch their scalps, proof that they are in fact bald. Thus both the viewer and Luke are prepared for his first meeting with a witch, which comes as he is playing in his tree house. The woman looks up at Luke, wiggling her nose in disgust. She offers him a snake, but noticing her purple eyes, Luke pulls back in fright. She demonstrates her control over the snake by wrapping it around her neck and holding its face close to hers so that its tongue nearly touches her face. Luke shouts for his grandmother, but the witch confidently tells him that she cannot hear him and frightens him even further by addressing him by name. With the offer of the snake unsuccessful, the witch turns to chocolate, but as she holds up the bar, Helga emerges from the house. Luke shouts to her and the witch hurries off, the snake magically appearing in her purse. Having climbed down the tree, Luke hurriedly tells his grandmother of what has happened. As she comforts him, the camera closes in on her finger stub.

The celebration of Luke's birthday seems a respite for the two, as the grandmother presents him with a pair of pet mice. Luke is busy thanking her and making plans for the mice when Helga leans on the cage in obvious pain. Looking in on the mice, Luke prophetically tells her that it "must be so neat to be a mouse." Only when she slumps onto the table, does Luke take notice and try vainly to wake her. The mice seem to sense the danger and run furiously in their cage. This is the darkest moment of the film, when it seems as if Luke will be cut off not only from his parents, but also from his grandmother. This pessimism is quickly dissipated in the next scene as a doctor pronounces Helga basically healthy, but says she has diabetes. She prescribes a diet for Helga that includes cutting out cigars, and she also recommends that Helga take a trip to the seaside. The doctor gone, Helga apologizes to Luke for having scared him. Relieved, he goes off to play with his mice, placing them on the intricate track he has set up. The sequence ends with a disturbing close-up of a mechanical skeleton, which is laughing maniacally.

Taking the doctor's advice, Helga and Luke visit the Hotel Excelsior. As isolated as the family's home in *Walkabout,* it sits by the sea with little around it. When Luke and his grandmother arrive, attendants quickly carry away their bags. Behind them another car arrives, and from it emerges Eva Ernst, who wears a tight black dress and a purple hat and speaks with a thick German accent. In the lobby, other women gather excitedly around Eva, who is the chairwoman of their organization, the Royal Society for the Prevention of Cruelty to Children. With Eva is her secretary, Miss Irvine, who is dressed in white. Having checked in, Eva glances approvingly at a painting, which has a small child in it. When she taps it, the figure disappears.

After Helga and Luke check into their room, he begins to explore the hotel. In the dining room he meets up with Bruno Jenkins, an obese boy who is sampling the rolls. "My dad's rich, but he's very tight," Bruno announces. He is pleased when one of the attendants brings out a cart with cookies. Back in his room, Luke's mice are discovered by a chamber maid, who runs off screaming to the owner, Mr. Stringer. He tells Luke and Helga that the mice must go, but she retorts that his hotel is already infested with mice. She remembers seeing a mouse run into the kitchen when they arrived, and Luke speaks up that the rolls in the dining room have been nibbled (actually the work of Bruno). Dismayed, Mr. Stringer agrees to let Luke keep his mice, provided they stay in the cage. This does not satisfy Luke, who wants to train his mice, but Helga tells him just to be careful not to get caught.

The guests sit down for tea, with Bruno's family seated at one table, Eva and her followers at another, and Helga and Luke at a third. At the buffet table, Mr. Stringer is carefully inspecting the rolls. Helga believes that Eva looks familiar, but fails to notice that she has just eaten some sugar. "Something very odd is going on," she observes. At her table, Eva's attention is on Bruno, who is sampling some chocolate as his parents admonish him for doing nothing but eating and watching television.

Luke wants to train his mice, but must first find a secure place to do it. The kitchen proves to be hostile: a maintenance man is setting up mouse traps under the watchful eye of Mr. Stringer. Finally making his way into a large conference room, Luke looks down the long line of red chairs toward an empty stage. He makes his way up the aisle to a partition set up beside the stage, behind which he begins to train his mice, William and Mary. Just as one of the mice starts across a small tightrope, the double doors burst in and a crowd of women hurry in, led by Mr. Stringer.

As the women are filling in the seats, Mr. Stringer tells Eva everything has been prepared. Looking through the partition, Luke is shocked to see that the women are scratching their scalps and that their eyes are purple.

With Stringer gone and the door locked, Eva takes center stage, telling the others that they may remove their shoes and wigs. With Miss Irvine's help, Eva removes her artificial face to reveal that she is the Grand High Witch, a hideous creature with a long crooked nose and misshapen teeth. Long strands of hair jut from her chin and her pointed ears hold long earrings, while her back is a large, bony hump. When she speaks, she gestures dramatically with her gnarled hands, pointing her long fingers accusingly at the women. Although less frightening, the members of her audience are also grotesque; they are all bald women (the scene is especially bizarre because Roeg includes men dressed as women). Among the audience is one of the maids, Elsie, as well as the witch Luke encountered while playing in his treehouse.

The Grand High Witch begins her speech by calling her audience a "disgrace" and "good for nothing worms." She sees wretched little children all over the place and complains that one child eliminated is not enough. The Grand High Witch unveils her plans to destroy all the children of England, but stops when she hears one of the women mumble that they cannot possibly wipe out all of them. As the other witches scramble to get away from her, the woman pleads for the Grand High Witch's forgiveness, but her pleas are in vain. While the other women lick their lips in anticipation, the Grand High Witch fires a purple beam at the witch who has offended her. A shower of sparks marks her demise, and all that remains is a pile of black ashes. In the lobby, papers from the desk blow around as if the very atmosphere has been altered. As the smoke gradually dissipates, the other witches laugh in glee while Eva continues, saying, "I hope nobody else is going to make me cross today."

The Grand High Witch outlines her plan, as she either leans on the table or gestures wildly with her hands. Her scheme is for the women to return to their homes, quit their jobs, and open candy shops, using money she has supplied to them. To create a dramatic effect, the Grand High Witch throws some money out into the aisle and the witches scurry for it. Gesturing for them to return to their seats, she tells them that they will also be given a secret potion to treat the candy. One stands up to say that the plan is brilliant because she presumes that they are to poison the children. The Grand High Witch grows furious, and she points out that then they would all be caught. Instead, Formula 86 contains a delay mechanism that lasts two hours if only one drop is used and reacts faster if more is digested. Intrigued, the women ask what it will do.

With all eyes focused on her, the Grand High Witch announces: "The child starts to shake, the child starts to grow fur. Starts growing a tail. All of this happens in precisely 25 seconds. Shrinking more. The child is no longer a child." She begins to laugh, playing with her wig as if it were fur and pausing momentarily for effect. "The child is a mouse," she says. All of the witches laugh and cheer, but the Grand High Witch gestures for them to return to their seats. To provide them with a demonstration, she has earlier given a piece of the treated chocolate to a boy in the hotel. The "repulsive" child is to meet her in two minutes to receive more. The women hurriedly replace their wigs and shoes, while Miss Irvine helps the Grand High Witch on with her mask. A knock at the door quiets them, and Elsie opens the door for Bruno, quickly locking it after him. As he walks up the center of the room toward the Grand High Witch, the women hold their noses. Pointing his finger at the Grand High Witch, Bruno tells the others that she has promised him six pieces of chocolate.

The Grand High Witch introduces Bruno to the others and has him come up to the stage. They begin to laugh, and he joins in, not sure what is going on, particularly when he is told he is in "for a treat." The women begin to gleefully count down, finally reaching zero as Bruno doubles over in pain. "Everyone look, it's fantastic," the women are told and indeed the transformation is fantastic: Bruno begins to shake violently and his teeth grow larger. Green smoke blows out of his mouth, then out of his ears. His hands are transformed into claws, and his ears grow outward. The witches cheer loudly, while Luke looks on in horror as Bruno's head begins to shrink, taking on the features of a mouse. Beginning to spin around as he grows smaller, Bruno is quickly lost in his clothing. Now a mouse, he runs away as the women applaud wildly.

The demonstration over, Eva and the women prepare to leave, and Luke relaxes, believing he is safe. It will be Elsie who first catches Luke's scent as she is straightening up the stage, and she shouts to the others that she smells dog droppings. Luke nervously crouches down as the others move around the stage, following their noses. Eva angrily tells the others that "it must be exterminated immediately." His hiding place discovered, Luke scrambles across the stage as the women converge on him. He manages to break free by crawling through overturned chairs and jumping off a piano. He rushes out into the pantry and then out of the building, as he narrowly avoids being caught. Luke hides himself on the beach, only to see Eva standing over a baby carriage while the mother sleeps on the bench beside her. Noticing his look, Eva pushes the carriage down the hill, where it begins to roll toward the cliff. The other women cheer in expectation of the child's death, but Luke breaks his cover to stop the carriage at the last moment. Once again Luke manages to escape the witches and finally makes his way back to the hotel. At this point the camera looks down on him from a great distance, in this way disconnecting the viewer from Luke's plight.

Running into their room, Luke finds his grandmother unconscious and he is unable to wake her. From the next room Eva emerges, calling Helga an old adversary. As Luke shouts to his grandmother, Eva grabs him.

She sweeps him up in her cape, and when it comes down he has been transported back to the auditorium. Luke is held down on a table, and his mouth is forced open while an entire bottle of potion is poured down his throat. When he is released, Luke staggers about as if drunk. Just as Bruno's transformation was shown from Luke's perspective so is his own. As Luke is undergoing his alteration, Helga awakens from her coma as if she is aware of her grandson's plight. Looking out through his clothes, Luke watches the witches as his form becomes smaller. It is as a mouse that Luke looks out from his discarded clothing, while Eva tells the others to kill him. The women stomp on his clothing, but Luke scurries away.

Having escaped into an air shaft, Luke is surprised to find he can still talk. He comes across Bruno, who is busy eating a discarded piece of cake; he is still disappointed that he did not receive his six bars of chocolate. Although Bruno is not surprised by Luke's appearance, he at first denies that he too is a mouse. He grudgingly accepts the fact only after looking down at his paws. "Well, I'm not too keen on being a mouse," he admits. Worried about his grandmother's health, Luke decides to go to her room, and with a promise of peanuts, Bruno agrees to go with him. They come across Luke's pet mice, William and Mary, but Luke is dismayed to find that they cannot talk. This small scene was one of the most difficult of the film to arrange, for it combines Henson's creations with real mice. Although the mechanical mice are noticeably different, they do not seem out-of-place in their surroundings.

Roeg's ability to make the normal seem abnormal is brought out once again. In *The Man Who Fell to Earth*, he was able to convey the perspective of an alien; here he conveys the perspective of a mouse. Luke and Bruno make their way across the now empty banquet room, with Bruno worrying about running on a full stomach. In the lobby they face new hazards, as they must avoid being spotted or accidently stepped on. Bruno sees his father, but Luke points out that his first reaction will be to step on them. They make it onto the elevator and hide under a discarded bag, while the human riders loom over them. Going down the hallway, Luke tells Bruno that they now have two enemies, humans and cats. Dismayed, Bruno tells Luke his family has three cats. Outside Helga's room they find a maid's cart, which they hide themselves on, only to be discovered by one of the maids. Hearing screams, Helga opens the door, but her attention is focused on Elsie. Seeing her purple eyes, Helga quickly closes the door, not noticing the two mice who have scurried in. When Luke calls to Helga from the nightstand, she is stunned to see what has happened. She sits down nervously on the bed (as well as on Bruno) as Luke tells her the Grand High Witch is in the hotel. Bruno finally makes his way out from under Helga and asks for the peanuts. While he nibbles them, Luke tells his grandmother that they must stop the witches.

In the lounge Eva finds herself cornered by Bruno's father, who ignores his wife's gesture to join her. The two engage in a conversation of misunderstanding as he first asks if she flew in and then remarks that he too is a philanthropist. Confused by the term, Eva asks if he collects stamps, but Miss Irvine quickly reminds her of their organization. Whenever Eva speaks the word *children,* she seems about to throw up, so that a panicked Miss Irvine is forced to hold a plate near her mouth. Mr. Jenkins mistakes it for a collection plate and drops in some change as he begins to recount his work in the Rotary Club. While Eva is trying to evade Bruno's father, Helga is lowering Luke (in a sock she is knitting) onto the balcony of Eva's room, where he hopes to retrieve the potion.

Luke gets safely out of the sock, but as he makes his way to the patio doors, he is confronted by Eva's cat. Chased up a potted plant, Luke screams for his grandmother as the weight of the cat pushes the plant over the edge. Helga quickly lowers the knitting again and lures the cat safely away, but Luke's size continues to make every little obstacle a major hurdle. Crossing a radio antenna becomes a high wire act, and even a lamp seems to dwarf him. Scaling one of Eva's trunks, he is momentarily frightened when he comes face to face with one of her masks. In the lobby, Eva manages to break free of Mr. Jenkins and begins to head for her room. Thus, without his yet realizing it, Luke is in danger of being discovered. Luke discovers the potion in the pages of a book, but as he wraps his tail about one of the vials, the door opens.

Stepping into the room, Eva and Miss Irvine immediately begin to look for her cat. They find it on the patio, still distracted by Helga and her knitting. Glaring up at her, Eva storms back into the room, promising to deal with her later. The past relationship between the two women is constantly alluded to, but never fully delineated. Roeg's omission of the past is not only uncharacteristic of his work, but is a minor flaw in the film. Luke's chance to escape comes when other witches enter the room. He runs out the door, and Eva's cat leaps after him, only to land in her arms. Luke makes his way along the carpet, trying to avoid the people and their belongings. He runs under the carpet, still pulling the vial behind him.

With a sample of the formula safely in hand, Helga decides it is time Bruno's parents were told what has happened. With the two mice hidden in her purse, she confronts Mr. and Mrs. Jenkins in the salon. Mr. Jenkins is not surprised to hear Bruno has gotten himself into trouble and quickly takes out his wallet to pay for the expected damages. When he is instead informed that his son has undergone an alteration, he is understandably confused. Helga opens her purse to produce Bruno, but on seeing the mice, Mrs. Jenkins becomes hysterical, jumping up on the chair in fright. Helga and her two companions flee as Mr. Jenkins shouts that he will call the manager and Bruno worries because "they don't recognize me."

While one of the maids (who is actually Mr. Stringer's mistress) is cleaning Eva's room, she too discovers the vials. Mistaking the contents for perfume, she puts some behind her ears and on her chest. The witches have gathered in the dining room, but Eva dismisses Miss Irvine, saying she is only there as her employee. Angered, the secretary storms off, threatening to quit. Eva enters the room to the applause of the others, while in the next room Helga is growing nervous. By reminding her of all the children who could be turned into mice, Luke finally convinces her to go on with their plan. With Luke hidden in her purse, she wanders into the kitchen, where she quickly releases him as the kitchen staff hurry her out. The kitchen is presented as a labyrinth, with obstacles like fire, spinning machines, and boiling grease which Luke must avoid. Learning that the witches are to be served watercress soup, Luke makes his way to the shelf above the kettle where it is being prepared.

Perhaps no film in Roeg's oeuvre contains as many distinctive characters as does this film. Mr. Jenkins is the stereotypical travelling Englishman, dissatisfied with the service and constantly demanding his way; his vanity reaches comical proportions. Mr. Stringer is his comical opposite, trying to maintain order amidst all the confusion. Even in the kitchen, where the characters are only briefly glimpsed, the personalities of the staff are well defined. When the chef is told that someone has complained about their meat, he pulls another piece from the trash, scrapes it clean, and tosses it on a plate to be taken back in. The cook preparing the watercress soup is equally defensive and ignores the chef's commands by adding more water. She too is a witch, as Luke discovers. Making his way precariously onto a ladle, he drops the vial into the kettle and then looks on helplessly as the cook samples it. In the pantry Mr. Stringer meets with his mistress, but as he kisses her neck, he pulls away in disgust. Confused by his response, she goes to the mirror. When she discovers hair growing in the areas where she applied the formula, she lets out a mouselike squeal.

To make his escape, Luke must first make his presence known, which he does, and he at once loses part of his tail when one of the cooks tries to strike him with a cleaver. Running across the floor, he makes his way up the chef's pants leg, causing the man to scream and bounce about as he tries to shake Luke loose. The man falls to the ground, laughing uncontrollably and trying to undo his pants. Mr. Stringer pulls the man's pants off, but Luke has already moved on and Mr. Stringer is confused about the reason for the fuss. Putting his pants back on, the chef gets up; he tries to remain composed, but is visibly shaken. He will soon take to drinking the cooking sherry and to surrounding himself with the mouse traps. The cook who ate some of the soup has now begun her transformation and avoids the others as she is altered. Having become a mouse, she races into the dining room to warn the others, but is immediately crushed by Eva; no trace is left of her but a green residue.

While the witches are being served the soup, Helga provides another distraction to allow Luke to escape from the kitchen. When she knocks over some drinking glasses, Mr. Stringer goes to the kitchen to retrieve a dust pan in which Luke is hiding. When Mr. Stringer is not looking, Helga puts Luke into her purse. When they are left alone, Luke tells her that he dumped the potion into the soup which the women are now spooning down. Mr. Jenkins's demands nearly get the best of him, for he has requested the same soup that the women received. Noticing that he is about to take a sip from the poisoned soup, Helga races over and knocks the spoon from his hand. When he starts to shout at her, Bruno finally makes his presence known, addressing both his parents from Helga's purse. His mother faints, while Mr. Jenkins looks on in shock as Bruno says, "Don't worry, Dad, it isn't all bad, just so long as the cat doesn't get me. No more school, no more homework, I'll live in the kitchen cupboard."

Mr. Jenkins tries to make the best of the situation while his wife sits up, staring blankly. Looking into the next room, Helga points to Eva, saying she is responsible for Bruno's alteration. The witches have begun their mass transformation, as first one, then all, begin to belch loudly. Eva begins to back away nervously, as Helga moves boldly toward her. Luke shouts for her to wait for the potion to take effect, but as Eva confronts Helga, Bruno leaps out at her. Helga quickly grabs him, just as Eva lets out a belch signaling her own demise. Her mask falls off to reveal a roaring animal that becomes an even more hideous mouse. Still defiant, the much smaller creature says she will get Helga yet.

The banquet room has become a scene of pandemonium. The witches are going through various stages of change: some have already become mice, others are still in the process of altering. Mr. Stringer and his staff race into the room armed with brooms and meat cleavers to dispose of their unwanted guests. A stunned Miss Irvine walks in on the confusion, her mouth open wide. Using a water pitcher, Helga traps the Grand High Witch and then calls to Mr. Stringer that she has captured an especially infectious mouse. As the creature lets out a scream, Mr. Stringer promptly destroys it with his cleaver, splattering himself in the process. Disgusted, he backs away as a green smoke issues from the carcass. Triumphant, Helga takes Bruno to his parents. Mr. Jenkins has already become resigned to his son's alteration, while Bruno tries to console his crying mother, saying, "Oh, Mom, you always wanted me to lose weight. Well look at me now." People begin to flee the hotel in panic, but Luke makes one more trip upstairs with a shipping tag in his paws.

Back at their home, Luke is excited by the arrival of a trunk, which two men unload as he makes his way down in a toy car, overcoming various

A scene from *The Witches*.

Rube Goldberg devices. After the men leave, Helga opens the trunk to find it filled with money, the money Eva had set aside for her grand plan. Luke hopes that it will be enough to get them to America, and as Helga looks at him he explains that the trunk also contains a list of witches in America. That night he prepares for bed, while Helga sings, "it doesn't matter who you are and what you are as long as somebody loves you." Luke is driving a toy car and is disappointed that he will never be able to drive a real one; then he wonders how long mice live. Having apparently accepted his fate, Luke settles down to sleep in a converted doll house.

This is how Dahl's story ends, with Luke living on as a mouse. The film, however, continues, with Miss Irvine arriving outside Luke's home as he sleeps. Smiling, she holds out her hand, sending through the window a ray which strikes Luke. He calls out to his grandmother, who awakes to find him in the midst of changing back into a boy. This transformation lacks the excitement of the first one; it is depicted mainly by means of a vibrating camera, light beams, and a shot of Luke crashing through the walls of the dollhouse. Running to the window, Luke and Helga look out to see Miss Irvine conjure up his glasses and make them appear on his face. She also returns for William and Mary, who take their place back in the cage. She looks at her hands, which are not the gnarled hands of a witch, but the normal hands of a woman. As Miss Irvine drives away, Luke shouts for her to do the same for Bruno. The intervention of Miss Irvine is not unexpected, as it had been foreshadowed by her appearance (she wears white) and her isolation from the other witches.

From the beginning, *The Witches* was hailed as an immediate classic, a children's story in the tradition of the *Wizard of Oz, Mary Poppins,* and *Who Framed Roger Rabbit?* It presented children with a new world, but did not talk down to them; thus it was as enjoyable for parents as for their children. One critic, Tom Milne, wrote: "The Witches resembles a brilliantly told bedtime story, though the teller of this children's tale may well be the slightly cracked relative who can't judge when scary stories become nightmares."[2] The fact, however, that the film was intended for children seemed enough for some critics to dismiss it as being beneath Roeg's ability. Tom Milne, long a Roeg supporter, thought *The Witches* was a "likable film, on balance, but a sad waste of time, one can't help feeling, for a director of Roeg's achievements and ambitions."[3]

To dismiss *The Witches* as a simple children's film is to overlook the time, effort, and imagination which went into it, not to mention the cost. Although it lacks the complexity of his other films, it remains one of Roeg's best works. For the first time he consciously made a film from the perspective of the lead character. The viewpoint is often from Luke's perspective: scenes are shot through objects or looking up at the adult characters. Thus viewers are drawn into Luke's adventure in a way that does not occur with Roeg's other protagonists. The film also contains some of Roeg's most sharply drawn characters, particularly Helga, Mr. Stringer, and Mr. Jenkins, but also the myriad of characters who move about the hotel. Angelica Huston's performance is the key to the film's success, however. Obviously relishing her role, Huston oozes with menace, but manages not to go too far. In fact, she is one of the few actors to be recognized for their performance in a Roeg film. In conjunction with her performance in *The Grifters*, Huston would win the Los Angeles Film Critics Award and the National Society of Film Critics Award for her work in *The Witches*.

One person who was dissatisfied with the film was Roald Dahl. His book had ended with Luke remaining a mouse, and there was no good witch. Roeg, however, was concerned that such a pessimistic ending might have a harmful effect on its younger viewers, as he explains, "It's all right when you are reading the book to a child because you can rationalize it if it seems to be distressing to their imagination. But in transferring it from page to screen, you can't go around to every child in the audience and explain what your intentions are. Dahl's ending on screen would have been painful to the spirit of the book."[4]

The Witches had been initiated by Lorimar Pictures, but halfway through production, the company was bought out by Warner Brothers. At the time, the transfer of power had little effect on the production, but it would be of key importance when it came time for the film's release. The film would be both a critical and commercial success in England, but its release was held up in the United States. This time the executives at Warner Brothers were not upset about the amount of sex in the picture or its confusing story line, as they had been with *Performance*. Instead the problem was similar to the one Roeg faced with *Eureka*. The executives had not initiated the project, and they seemed confused about how to advertise it and had little incentive to create a success out of another studio's project. In the end the film would barely cover its cost at a time when a more mediocre film like *Teenage Mutant Ninja Turtles* would make ten times more money.

Notes

1. *Cinefantastique*, December 1990, p. 50.
2. *New York Times*, August 24, 1990, p. 13.
3. *Monthly Film Bulletin*, May 1990, p. 147.
4. *Cinefantastique*, December 1990, p. 50.

THIRTEEN

Cold Heaven

In 1988 Roeg served as executive producer of Sandra Bernhard's *concert vérité* titled *Without You I'm Nothing*. The work is the most extreme example of Roeg's predilection for protagonist as performer because it culminates with Bernhard standing naked in an empty nightclub. One's tolerance of the film must be based on one's acceptance of Bernhard's unique comic persona. Although some of her comments are insightful, most are simply strident. Roeg's involvement seems to have been negligible because he was already involved in his next film, an adaptation of Brian Moore's *Cold Heaven*. Alan Scott, who initiated the project, was again to serve as screenwriter, but he also functioned as producer. The similarities between this film and *Don't Look Now* are obvious: the apparition which both protagonists try to deny, the death associated with water, and the religious symbolism which runs throughout the film.

Marie and Alex Davenport are in Europe for a medical convention and conclude their trip in Nice. Involved in an extramarital affair, Marie is preparing to dissolve her marriage to Alex when she is informed he is killed in a boating accident. When Marie goes to the morgue, however, she finds his body is missing, and she gradually determines that he has somehow returned to the United States. When she finally locates him in California, he does, in fact, seem near death. He is feverish and his vital signs completely stop, then hours later he is back to normal. The story deals with Marie's confusion over her husband's health and her conflicting feelings about a vision she once witnessed, a vision she believes is influencing her present life.

In the past Roeg had often adapted works by opening them up, the most extreme example being *The Man Who Fell to Earth*. Although in the case of *Cold Heaven* Roeg and Scott remain relatively faithful to the original, they do omit many things and the few direct changes that have

187

been made significantly alter the work, so that the final result is more in keeping with Roeg's obsessions. The most crucial revision will be in the ending. Moore leaves the relationship between Alex and Marie unresolved, although there is a sense of hope. In the film the relationship will be fully resolved.

The film would once again star Russell. Her acting has been important to Roeg's career, but some critics believe he has inhibited her potential success. All of the films she has starred in with Roeg have been, for the most part, commercial failures. She is best known for her numerous talk show appearances and her roles in thrillers such as *Black Widow* and *Impulse*. She has also demonstrated a willingness to take on risks with other directors by appearing in Steven Soderbergh's *Kafka* and Ken Russell's *Whore*. The latter presented Russell with one of her most difficult roles, requiring her to relate directly to the camera, but the film ultimately fails. It was billed as a response to *Pretty Woman,* but each film simply presents its own fantasy of what prostitution is like.

Whore is of particular interest in the present context because it once again unites the careers of Ken Russell and Roeg. Because of their similar backgrounds, the two directors are often mentioned in the same breath in film histories. Both have taken the British cinema away from the literary tradition which has so long characterized it and have incorporated many of the experiments begun by the French New Wave. Like Roeg, Ken Russell is known most for the look of his films, but he has also demonstrated how technique can overtake a film. His films are always of interest, but too often he takes a sledgehammer approach to his material. Roeg's predilection has always been to examine characters and relationships, and the effects he utilizes are simply another layer he employs in this examination. Ken Russell's goal seems more to shock or parody.

It is Theresa Russell's work with Roeg which remains of the most interest in the present context, however. Roeg understood how they complemented one another: "Think of Theresa as the most important actor in my rep company. I like women in film. I like women in general, but I especially like to show them on film. They are not ciphers. There just isn't much latitude for them these days in movies. Theresa is an actress. These days she can play someone's wife or stand starry-eyed looking at her lover, or she can carry the fucking movie, like she does in *Cold Heaven*."[1]

In *Cold Heaven* Russell is once again called upon to create a complex character. Each of the characters she has portrayed for Roeg is distinctively different from the others, but small characteristics carry over. In the other films, Russell was part of an ensemble, but here she is the central figure, with everyone else functioning simply as supporting characters to her conflict. Marie Davenport is a woman wasting away in a marriage, but she is not the hostile spouse that Linda Henry was. When she becomes bored with her husband, she deals with the situation by falling in love with a man who is nearly his double (both are respected physicians).

As the credits are run, a series of wedding photographs are displayed from the weddings of Alex and Marie Davenport and Daniel and Anna Corvin. In a sequence which recalls the opening of *Psycho,* the camera moves out a window and pans across a city. There follows a series of seemingly disjointed shots of an airport, an elevator opening, and of the city, all of which give the viewer a sense of dislocation. The next sequence shows that the happiness captured in the photographs has long since dissipated, for Marie and Daniel are involved in an affair. While she is dressing, Daniel looks out the window of their hotel room. It is significant that he is watching a plane land at a nearby airport because a plane is used to open *Performance* and *The Man Who Fell to Earth* to anticipate journeys. A butterfly passes by the window, a motif which will run throughout the film.

Music has always been important in Roeg's films, but never more so than in this one. Stanley Myers's music imbues the film with an elegiac quality which adds to the feeling of a melancholy that imbues the film. Marie and Daniel stand in front of a mirror, their pose resembling that of their respective wedding photographs, but as always with Roeg, the characters must confront themselves in the reflection. He asks her to promise to tell Alex of their relationship, but she is hesitant and says, "I always make promises I can't keep. I hate it when I fail." She and Alex are to depart for Acapulco the next day for a conference which she hopes will provide her with the opportunity. Daniel wonders if she is happy and although she replies yes, the camera holds on her as they embrace, her face already reflecting her confusion.

In Acapulco, Marie struggles to tell Alex of her affair as they are riding in a pedal boat. Their relationship resembles that of the Henrys in *Track 29,* even to the husband's profession. While Marie tries to find words to tell Alex of her affair, he talks of clogged arteries and overweight patients. They recall happier times, and then he makes a reference to her disfigured hand. (This disfigurement is alluded to in another scene, but its significance is never brought out.) The two have stopped pedaling, and he goes overboard to relieve himself. Nearby, a man is racing his boat while struggling with his son, and in the process he fails to notice Alex swimming in front of him. The association of death and water is not all that unites this sequence with the opening of *Don't Look Now.* The daughter's death was filmed in slow motion to give the father's perspective and his sense of helplessness; here the presentation resembles a nightmare to intensify Marie's anxiety. The natural sounds have been replaced by Myers's music.

After Alex is struck, he floats face down in the water as it gradually turns red. Marie swims to him and with the help of others manages to get him to shore. Only as his body is lifted onto the beach does the speed of the action return to normal. An ambulance arrives and takes Alex away, while Roeg cuts to Marie's belongings floating in the water; a photograph of Daniel gradually sinks, thus uniting Alex's tragedy with her infidelity. The arrival at the hospital recalls *Bad Timing*: an attendant questions Marie about what has happened and she is surrounded by foreign voices she does not understand. In Roeg's oeuvre, hospitals are cold, sterile environments where characters are often forced into isolation.

In *Bad Timing* Roeg also instituted the use of a voice-over for one scene, but in *Cold Heaven* he goes even further. While she is sitting in the waiting room, Marie thinks not just about the accident, but about whether she should have told Alex of her affair and whether her belongings have been lost. When she learns the date, however, her thoughts focus on its significance. An inset shows Marie overlooking a cliff and seeing a light coming up from the water. Alex's accident has occurred on the anniversary of the vision she witnessed at Mt. Carmel. When Marie is called into the doctor's office, she already anticipates Alex's death. ("It's over. This is what it feels like.") She is confused about what she should feel—relief that it is over or regret for what she has lost.

When Marie is taken to Alex's room, she is shocked when the curtain is pulled back to reveal his body. Her sense of loss is not felt, however, until she returns to her hotel room. She examines herself in the mirror and finds that her bloodied clothing is all that ties her to Alex ("I'm closer to him now than before"). In the bathroom she comes across Alex's razor, cutting herself; the setting is a reminder of *Don't Look Now*, the only Roeg film in which a couple experiences both sexual intimacy and love. When Marie sleeps alone in her bed, she holds a pillow close to her chest while she looks at the space Alex would have occupied. In Los Angeles, Daniel is also awake, and although his wife lies against him, his mind is on Marie.

The next morning Marie is contacted by an American diplomat who escorts her to the hospital to meet with Alex's physicians. Her husband's body has disappeared, and there is no trace of it having been removed. Shocked by this news, Marie is asked about Alex's death, and she tells them that it was an accident, a statement she will repeat throughout the film. The doctors agree that there is no chance that her husband is alive and say that he would have contacted her if he was. Marie returns to her bedroom and while she lies on the bed, a shadow passes across her; at that moment, Daniel is telling his wife of his affair. Anna's reaction is first shock, then anger, and even as she tries to hold Daniel back, Marie is on the phone trying to reach him.

Marie looks about her room and in the process discovers that Alex's belongings are missing, including his passport and airline ticket. In the bathroom she finds a hospital gown lying on the floor. Instinctively, she goes to the airport, but the plane Alex could be on is already taking off.

Marie returns alone to Los Angeles, but finds no trace of him there. The apartment consists of a series of rooms which are sealed off from the outside; the curtains are always closed and only Daniel will ever show interest in his surroundings. There is no reply when Marie calls out her husband's name. Unable to reach Daniel, Marie calls her answering service to get her messages, but finds all but one have been picked up. The remaining message, which is not directly addressed to her, is unsigned, and on a nightstand she finds the impression of a note with the name of a hotel name also written on it.

The drive to Mt. Carmel is a beautiful sequence and makes strikingly clear how different this film is from most of Roeg's work. The colors are more muted and subdued, in keeping with the haunting ambience. Roeg's propensity for the color red is kept to a minimum, the only instance being the blood from Alex's accident. The landscape seems to mirror the emotions of the participants, with dark clouds dominating the skyline. As in *Eureka,* the emotions of the characters are aligned to the happenings of nature.

On checking in, Marie learns that Daniel will not arrive until the next day, so to occupy her time she walks about the grounds. Her haunting memories seem to overwhelm her. A jet flies overhead in a shot which duplicates the opening of *Performance* as well as other opening scenes Roeg has used. The leitmotif of this film involves butterflies, and several begin to encircle Marie as her anxiety grows. The butterflies are also integral to Moore's work, in which he writes: "Like a somnambulist she turned toward the redwood sign. As she did, there came into her vision three monarch butterflies, hovering like tiny kites, moving ahead of her towards the cliffs and sea. The butterflies were not innocent. They had come to the grounds of the inn to lead her on and now they glided ahead of her, enticing her as she stepped out obstensibly toward the beach."[2]

Continuing her walk, Marie arrives at the Lady of Carmel Convent, where Sister Martha looks at her with a sense of déjà vu. Going into the church, Marie automatically puts her hand into the holy water, but pulls back when she realizes what she has done. While she looks about the church, a lecturer can be heard relating its history (another reference to *Don't Look Now*), and the relationship of the butterflies and the church is brought out. "Our Lady of Carmel among the butterflies," the lecturer says. The Carmelites are an order of nuns devoted to penance and founded on the principles of the Virgin Mary. Behind Marie, Sister Martha silently passes by like a specter. Religious icons permeate the film from the beginning. When Alex dives into the waters off Acapulco, a statue of the Virgin Mary rests at the bottom. One of the ambulance drivers wears a cross about his neck, and on a wall of Marie's apartment, there is a photograph of her with a nun. The church at Mt. Carmel is laden with memories for Marie, not just of her vision, but of her own mother's death, and she eventually runs off in terror.

Returning to her room, Marie finds a note telling her to come to room 332. Believing it is from Daniel, she runs excitedly to the room, but when the door opens it is Alex who greets her, his skin a ghostly white and his head bandaged. Like a nocturnal creature he pulls back from the door, frightening her even further. "I don't want anyone touching me," he tells her. When she tries to ask him what has happened, he shouts for her to sit down and insists on asking the questions. First he wants to know if she left him the message they'd both found at their apartment; then he asks if his mishap really was an accident. She tells him she is glad he is alive and then asks why he left as he did. He remembers waking in the dark and knowing from the smell that he was in a morgue. Alex is worried that he will become a medical freak, and our awareness of how the alien in *The Man Who Fell to Earth* was treated gives this statement substance. Alex's manner is that of a person drained of life; he constantly checks his pulse, while struggling to remain conscious. He asks Marie to leave and lies back on the bed to sleep. Outside the sky grows darker.

When Marie returns, Alex has the appearance of a corpse and does not even move when she touches his hand. On the nightstand she finds a notebook in which he is recording his medical information. His vital signs often drop to those of a corpse. In the book Alex's propensity to die on various occasions is integral to the story, but in the film it is only alluded to ("You left me again," Marie remarks at one point). It is while Alex is still asleep that Daniel finally gets through to Marie. Her conversation is purposely guarded because she is fearful that Alex will overhear. He does, in fact, ask her who the caller was. He repeats her response ("The desk, no one") as if mocking her. "Sometimes, Marie, I've heard things. I've seen things that I can't remember after," he says.

While Alex sleeps, Marie returns to the church. Monsignor Cassidy, anxious to make his golf appointment, reluctantly agrees to meet with her. As she talks to him, he constantly glances at his watch or fidgets with his hands. She begins by saying that he probably will not believe what she has to say and tells him that she is no longer religious, a point she feels is important. She lost her faith when she was fifteen because she felt God had ignored her prayers to save her mother. One year ago she had come to Mt. Carmel with Alex and in the process had met Daniel. While the men attended a conference, she had explored the surroundings. Coming to Cliff Walk, she had looked out at the water, and it was then that she experienced a vision. The cypress trees began to move, and from the water a young woman arose. The woman, presumably the Virgin Mary, asked Marie to tell the priests of the miracle and to have them build a sanctuary at the spot. When it began to rain, the vision disappeared and although she was fearful of what had occurred, Marie had also laughed to think she had been the one chosen. She now believes she has been forced to come to the priests. "It's threatening my husband," she tells Monsignor Cassidy.

Believing she has now met her obligation to the apparition, Marie asks if her role is over. Monsignor Cassidy nods his head yes, but his manner indicates he is only tolerating her speech. He is the opposite of Bishop Barbarrigo in *Don't Look Now*, who had been sympathetic to John Baxter's vision. Although a painting of Christ is on his wall, it is flanked by a gold trophy, indicating that the monsignor's faith is divided. He doubts that there will be an investigation into her vision, but Roeg cuts to Alex having a convulsion, thus demonstrating this assertion to be false.

When Marie returns to Alex, he seems to be in a daze. The resulting conversation, which demonstrates Alex's confusion and Marie's anxiety, is typical of a Roeg film:

> ALEX   I went to a place. I found a place. I knew everything. I can't remember what it was. (*The camera closes on a painting of an ocean.*)
> MARIE   A dream?
> ALEX   No. Yes. (*The camera moves in on the painting and the sound of the ocean can be heard.*) A very bright dream.
> MARIE   I went to tell . . . I'm helping you now, Alex.
> ALEX   I can't remember.
> MARIE   What?
> ALEX   It's as if you were there with me. Like you always are and I knew everything I'll ever know. (*Alex goes to Marie and as he finishes his line he seems to collapse.*) I remember now. (*The sequence ends on the painting, as we again hear the sound of waves breaking.*)

Roeg's films are often based on doubles, or doppelgangers; in this case Marie's double is Sister Martha. Sister Martha has gone to confession, but instead of confessing her sins, she relates a dream she has had for the past year. In the dream she sees Marie and her vision. While she speaks, she clutches at the confessional mesh in front of her, and in the next shot, Marie is photographed through the frame of a window. She is waiting for Daniel, and when he arrives she takes him to her room. She tries to tell him what has happened, but he is angered that she has not told Alex the truth. She admits her feelings have already changed, that she finds it difficult to turn her back on Alex or to forget the past. She takes Daniel to examine Alex, but the two men are wary of one another. Daniel begins his examination, but Alex does not respond to his inquiries and looks instead at Marie.

The priest whom Sister Martha had confessed to, Father Niles, now comes looking for Marie, but learns she has taken Alex to San Francisco. In a hotel room, Marie is angrily tossing aside her clothing as Daniel comes in. The two attempt to make love, but each is burdened by the past, and once again Roeg equates lovemaking with violence. Marie grows hysterical, and her cries are like Tracy's in *Eureka*, "love me, love me." Marie is shocked when she opens the door and finds Father Niles; she tries to block him out, saying it is over. At the hospital Alex goes into a convulsion, his response seemingly tied to Marie's actions (further echoing *Bad Timing*).

The doctors are confused by Alex's condition because his temperature has dropped below that of a corpse. When Marie visits Alex, his vision is cloudy and he pleads for her help ("What's happening, Marie?"). She tries to comfort him but he goes into another convulsion and spews blood out at her. Through the window, Father Niles is watching as Marie is hurried out, while the attendants begin to work on Alex. The character of Father Niles has been significantly altered by Roeg. In the book, he is more intrusive, serving more the role of an investigator than of a theologian. He is constantly checking the validity of Marie's story, even going to Alex's hospital room to question him about his accident. Marie considers him an emissary who is influencing what is happening. In fact, much of the book is a study of paranoia. Marie assumes each person and event is part of some giant scheme of which she is the ultimate victim.

In the film, however, Roeg uses the character of Father Niles to console Marie and serve as her confessor. He takes Marie away from the commotion of Alex's hospital room and cleans her up, as she worries that she has no control over her life. She remembers trying to tell Alex of her affair and equates herself with an assassin. Father Niles tries to comfort her by saying: "We are not made or unmade by things that happen to us. It is our reaction to them that matters. That's all God cares about." Realizing she is still confused, he says he believes her vision was a miracle, but that it is not related to Alex's illness. He muses that the illness sounds more like a demonic possession, but says that "life and death belong to God and everything else, everything, is ours—yours and mine—to decide."

This is Roeg's most extreme example of the "watcher," the character who often looks on as the protagonists act. This conversation between Marie and Father Niles encapsulates the themes which attracted him to the project, as he explains:

> We are all being watched by some larger vision. And when we don't look at the signs, there's trouble later. That's the mood behind *Cold Heaven*, that and the feeling the woman has that just when she is about to make a decision, that decision is taken from her hands and although she should feel relieved, what she really feels is fear. She is about to tell Mark [the actor who plays Alex] that she wants to leave him, but his accident comes in the way.[3]

During Marie's conversation with Father Niles, Roeg juxtaposes scenes of the doctors and nurses caring for Alex, who seems to be gaining strength. When Father Niles leaves, Marie sits in the dark, but the arrival of dawn anticipates a renewal. A seemingly rejuvenated Alex comes into the room and wants to leave and return to Mt. Carmel. On the drive, Alex is angered that Marie broke her promise not to tell anyone, but he gradually realizes that she had no one else to turn to. In their room, Marie is showering as Alex whispers that he would like to make love to her once more. When she comes out, he asks her to lie beside him, saying, "Know what I wish? I wish we could go on." Their positioning recalls the earlier scene of her sleeping alone on the night of his death. It is the film's most tender scene, but as always with Roeg such a scene precedes a cataclysm. A cloud passes across the moon as Alex begins to convulse and shouts for her to bring the priest, his body now serving as a vessel for the vision. The window overhead shatters, while at the rectory a shelf collapses. When Sister Martha picks up the statues that have fallen, she is cut on a piece of glass. This accident duplicates the scene when Marie cuts her finger on Alex's razor and thus further unites the women. As Marie hurries from the bedroom, the camera focuses on a sign announcing the Cliff Walk.

Having contacted Father Niles, Marie races to the church, its red interior illuminated by candles. Marie finds Sister Martha lying at the base of the altar, and the women return to the site of Marie's vision. Sister Martha recognizes it as the place in her dream, and as she kneels on the red earth, the sun shifts in the sky, as if the very universe if being displaced. Frightened by what is already happening and her anticipation of what will occur, Marie drops to the ground, covering her ears as a choir of voices call out her name. Clouds hurtle across the horizon, and the moon and sun align in the heavens. The figure in the water is juxtaposed with Alex floating in the ocean, and on the side of the hill, a cross appears on the ground. It is this sequence alone which is disappointing, resembling something from a Cecil B. DeMille epic with the shaking earth, the choir of voices, and the lightning which leaves a cross on the ground. Roeg's presentation of the earlier vision is much better; he utilizes a brief inset that leaves us with a sense of wonder.

The experience over, Sister Martha runs up to Marie, who is still writhing on the ground with her ears covered by her hands. She asks Marie if she witnessed it, but Marie denies seeing anything. Her cries grow louder until she finally admits she saw Christ. At that moment, Alex awakes in the room, calling her name. The relationship between his health and the apparition is clear because the blood from his ear magically disappears. At the cliff, Father Niles and Monsignor Cassidy arrive, and the latter comments ironically that Marie has finally brought the priest. His skepticism ends when Sister Martha points out the cross. She admits she did not view the apparition, but says, "I felt a presence."

Already Roeg has departed from the original work by not having Sister Martha witness the miracle. The remainder of the film is also his and Scott's creation. Monsignor Cassidy speaks to Marie, but Daniel's face is superimposed over his, as if she recognizes the two men to be the same. Father Niles walks away with Marie, talking to her of the miracle that has occurred. She assumes her experience to be over, but he argues that it is only beginning. In a statement which comments ironically on Roeg's own past, Father Niles admits that "none of us are obliged to believe in miracles any more than in aliens from outer space, unless we see them." He reminds Marie that the figure in the vision spoke of a sanctuary, and he asks, "Isn't marriage a sanctuary? That too is a holy place." His intimation that she is being given a second chance seems to give Marie renewed hope. It was not her infidelity which brought on the vision, but her lack of faith in anything, marriage or religion. She has now been given a chance to rediscover both.

When Marie returns to the hotel, her burden has been lifted. She is smiling as she runs to their room and does not even hear Daniel as he calls her. She runs expectantly into the room, but finds it empty. When she turns around, however, Alex is standing in the doorway. The two embrace as Daniel stands in the hall, aware that his part is over. Marie and Alex continue to kiss; then Roeg cuts to Father Niles sitting on the grass.

Is the ending a concession on Roeg's part to making a more accessible work? Roeg's choice of subject matter alone seems to negate this. The change in attitude anticipated in *The Witches* may be a sign of Roeg's own personal growth. As a father he had realized the effect *The Witches* could have had if Luke had not been changed back, and similarly it could be his marriage to Russell which influenced *Cold Heaven*. Their relationship had lasted over twenty years, and perhaps this created in Roeg an awareness that marriages could survive. Most of Roeg's films focus on the dissolution of a couple, but with *Cold Heaven* the inverse occurs. Yet, even in these earlier films, however, there was a sense of a couple discovering their love for one another. Alexandra genuinely loves Chance Wayne even though she leaves him to his fate; Jack McCann makes love to his wife before sending her off; and Gerald and Lucy discover their relationship does have more meaning than being a simple contractural arrangement. Roeg has been criticized by some as producing films devoid of emotion, but at the heart of all his works is a relationship.

In the twenty years since the release of *Performance*, Roeg has remained committed to the themes and experiments which first attracted him to film. *Cold Heaven* is not the kinetic mind experience *Performance* was, but it is unmistakably the work of the same director. The influence of Borges remains; Marie is convinced that it is her past which is influencing her present. Like Chas, she is also confronted with an experience her mind has trouble comprehending, and she becomes humanized because of it. Finally, the techniques which characterized the earlier film also continue; the superimposition of one character's face over another, the sexual encounter infused with violence, and most importantly, the small details which often contain the key to understanding the film. As John Izod has pointed out, Marie's small deformity is not simply a detail to humanize her.

> A covert pointer to this optimistic outcome is present, barely visible throughout the film—a precognition of the more complete knowledge that will follow Marie's confrontation with both the dark and bright aspects of the unconscious. Unlike Brian Moore's character, she has a slight deformity to her right hand. It recalls Helga's hand in *The Witches*, and also foretells the encroachment of demonic powers. Very early in our acquaintance with her, Marie declines Alex's advice to have the problem rectified by a surgeon, saying that she quite likes her crooked finger. In this small acceptance she acknowledges her mortality, and the inescapable fact of being made like all humanity in the image of both our demons and our gods—those kaleidoscopic yet constant figures who shape and transform us all. So her miraculous rebirth is clearly signalled when finally she strokes Alex's head, and her bent finger straightens.[4]

Ironically, little has changed for Roeg since his first film. Like *Performance* and *Eureka*, the release of the film was held up in the United States, as if distributors were unsure how to market such a complex work. When it was finally released, little attention was paid to it by critics, either in the United States or England. Those that did review, such as Janet Maslin, dismissed it as another failure for Roeg. "The beginning is promising, especially for someone with Mr. Roeg's flair for swirling intimidations of eroticism, danger and mysticism into an insinuating blend. But *Cold Heaven* proves to be surprisingly graceless and literal, especially when faced with the questions of faith that are raised in Mr. Moore's book."[5]

If *Cold Heaven* continues the pattern of Roeg's previous films, then it will eventually find an audience as all his films have. Roeg has already established himself in the pantheon of directors at work today who create films that challenge audiences and explore the realm of cinema. That he has done this without any widespread public recognition for his talent is a problem even he would have difficulty answering. Roeg does have advice for those willing to experience his films: "I want to write on the front of the camera, 'Abandon all preconceptions, ye who enter here. Let it get to you, let it happen. Then it will be exciting.'"[6]

Notes

1. *Movieline*, January 1991, p. 84.
2. Brian Moore, *Cold Heaven*, 1983, p. 61.
3. *Movieline*, January 1991, pp. 38–40.
4. John Izod, *The Films of Nicolas Roeg*, pp. 246–248.
5. *New York Times*, May 29, 1992, p. C15.
6. *Vogue*, August 1985, p. 333.

ANNOTATED BIBLIOGRAPHY

Articles and Reviews of Roeg's Films

Performance

Cocks, Jay. "Mick's Duet." *Time*. August 24, 1970, p. 61.

Dawson, Jan. "*Performance*." *British Film Institute Monthly Bulletin* (February 1971): 27–28.

Farber, Stephen. *Performance: The Nightmare Journey Cinema* (Fall 1970): 20–24.

French, Philip. "*Performance*." *Sight and Sound* (Spring 1971): 67–69.

Gomez, Joseph A. "*Performance* and Jorge Luis Borges." *Film Literature Quarterly* (Spring 1977): 147–53.

Greenspun, Roger. "Jagger and Fox Shape Tone of the Action." *New York Times*. August 4, 1970, p. 21.

Gross, Larry. "Film Après Noir." *Film Comment* (July 1976): 44–49. Gross examines four films: *Alphaville, Point Blank, Performance*, and *The Long Goodbye*.

Knight, Arthur. "A Matter of Taste." *Saturday Review*. August 22, 1970, p. 61.

Kroll, Jack. "A Last Word on *Performance*." *Art in America* (March 1971): 114–15.

Murf. "*Performance*." *Variety*. August 5, 1970, p. 20.

Schjeldahl, Peter. "One Emerges Feeling a Little Scorched, But. . ." *New York Times*. August 17, 1970, pp. 1, 5.

Simon, John. "The Most Loathsome Film." *New York Times*. August 23, 1970, Sec. II p. 1.

Zimmerman, Paul D. "Under the Rock." *Newsweek*. August 17, 1970, p. 85.

Walkabout

Alpert, Hollis. "Studies in Survival." *Saturday Review*. June 5, 1971, p. 12.

Brackman, Jacob. "Films." *Esquire* (August 1971): p. 42.

Canby, Vincent. "The Screen: Reflections on an Aborigine Ritual." *New York Times*. July 26, 1971, p. 26.

Dawson, Jan. *"Walkabout." British Film Institute Monthly Film Bulletin* (February 1971): 227.

Geist, Kenneth. "Cinematic Poem Down Under." *Village Voice.* May 20, 1971, p. 66.

Gillaitt, Penelope. "Split." *New Yorker.* July 10, 1971, p. 55.

Gomez, Joseph. "Two Images of the Aboriginal: *Walkabout,* the Novel and Film." *Film Literature Quarterly* (Spring 1979): 67–83.

Greenway, John. "No Sex, No Bushman." *National Review.* October 24, 1975, pp. 1179–80.

Held, Leonard. "Myth and Archetype in Nicolas Roeg's *Walkabout." Post Script* (Fall 1986): 21–45.

Izod, John. *"Walkabout:* A Wasted Journey." *Sight and Sound* (Spring 1980): 113–16.

Kaufman, Stanley. *"Walkabout." New Republic.* July 3, 1971, p. 34.

McGregor, Craig. *"Walkabout:* Beautiful but Fake?" *New York Times.* July 18, 1971, pp. B1, B11.

Miller, Gavin. *"Walkabout." Sight and Sound* (Winter 1971): 40.

Murf. *"Walkabout." Variety.* May 19, 1971, p. 17.

Nichols, Bill. *"Walkabout." Cinema* (Fall 1971): 18.

Schickel, Richard. "Coming of Age in the Outback." *Life.* June 4, 1971, p. 16.

Don't Look Now

Allombert, Guy. "Ne Vous Retournez Pas." *La Revue du Cinéma* (November 1977): 108–9.

Baumbach, Jonathan. *"Don't Look Now." Partisan Review* (v. 41 n. 2): 274–76.

Canby, Vincent. "Film: *Don't Look Now,* a Horror Tale." *New York Times.* December 10, 1973, p. 56.

Carlsen, Ebsen Hollund. "Pa Vej Mod et Nyt Filmsprog." *Kosmoroma* (Spring 1987): 16–19.

Cocks, Jay. "Second Sight." *Time.* December 10, 1973, p. 104.

Cowie, Peter. *"Don't Look Now. Focus on Film* (Autumn 1973): 7.

Dawson, Jan. "Journals-London." *Film Comment* (January 1974): 2, 4.

Dempsey, Michael. *"Don't Look Now." Film Quarterly* (Spring 1974): 39–43.

Farber, Stephen. *"Don't Look Now* Will Scare You Silly." *New York Times.* December 23, 1973, pp. 15, 20.

Frumkes, Roy. *"Don't Look Now." Films in Review* (January 1974): 49.

Gifford, James. "Previews and Postviews." *Photon* (1974): 11.

Glacci, Vittorio. "A Venezia . . . Un Dicembre Rosso Shoking." *Cineforum* (May 1974): 370–73.

Gow, Gordon. *"Don't Look Now." Films and Filming* (November 1973): 45–46.

Grisolia, Michel. "Ne Vous Retournez Pas!" *Cinéma 74* (November 1974): 139.

Haskell, Molly. "Little Red Herring Hood." *Village Voice.* December 20, 1973, p. 85.

Hawk. *"Don't Look Now." Variety.* October 24, 1973, p. 16.

J.M.S. *"Ne Vous Retournez Pas." Revue du Cinéma* (October 1975): 261–62.

Kael, Pauline. "Labyrinths." *New Yorker.* December 24, 1973, p. 68.

Kanon, Joseph. "Death in Venice." *Atlantic* (January 1974): 94–96.

Landau, Jon. "Nicholas Goes Belly Up." *Rolling Stone.* February 28, 1974, pp. 60–61.

Lavery, David. "The Horror Film and the Horror of Film." *Film Criticism* (Fall 1982): 47–55.

Lindberg, Ib. "Doden i Venedig." *Kosmoroma* (June 1974): 242–43.

Milne, Tom. *"Don't Look Now." Sight and Sound* (Winter 1973): 237–38.

Runefelt, Eva. "Stillbiden." *Chaplin* (June 1986): 140–41, 162.

Samuels, Charles Thomas. "Films About Film." *American Scholar* (Summer 1974): 467.

Schupp, Patrick. *"Don't Look Now." Sequences* (July 1974): 35–36.

Simon, John. "Films." *Esquire* (March 1974): 70–71.

Turan, Kenneth. "Films: Unbelievable Horror." *The Progressive.* (March 1974): 54.

Walsh, Moira. "I Don't Want to Look." *America.* February 23, 1974, p. 134.

Westerbeck, Colin L., Jr. "Don't Look at All." *Commonweal.* January 25, 1974, p. 416.

Zimmerman, Paul D. "Vertigo in Venice." *Newsweek.* December 17, 1973, p. 91.

The Man Who Fell to Earth

Allen, Tom. "Three Sci-Fi Films for Three Audiences." *America.* July 10, 1976, pp. 19–20.

Bartholomew, David. *"The Man Who Fell to Earth." Film Heritage* (Fall 1976): 18–25.

Cocks, Jay. "Heavenly Body." *Time.* June 14, 1976, p. 66.

Coleman, John. "Films." *New Statesman.* March 18, 1976, p. 380.

Combs, Richard. "Buck Henry's Voices." *Sight and Sound* (Summer 1976): 154–55. A brief interview with Buck Henry about the film.

Comuzio, Ermanno. *"L'Uomo Che Cade sulla Terra." Cineforum* (April 1976): 233–35.

Crist, Judith. "A Bicentennial Buffalo Bill." *Saturday Review.* July 10, 1976, p. 63.

Dagneau, Gilles. *"L'Homme Qui Venait d'Ailleurs." Revue du Cinéma* (September 1977): 101–2.

Eder, Richard. *"Man Who Fell to Earth* Is Beautiful Science Fiction." *New York Times.* May 29, 1976, p. 4.

Farren, Jonathan. *"L'Homme Qui Venait d'Ailleurs." Cinéma 77* (August 1977): 190–91.

Gressard, G. *"L'Homme Qui Venait d'Ailleurs." Positif* (October 1977): p. 74.

Gillaitt, Penelope. "Guernica." *New Yorker.* June 17, 1976, pp. 120–24.

Greenspun, Roger. "Time Machines." *Penthouse* (September 1976): 46–47.

Hawk. *"The Man Who Fell to Earth." Variety.* March 24, 1976, p. 22.

Hatch, Robert. "Films." *Nation.* June 19, 1976, p. 765.

Kael, Pauline. "Notes on Evolving Heroes, Morals, Audiences." *New Yorker.* November 8, 1976, pp. 140–42.

Kroll, Jack. "Saint from Space." *Newsweek.* June 14, 1976, pp. 89–90.

Leach, James. *"The Man Who Fell to Earth*: Adaptation by Omission." *Film Literature Quarterly* (Fall 1978): 371–78.

McVay, Douglas. *"The Man Who Fell to Earth." Film* (May 1976): 8.

Mayersburg, Paul. "The Story So Far. . ." *Sight and Sound* (Autumn 1975): 225–227, 230–1. A commentary by Mayersburg on his first film; interesting both for the alterations that occurred and for Mayersburg's interpretation of the film.

Milne, Tom. *"The Man Who Fell to Earth." Sight and Sound* (Summer 1976): 145–47. One of the best essays written on the film; it examines the primary motifs of the train and incarceration.

Morgan, Jane. *"The Man Who Fell to Earth." Films in Review* (August 1976): 442.

Nelson, Paul. "Bowie Film Falls Flat: Too Much of Nothing." *Rolling Stone.* July 13, 1976, p. 22.

Olsson, Sven E. *"Mannen utan Ansikte." Chaplin* (November 1976): 147.

P. E. *"The Man Who Fell to Earth." Independent Film Journal.* June 11, 1976, p. 9.

Pedral, René. *"L'Homme Qui Venait d'Ailleurs." Jeune Cinéma* (September 1977): 48–50.

Phillips, Harvey E. "Futures Past." *National Review.* November 12, 1976, p. 129.

Rosenblaum, Jonathan. *"Man Who Fell to Earth." British Film Institute Monthly Bulletin* (April 1976): 86–87.

Schupp, Patrick. *"The Man Who Fell to Earth." Sequences* (October 1976): 53–54.

Simon, John. "Head Ache." *New York.* June 14, 1976, pp. 63–64.

Stuart, Alexander. *"The Man Who Fell to Earth." Films and Filming* (May 1976): 28–29.

Turan, Kenneth. "The Future Revisited." *Progressive* (September 1976): 53–54.

Van Wert, William F. "Film as Science Fiction: Nicolas Roeg's *The Man Who Fell to Earth." Western Humanities Review* (1979): 141–48.

Weightman, John. "Mythmash." *Encounter* (June 1976): 30–34.

Westerbeck, Colin L., Jr. "Spaceship Earth." *Commonweal.* July 16, 1976, pp. 463–64.

Bad Timing: A Sensual Obsession

Ansen, David. *"Bad Timing." Newsweek.* October 6, 1980, p. 72.

Barber, Susan. *"Bad Timing." Film Quarterly* (Fall 1981): 46–50. A long essay on the film which examines how Roeg's perspective influences the way the viewer responds to the film.

Billanti, Dean. *"Bad Timing." Films in Review* (November 1980): 568.

Carlo, Scarrone. "Illusions e Maschera." *Filmcritica* (February 1981): 85–88.

Coleman, John. *"Bad Timing." New Statesman.* April 18, 1980, p. 600.

Coulsen, Esben Hoilund. "Omridset af Uopfyldt." *Kosmorama* (June 1983): 67–69.

Crist, Judith. *"Bad Timing." Saturday Review* (September 1980): 90.

D. D. "Enquête sur une Passion." *Cahiers du Cinéma* (September 1980): 55.

Dawson, Jan. *"Bad Timing." Cinema Papers* (August 1980): 226–29. Dawson's article is in response to John Pyn's essay in *Sight and Sound.* Interesting for presenting a feminine perspective of the film: "What Roeg dramatizes in *Bad Timing* is the conflict between love as an acceptance of the other [person] and love as a Svengalian desire to change it."

de Laurentis, Teresa. "Now and Nowhere: Roeg's *Bad Timing." Discourse* (Spring 1983): 21–40. Adapts the writings of Michael Foucault to film, in particular to *Bad Timing.*

Denby, David. *"Bad Timing." New York.* September 29, 1980, p. 59.

Gault, John. "A Festival Date with an Ill-Fated Love Affair." *MacLeans* (September 1980): 61.

Gow, Gordon. *"Bad Timing." Films and Filming* (September 1980): 29–30.

Hatch, Robert. *"Bad Timing." The Nation.* October 25, 1980, p. 420.

Kaufmann, Stanley. "Milder and Muddler." *New Republic.* October 4, 1980, pp. 26–27.

Lenne, Gérard. "Enquête sur une Passion." *La Revue du Cinéma* (July 1980): 35–36.

McCourt, James. "British Film Now and Retrospectives." *Film Comment* (November 1980): 59.

Milne, Tom. *"Bad Timing." British Film Institute Monthly Bulletin* (March 1980): 46–47.

Morton, James. "Quarterly Film Review." *Contemporary Review* (August 1980): 103–4.

Penman, Ian. *"Bad Timing:* A Codifying Love Story." *Screen* (1980): 107–9.

Porro, Maurizio. "Il Lenzuolo Viola." *Cineforum* (September 1980): 588–603. A long essay on *Bad Timing.*

Pyn, John. "Ungratified Desire." *Sight and Sound* (Spring 1980): 111–12.

R. F. "Enquête sur une Passion." *Positif* (September 1980): 67–68.

Rabourdin, Dominique. "Enquête sur une Passion." *Cinéma 80* (July 1980): 114–15.

Rickey, Carrie. *"Bad Timing." Village Voice.* September 24, 1980, p. 52.

Schickel, Richard. *"Bad Timing." Time.* November 11, 1980, p. 108.

Simo. *"Bad Timing." Variety.* February 20, 1980, p. 22.

T. J. *"Bad Timing: A Sensual Obsession." Film Journal* (October 1980): 42.

Wall, James W. "Current Cinema." *Christian Century.* November 12, 1980, p. 1106.

Young, Vernon. "Film Chronicle: The Bloody British Cinema." *Hudson Review* (1980): 560–64.

Eureka

Coleman, John. "Love's Labour Lost." *New Statesman.* May 20, 1983, p. 31.

Combs, Richard. "A Miner and His Daughter." *Sight and Sound* (Spring 1983): 134–36.

Elley, Derek. *"Eureka." Films and Filming* (May 1983): 33–35.

Ferrario, Davide. "Sul Festival di Rotterdam." *Cineforum* (April 1984): 23. An analysis of the films which appeared at the festival, including *Eureka*.

Goodman, Walter. "Screen: *Eureka* by Nicolas Roeg." *New York Times*. August 30, 1985, p. C5.

Martineau, Richard. "*Eureka*." *Sequences* (April 1986): 67–68.

Meise, Myron. "*Eureka*." *Film Journal* (October 1985): 68, 280–85. An interview with Mayersburg about working with Roeg and the writing of the film.

―――――. "*Eureka*." *British Film Institute Film Monthly Bulletin* (May 1983): 115–16.

Milne, Tom. "*Eureka*." *Sight and Sound* (Autumn 1982) 280–85. An interview with Mayersburg about working with Roeg and the writing of the film.

Pit. "*Eureka*." *Variety*. June 8, 1983, p. 20.

Pursell, Michael. "From Gold Nugget to Ice Crystal: The Diagnetic Structure of Roeg's *Eureka*." *Film Literature Quarterly* (October 1983): 215–20.

Russell, Mike. "What It Means to Be Gene Hackman." *Photoplay* (October 1982): 25–26. An interview with the star on working with Roeg and what attracted him to the film.

Stein, Elliott. "*Eureka*." *Village Voice*. September 10, 1985, p. 61.

Sterritt, David. "*Eureka*." *Christian Science Monitor*. September 11, 1985, p. 23.

Ward, Robert. "I'm Not a Movie Star; I'm an Actor." *American Film* (March 1983): 40–45. An interview with Hackman during the filming of *Eureka*.

Insignificance

Baxter, Brian. "*Insignificance*." *Monthly Film Bulletin* (August 1985): 37.

Bonneville, Leo. "*Insignificance*." *Sequences* (July 1985): 9–10.

Canby, Vincent. "Screen: *Insignificance*, Mythic Tale of the 50's." *New York Times*. August 11, 1985, p. 57.

Caron, Alain. "*Une Nuit de Réflexion*." *Jeune Cinéma* (March 1986): 40–41.

Coleman, John. "*Insignificance*." *New Statesman*. August 9, 1985, p. 28.

Combs, Richard. "*Insignificance*." *British Film Institute Monthly Bulletin* (August 1985): 235.

―――――. "Relatively Speaking." *British Film Institute Monthly Bulletin* (August 1985): 237–38. An interview with both Roeg and Terry Johnson concerning their work on the adaptation. Johnson states, "My interest in film, which is now quite strong, came out of the experience of adapting the play for Roeg."

Corliss, Richard. "Such Fun Singing the Blahs." *Time*. August 19, 1985, pp. 70–71. Corliss examines three British films (*Wetherby, Dance with a Stranger, Insignificance*) which he believes represent a resurgence in the British cinema.

Du. P. "*Une Nuit de Réflexion*." *Cinéma 85* (June 1985): 13.

Hoberman, J. "*Insignificance*." *Village Voice*. August 20, 1985, p. 61.

Japa. "*Insignificance*." *Variety*. May 15, 1985, p. 20.

Kruger, Barbara. "*Insignificance*." *Artforum* (December 1985): 89.

M. C. "*Insignificance*." *Cahiers du Cinéma* (June 1985): 30–31.

_____. *"Insignificance." Positif* (July 1985): 97.

Manceau, Jean-Louis. *"Une Nuit de Réflexion." Cinéma 86* (February 1986): 22.

Milne, Tom. "Shape of the Universe." *Sight and Sound* (Summer 1985): 218–19.

Piccardi, Adriano. *"Insignificance." Cineforum* (June 1985): 16–17.

Roddick, Nick. "Countries of the Mind." *Cinema Papers* (September 1985): 63–64.

Soullard, Catherine. *"Une Nuit de Réflexion." Cinématographe* (February 1986): 38.

Sterritt, David. *"Insignificance." Christian Science Monitor.* September 11, 1985, p. 23.

Tessier, Max. *"Insignificance." La Revue du Cinéma* (October 1985): 75–77.

Toumarkine, Doris. *"Insignificance." Film Journal* (August 1985): 20.

Zimmer, Jacques. *"Une Nuit de Réflexion." La Revue du Cinéma* (1986): 125.

Castaway

Adams. *"Castaway." Variety.* December 10, 1986, p. 13.

Combs, Richard. "Time Away." *Sight and Sound* (Winter 1986): 70–71.

Cook, Pam. *"Castaway." Monthly Film Bulletin* (October 1987): 42–43.

Dewson, Lisa. "Undressed to Kill." *Photoplay* (March 1987): 16–18. A profile of Amanda Donohoe, in which she discusses her first film, *Castaway,* and how she handled the nudity.

Doyle, Terence. *"Pages as Pictures." Films and Filming* (December 1986): 20. An interview with various screenwriters, including Alan Scott, who discusses his work on *Castaway.*

Kelleher, Ed. *"Castaway." Film Journal* (November 1987): 53–54.

Kockenlocker. "Desert Island." *Sight and Sound* (Winter 1985): 31. An account of a meeting between Lucy Irvine and Amanda Donohoe.

McVay, Douglas. *"Castaway." Film* (February 1987): 7–8.

Martini, Emanuela. *"Castaway." Cineforum* (September 1987): 94.

Pulleine, Tim. "Nature's Call." *Lighting Dimensions* (September 1987): 55–57, 73–74. Pulleine, like Valentine, discusses the making of the film, but his article is less technical and of more interest than Valentine's.

Schickel, Richard. "The War Between the Mates." *Time.* September 28, 1987, p. 69.

Valentine, Mike. "Down to the Sea for *Castaway. American Cinematographer* (December 1987): 20–24. Valentine talks about working on his first feature film. More of interest to cinematographers than to admirers of Roeg.

Track 29

Barker, Adam. "What the Detectives Saw or a Case of Mistaken Identity." *British Film Institute Monthly Bulletin* (July 1988): 193–95. Examines the similarities and differences between Dennis Potter and Roeg.

Bartholomew, David. *"Track 29." Film Journal* (September 1988): 72.

Bernhard, Sandra. "Right on Track." *American Film* (April 1988): 31, 51–53.

Bernhard's account of her experience on *Track 29*. She seems in awe of both Roeg and Theresa Russell.

Combs, Richard. "*Track 29*." *British Film Institute Monthly Bulletin* (July 1988): 191.

Corliss, Richard. "Adventures of a Career Kid." *Time*. September 19, 1988, p. 97.

Emanula, Martini. "*Track 29*." *Cineforum* (July 1988): 49.

Fuller, Graham. "Room at the Top." *American Film* (April 1988): 24–30.

Maslin, Janet. "Curious Scenes from a Southern Marriage." *New York Times*. September 8, 1988, p. 3.

Moore, Suzanna. "Tricks on the Track." *New Statesman*. August 12, 1988, p. 40.

Sante, Luc. "Potter's Clay." *Interview* (October 1988): 145. Sante examines both *Track 29* and *The Singing Detective* and lays all the blame for any problems with the former on Roeg.

Stein, Elliott. "*Track 29*." *Village Voice*. September 13, 1988, p. 89.

Yung. "*Track 29*." *Variety*. May 25, 1988, p. 19.

Aria

Blau, Eleanor. "*Aria* Coming to U.S." *New York Times*. January 1, 1988, p. 18. A brief interview with producer Don Boyd on his compilation film, *Aria*. No mention is made of Roeg.

Chion, Michel. "Opéra, Sirènes et Sorcières." *Cahiers du Cinéma* (July 1987): 50–51.

Corliss, Richard. "Opera for the Inoperative." *Time*. May 2, 1988, p. 79.

Jabr. "*Aria*." *Variety*. May 27, 1988, p. 11.

Jenkins, Steve. "*Aria*." *British Film Institute Monthly Bulletin* (November 1987): 328–29.

Maslin, Janet. "Director's Daydreams Become the Stuff of Opera." *New York Times*. May 21, 1988, p. 54.

O'Conner, Patrick. "Viewpoint." *Opera News*. April 9, 1988, p. 4.

Phelps, Guy. "Omnibus or What's Opera Done?" *Sight and Sound* (Summer 1987): 188–90. The article examines how the film came into being and how the directors approached their work.

Schupp, Patrick. "*Aria*." *Sequences* (November 1988): 85–86.

Taubin, Amy. "*Aria*." *Village Voice*. May 31, 1988, p. 69.

Valot, Jacque. "*Aria*." *La Revue du Cinéma* (1987): 18–19.

Walsh, Michael. "*Aria* Opportunities." *Film Comment* (May 1988): 76–77.

Sweet Bird of Youth

Durbano, Art. "This Week's Movies." *T.V. Guide*. September 30, 1989, p. 57.

Farber, Stephen. "A Stellar Cast Films a Steamy Williams Play." *New York Times*. July 29, 1989, pp. 27–28. Most of the principals are interviewed for this piece, including the producers, writer, director, and Elizabeth Taylor.

Warren, Elaine. "On *Sweet Bird* Liz Is the 600-Pound Canary." *T.V. Guide*.

September 30, 1989, pp. 10–12. Primarily a profile of Elizabeth Taylor and her work on the television film.

The Witches

Ansen, David. "Wicked Witchcraft." *Newsweek.* September 24, 1990, p. 70.

James, Caryn. "When the Ladies Take off Their Wigs, Head for Home. Fast." *New York Times.* August 24, 1990, p. C12.

Jones, Alan. "Nicolas Roeg on Directing *The Witches.*" *Cinefantastique* (December 1990): 50–51. A good article on the background of the making of the film.

Lodato, Nuccio. "Chi Ha Paura delle Streghe?" *Cineforum* (October 1990): 92–93.

Milne, Tom. "*The Witches.*" *Monthly Film Bulletin* (May 1990): 146–47.

Toumarkine, Doris. "*The Witches.*" *Film Journal* (October 1990): 65.

Cold Heaven

Maslin, Janet "*Intimations of Danger, Musticism and Sex*" New York Times. (May 29, 1992): C15.

Articles on Roeg

Alvarez, Al. "Roeg Time." *Interview* (July 1988): 63–64. An interview with Roeg on his latest film, *Track 29,* and on his career. He comments, "I like to feel that the plot is just the shell within which the characters can act, and react, as they wish."

Baxter, Brian. "The Significance of Mr. Roeg." *Films and Filming* (August 1985): 14–16. An interview with Roeg concerning *Insignificance* and his career as a whole.

Birkvard, Soren. "Mystiker of Modernist." *Kosmorama* (Summer 1986): 11–14.

Buckley, Tom. "The Man Behind *Bad Timing.*" *New York Times.* September 19, 1980, p. C6. Presents nothing exceptional on Roeg or the film, except for how he handles actors: "It's really very simple. I just mind my own business and stay as far away from the actors as possible."

Cohen, Georges. "Entretien avec Nicolas Roeg." *Cinéma 76* (June 1976): 22–25. An interview with Roeg at the time *The Man Who Fell to Earth* was released.

Combs, Richard. "Looking at the Rubber Duck." *Sight and Sound* (Winter 1984): 42–43. Roeg discusses his work on *Farenheit 451* and his relationship with François Truffaut.

Cros, Jean-Louis, and Raymond Lefèvre. "Pour Réhabiliter Nicolas Roeg." *La Revue du Cinéma* (June 1981): 61–76. A collection of essays on Roeg's films and his career.

Dempsey, Michael. "*Insignificance, Eureka.*" *Film Quarterly* (Winter 1985): 49–56. Obstensibly a review of *Insignificance* and *Eureka,* but a good overview of Roeg's entire career. "The first part of *Eureka* has an enraptured, visionary tone that is already classic."

Fierberg, Steven. "Roeg on Roeg." *Lighting Dimensions* (September 1987): 56, 74–77. "If I couldn't direct, I don't think I'd go back to being a DP; I'd be an extra or something."

Frankel, Martha. "Nic at Noon." *Movieline* (January 1991): 36–41, 84.

Gomez, Joseph. "Another Look at Nicolas Roeg." *Film Criticism* (Fall 1981): 43–54.

Gow, Gordon. "An Interview with Nicolas Roeg." *Films and Filming* (January 1972): 18–25.

Guerif, Francois. "Entretien avec Nicolas Roeg." *La Revue du Cinéma* (October 1985): 77–82. An extensive interview with Roeg.

Gussow, Mel. "Roeg: The Man Behind *The Man Who Fell to Earth*." *New York Times.* August 22, 1976, p. 11. Interviews both Roeg and Donald Ruggoff, the distributor who edited twenty minutes out of the film for its American release.

Hay, David, and Elliot Davis. "Nicolas Roeg." *Cinema Papers* (April 1974): 174–77.

Heaton, Louis. "A True Castaway." *Photoplay* (February 1987): 32–35. An examination of Roeg's career up through his latest film, *Castaway.*

Kennedy, Harlan. "The Illusions of Nicolas Roeg." *American Film* (January 1980): 22–27.

―――――. "Roeg: Warrior." *Film Comment* (April 1983): 20–23. Kennedy is one of the few to analyze *Eureka* successfully and is able to incorporate Roeg's interview into his examination.

―――――. "The Time Machine." *Film Comment* (January 1984): 9–16. Kennedy examines how film is able to manipulate time; he focuses on various genres and directors, including Roeg.

Kinder, Marsha, and Beverle Houston. "Insiders and Outsiders in the Films of Nicolas Roeg." *Quarterly Review of Film Studies* (Summer 1978): 317–43. Would later be expanded into a chapter in *Self and Cinema.*

Kleinhans, Chuck. "Nicolas Roeg: Permutations Without Profundity." *Jump Cut* (September 1974): 13–17.

Kolker, Robert Phillip. "The Open Texts of Nicolas Roeg." *Sight and Sound* (Spring 1977): 82–84, 113.

Lahr, John. "Nicolas Roeg Dazzles Us." *Vogue* (August 1985): 333, 380. An interview with Roeg at the time of the release of *Insignificance.*

"Lands of Lost Content." *Economist.* January 26, 1985, pp. 85–86.

Lifflander, John, and Stephan Shroyer. "Nick Roeg . . . and the man who fell to earth." *Interview* (March 1976): 34–36. An interview with Andy Warhol.

Milne, Tom, and Penelope Houston. "Don't Look Now." (Winter 1973): 2–8. An interview with Roeg covering his career up to the release of *Don't Look Now.*

Norman, Neil, and Davis Starr. "The Face Interview: Nicolas Roeg." *The Face* (1983): 60–64.

Padroff, Jay. "The Effects of International Locations on the Films of Nicolas Roeg." *Millimeter* (March 1981): 171–79.

Roddick, Nick. "None of the Above." *Cinema Papers* (September 1985): 41–44. Talks to Roeg about *Insignificance* and his taking it to the Cannes Film Festival.

Roeg, Nicolas, and Jeremy Thomas. "Mad Dogs and Englishman." *British Film Institute Monthly Bulletin* (May 1983): 116–19. Actually two articles, one an interview with Roeg and the other an interview with the producer of the film, Jeremy Thomas.

Wagner, Richard. "The Search for Self in the Films of Nicolas Roeg." *Velvet Light Trap.* November 13, 1974, pp. 31–35. An examination of Roeg's first three films.

Waller, Nick. "Nicolas Roeg: A Sense of Wonder." (Summer 1976): 25–29. An interview with Roeg, his interpretations of his films and a discussion of projects which never came to fruition.

Williams, Hugo. "Snap." *New Statesman.* May 27, 1983, 22–23. An account of Roeg's appearance on "The Guardian Lecture," which was made difficult by his just having had his jaw wired shut.

Yakir, Da. "The 401st Blow." *Film Comment* (January 1985): 42–43. Part of an extensive tribute to Truffaut; interviews seven of Truffaut's colleagues, including Roeg.

Books

Cowie, Peter. *International Film Guide.* London: Tantivy, 1981, pp. 37–41.

Feineman, Neil. *Nicolas Roeg.* Boston: Twayne, 1978.

Fitzgerald, F. Scott. *Great Gatsby.* New York: Macmillan, 1988.

Fox, James. "Performance." Chapter 9 in *Comeback*, pp. 105–11. London: Hodder and Stoughton, 1983. Fox writes of his experience on what would become one of his last films.

Hacker, Jonathan, and David Price. *Take 10: Contemporary British Film Directors*, pp. 350–77. New York: Oxford University Press, 1991. Two chapters on Roeg, one an essay on his career, the other an extensive interview with him.

Izod, John. *The Films of Nicolas Roeg: Myth and Mind.* New York: St. Martin's Press, 1992. 295 p.

Kinder, Marsha, and Beverle Houston. "Insiders and Outsiders in Roeg's Films." Chapter 4 in *Self and Cinema: A Transformalist Perspective.* New York: Redgrave Publishing, 1980.

_____. "The Ultimate Performance." Chapter 9 in *Close-up: A Critical Perspective on Film*, pp. 359–76. New York: Harcourt Brace Jovanovich, 1972. A discussion of *Performance.*

Lanza, Joseph. *Fragile Geometry: The Films, Philosophy, and Misadventures of Nicolas Roeg.* New York: PAJ Publications, 1989. 171 p.

Norman, Neil, and Jon Barraclough. *Insignificance the Book.* London: Sidgwick and Jackson. Although it contains the complete screenplay of the film, most of the book concerns the myths about the real-life counterparts of the characters in the film.

Poe, Edgar Allan. *Eureka: A Prose Poem.* Harmondsworth: Penguin, 1979.
Sinyard, Neil. The *Films of Nicolas Roeg.* London: Charles Lett & Co., Ltd., 1991. 167 p.
Sontag, Susan. *Styles of Radical Will.*
Walker, John. "Rogue Talents." Chapter 9 in *The Once and Future Film,* pp. 95–98. London: Metheun, 1986. The chapter examines the careers of Roeg and Ken Russell.

FILMOGRAPHY

Performance

Production: Goodtimes Enterprises. Producer: Sanford Lieberson. Associate Producer: Donald Cammell. Co-director: Donald Cammell. Screenplay: Donald Cammell. Director of Photography: Nicolas Roeg. Editors: Anthony Gibbs, Brian Smedley-Aston. Music: Jack Nitzsche. Songs: "Performance," "Poor White Hound Dog," by Merry Clayton; "Turner's Murder" by Merry Clayton Singers; "Dyed, Dead, and Red" by Buffy Sainte-Marie, "Wake Up Niggers" by Jack Nitzsche, performed by Last Poets; "Gone Dead Train" by Jack Nitzsche, Randy Newman, performed by Newman; "Memo from Turner" by Mick Jagger, Keith Richards, performed by Jagger. Sound: Alan Pattillo, Ron Barron. Technical Advisor: David Litvinoff. Art Director: John Clark. Sets: Peter Young. Assistant Director: Richard Burge. Design Consultant for Turner's house: Christopher Gibbs. Released 1970. Running Time: 102 minutes.

Leading Players: James Fox (Chas Devlin), Mick Jagger (Turner), Anita Pallenberg (Pherber), Michele Breton (Lucy), Ann Sidney (Dana), John Bindon (Moody), Stanley Meadows (Rosebloom), Allan Cuthbertson (lawyer), Antony Morton (Dennis), Johnny Shannon (Harry Flowers), Anthony Valentine (Joey Maddocks), Ken Colley (Tony Farrell), John Sterland (chauffeur), Laraine Wicks (Lorraine).

Walkabout

Production: Max L. Raab-Si Litvinoff Films. Executive Producer: Max L. Raab. Producer: Si Litvinoff. Associate Producer: Anthony J. Hope. Screenplay: Edward Bond, from the novel by James Vance Marshall. Director of Photography: Nicolas Roeg. Special Photography: Tony Richmond. Editors: Anthony Gibbs, Alan Pattillo. Music: John Barry. Songs: "Electric Dance" by Billy Mitchell; "Gasoline Alley" by Rod Stewart; "Los Angeles" by Warren

211

Morley; excerpts from Stockhausen's "Hymnen." Art Director: Terry Gough. Assistant Director: Kevin Kavanagh. Production Design: Brian Eatwell. Relelased 1971. Running Time: 95 minutes.

Leading Players: Jenny Agutter (girl), Lucien John (brother), David Gumpilil (aborigine), John Meillon (father), Peter Carver (no hoper), John Illingsworth (husband), Barry Donnelly (Australian scientist), Noelene Brown (German scientist), Carlo Manchini (Italian scientist), Hilary Bamberger, Robert McDara.

Don't Look Now

Production: Casey Productions/Eldorado Films. Executive Producer: Anthony B. Unger. Producer: Peter Katz. Associate Producer: Frederico Mueller. Screenplay: Allan Scott, Chris Bryant, from the story by Daphne du Maurier. Director of Photography: Anthony Richmond. Editor: Graeme Clifford. Music: Pino Donaggio, directed by Giampiero Boneschi. Art Director: Giovanni Soccol. Sets: Francesca Chinanese. Assistant Director: Francesco Cinieri. Released 1973. Running Time: 110 minutes.

Leading Players: Julie Christie (Laura Baxter), Donald Sutherland (John Baxter), Hilary Mason (Heather), Clelia Matania (Wendy), Massimo Serato (Bishop Barbarrigo), Renato Scarpa (Inspector Longhi), Giorgio Trestini (workman), Leopoldo Trieste (hotel manager), David Tree (Anthony Babbage), Ann Rye (Mandy Babbage), Nicholas Salter (Johnny Baxter), Sharon Williams (Christine Baxter), Bruno Cattaneo (Detective Sabbione), Adelina Poerio (dwarf).

The Man Who Fell to Earth

Production: British Lion. Executive Producer: Si Litvinoff. Producers: Michael Deeley, Barry Spikings. Associate Producer: John Peverall. Screenplay: Paul Mayersberg, from the novel by Walter Tevis. Director of Photography: Anthony Richmond. Editor: Graeme Clifford. Music: John Phillips. Songs: "Poker Dice," "Thirty-three and a Third," "Mandala," "Wind Words," Stomo Yamashta; "Blueberry Hill," Louis Armstrong; "Make Our World Go Away," "A Fool Such as I," Jim Reeves; "Stardust," Artie Shaw; "True Love," Bing Crosby; "Try to Remember," Kingston Trio; "Boys from the South," "Bluegrass Breakdown," John Phillips; "Hello Mary Lou," John Phillips, Mick Taylor; "Love Is Coming Back," Genevieve White; "Silent Night," Robert Farnon. Sound: Stomo Yamashta. Art Director: Brian Eatwell. Assistant Director: Robin Gregory. Released 1976. Running Time: 138 minutes for British release; cut to 116 minutes for American release.

Leading Players: David Bowie (Thomas Jerome Newton), Rip Torn (Nathan Bryce), Candy Clark (Mary Lou), Buck Henry (Oliver Farnsworth), Bernie Casey (Peters), Jackson D. Kane (Professor Canutti), Rick Riccardo (Trevor), Tony Mascia (Arthur), Linda Hutton (Elaine), Hillary Holland (Jill), Adrienne Larussa (Helen), Lilybelle Crawford (jewelry store owner), Albert Nelson (waiter), Peter Prouse (Peters's associate), Captain James Lovell (himself), preacher and congregation of Presbyterian Church, Artesia, New Mexico.

Bad Timing: A Sensual Obsession

Production: Rank Organizations. Producer: Jeremy Thomas. Screenplay: Yale Udoff. Director of Photography: Anthony Richmond. Editor: Tony Lawson. Music: Richard Hartley. Songs: Berceuse," Vernon Midgley; "Dreaming My Dreams," Billy Kinsley; "Time Out," Zoot Money; "An Invitation to the Blues," Tom Wait; "I'll Be Seeing You," "It's the Same Old Story," Billie Holiday; "The Koln Concert," Keith Jarret; "Who Are You?" Who; "Daphne of the Dunes," "Delusion of Fury," Harry Patch. Sound: Paul Le Mare. Art Director: David Brockhurst. Assistant Director: Veil Vine Miller. Production Designer: Brian Eatwell. Released 1980. Running Time: 123 minutes.

Leading Players: Art Garfunkel (Dr. Alex Linden), Theresa Russell (Milena Flaherty), Harvey Keitel (Inspector Fredrich Netusil), Denholm Elliot (Stefan Vognic), Daniel Massey (foppish man), Dana Gillespie (Amy), William Hootkins (Colonel Taylor), Eugene Lipinski (hospital policeman), George Roubicek (first policeman), Stefan Gryff (second policeman), Sevilla Delofski (Czech receptionist), Robert Walker (Konrad), Gertan Klauber (ambulance man), Ania Marson (Dr. Schneider), Lex van Gelden (young doctor), Rudolph Bisseger (Giovanni), Hans Christian (Czech consul), Ellan Fartt (Ulla), Fritz Gublirsch (drunken man), Nino La Rocca (Arab in truck), Roman Scheidl (angry student).

Eureka

Production: Recorded Picture Company/JF Productions/Sunley Feature for MGM/UA Classics. Producer: Jeremy Thomas. Associate Producer: Tim Van Rellim. Screenplay: Paul Mayersberg, from the novel *Who Killed Sir Harry Oakes* by Marshall Houts. Director of Photography: Alex Thomson. Editor: Tony Lawson. Music: Stanley Myers. Sound: Paul Le Mare, John Richards. Art Director: Les Dilley. Sets: Michael Seirton. Assistant Director: Anthony Waye. Production Designer: Michael Seymour. Special Effects: Peter Hutchinson, J. B. Jones. Released 1982. Running Time: 129 minutes.

Leading Players: Gene Hackman (Jack McCann), Theresa Russell (Tracy McCann), Rutger Hauer (Claude Maillot van Horn), Jane Lapotaire (Helen McCann), Ed Lauter (Charles Perkins), Mickey Rourke (Aurelio D'Amato), Joe Pesci (Mayakofsky), Helen Kallianiotes (Frieda), Corin Redgrave (Worsley), James Faulkner (Roger), Tim Scott (Webb), Cavan Kendall (Pierre de Valois), Joe Spinell (Pete), Frank Pesce (Stefano), Michael Scott Addis (Joe), Norman Beaton (Byron Judson), Emrys James (judge), Ann Thornton (Jane), Emma Relph (Mary), John Vine (Julian), Tim Van Rellim (police chief), Ellis Dale (jury foreman), Lloyd Berry (Olaf), Tom Heaton (man blowing off head), Timothy Scott (Jim Webb), Geri Dewson (whore), Annie Kidder (Rita), Ian Tracey (Joey), Brad Sakiyama (Phil), Sandra Friesen (mother), Raimund Stamm (patron), Suzette Collins (Esther), Tommy Lane (Miami chauffeur),

Mico Blanco group, accompanied by the Aklowa Master Drummers (Tonnelle Dancers).

Insignificance

Production: Zenith Productions/Recorded Picture Company. Executive Producer: Alexander Stuart. Producer: Jeremy Thomas. Screenplay: Terry Johnson, from his play. Director of Photography: Peter Hannan. Editor: Tony Lawson. Music: Stanley Myers. Songs: "Wild Heart," by Roy Orbison; "Life Goes On" by Stanley Myers, Will Jennings, performed by Theresa Russell; "When Your Heart Runs Out of Time" by Will Jennings; "America" by Stuart Albright. Sound: Paul LeMare, Hugh Strain. Art Director: Arthur Max Shafransky. Sets: Diana Johnstone. Assistant Directors: Michael Zimbrich, Zsuzsanna Mills, Lee Cleary, Joe Reidy, Ann Egbert. Production Designer: David Brockhurst. Special Effects: Alan Whibley. Calendar designed by David Hockney. Released 1985. Running Time: 109 minutes.

Leading Players: Michael Emil (professor), Theresa Russell (actress), Tony Curtis (senator), Gary Busey (ballplayer), Will Sampson (Cherokee elevator operator), Patrick Kilpatrick (driver), Ian O'Connell (assistant director), Richard Davidson (director of photography), Mitchell Greenberg (technician), Raynor Scheine (autograph hunter), Jude Ciccolella (gaffer), Lou Hirsch (Charlie), Ray Charleson (Bud), Joel Cutrara (bar drunk), Raymond Barry (ballplayer's father), John Stamford (young ballplayer), Desiree Erasmus (prostitute), George Holmes (actor), David Lambert (young professor), Cassie Stuart (young actress), Meachell Dunsmoor (actress as a child), Daniel Benzalli (first theatrical agent), R. J. Bell (second theatrical agent), Shinobu Kanai (Japanese woman), David Montagu (young senator).

Castaway

Production: Castaway Films/Cannon Group. Executive Producer: Peter Shaw, Richard Johnson. Producer: Rick McCallum. Screenplay: Allan Scott, from Lucy Irvine's biography. Director of Photography: Harvey Harrison. Additional Photography: Michael Valentine. Editor: Tony Lawson. Music: Stanley Myers, Hans Zimmer, Barry Guy. Songs: "Chemistry," Brian Eno; "Be Kind to My Mistakes," Kate Bush; "Nessun Dorma" from Puccini's *Turandot*, performed by Luciano Pavarotti; "In Tangier Down a Winding Street" by David Mills, performed by Herbie Mann; "Sleepy Lagoon" by Eric Coates; "Please Remember Me"; "No Mad Warning Chant"; "Music from South New Guinea"; "Songs of Aboriginal Australia and Torres Straight." Sound: Paul LeMare. Art Directors: Stuart Rose, George Galitzine. Assistant Directors: Michael Zimbrich, Waldo Roeg, Lee Cleary. Production Designer: Andrew Sanders. Special Effects: Alan Whibley. Released 1987. Running Time: 120 minutes.

Leading Players: Oliver Reed (Gerald Kingsland), Amanda Donohoe (Lucy Irvine), Georgina Hale (Sister Saint Margaret), Frances Barber (Sister Saint Winifred), Tony Richards (Jason), Todd Rippon (Rod), John Sessions (man in pub), Virginia Hey (Janice), Sorrell Johnson (Lara), Len Peihopa

(Ronald), Paul Reynolds (Mike Kingsland), Sean Hamilton (Geoffrey Kingsland), Sarah Harper (swimming teacher), Stephen Jenn (shop manager), Joseph Blatchley (registrar), Simon Dormandy (Jackson), Ruth Huddson (receptionist), Gordon Honeycombe (TV newsreader).

Aria—*"King Zog Shot Back"*

Production: Boyd's Co. Film Productions/Lightyear Entertainment. Executive Producers: Jim Mervis, Tom Kuhn, Charles Mitchell. Producer: Don Boyd. Associate Producers: Richard Bell, Luc Roeg. Screenplay: Nicolas Roeg. Director of Photography: Harvey Harrison. Editor: Tony Lawson. Coordinating Editors: Marie Therese Boiche, Mike Cragg. Music Supervisor: Ralph Mace. Music: *Un Ballo in Maschera* (extracts) by Giuseppi Verdi. Singers: Leontyne Price, Carlo Bergonni, Robert Merrill, Shirley Verrett, Reni Crist. Orchestra: RCA Italian Opera Orchestra conducted by Erich Leinsdorf. Assistant Directors: Waldo Roeg, Iain Patrick, Layla Alexandra. Production Designer: Diane Johnstone. Location Work: Vienna, London. Released 1987. Running Time: 98 minutes.

Leading Players: Theresa Russell (King Zog/woman in window), Stephanie Lane (baroness), Roy Hyatt (chauffeur), Sevilla Delofski (maid), Ruth Halliday (companion), Arthur Cox (major), Dennis Holmes (colonel), Paul Brightwell, Frank Baker, Chris Hunter (assassins), Paul Collard (valet), George Ellis Jones (chauffeur), Danny Fitzgerald (Mercedes man), Johnny Boyle (blind balloon man), David Ross (doorman), Lucy Oliver (woman in background), Gordon Winter (man in background), Derek Farmer (motorbike man), Michelle Read (nanny), Maximillian Roeg (baby). Other segments directed by Charles Stutteridge, Jean Luc Godard, Julian Temple, Bruce Beresford, Robert Altman, Franc Roddam, Ken Russell, Derek Jarman, and Bill Bryden.

Track 29

Production: Island Pictures. Executive Producers: George Harrison, Denis O'Brien. Producer: Rick McCallum. Screenplay: Dennis Potter. Director of Photography: Alex Thomson. Editor: Tony Lawson. Music: Stanley Myers. Songs: "M.O.T.H.E.R." by Theodore Morse, Fiske O'Hara; "Mother" by John Lennon; "When the Red Red Robin Comes Bob Bob Bobbin' Along" by Harry Woods; "Chattanooga Choo Choo" by Harry Warren, Mack Gordon; "Young at Heart" by John Richards, Carolyn Leigh, performed by Rosemary Clooney. Sound: Rodney Glenn, Colin Chapman. Art Directors: Curtis Schnell, Francine Mercadante. Sets: Douglas A. Mowat. Assistant Directors: Bruce Moriarty, Jay Tobias. Production Designer: David Brockhurst. Released 1988. Running Time: 90 minutes.

Leading Players: Theresa Russell (Linda Henry), Gary Oldman (Martin), Christopher Lloyd (Dr. Henry Henry), Colleen Camp (Arlanda), Sandra Bernhard (Nurse Stein), Seymour Cassel (Dr. Bernhard Fairmont), Leon Rippy (trucker), Vance Colvig (Mr. Ennis), Kathryn Tomlinson (receptionist), Jerry

Rushing (redneck), Tommy Hull (counterman), J. Michael Hunter (waiter), Richard K. Olsen (delegate), Ted Barrow (old man).

Sweet Bird of Youth

Production: Linda Yellen Company/Kushner-Locke Company. Executive Producers: Linda Yellen, Laurence Mark, Peter Locke, Donald Kushner. Producer: Fred Whitehead. Screenplay: Gavin Lambert, from the Tennessee Williams play. Director of Photography: Francis Kenny. Editor: Pamela Malouf-Cundy. Music: Ralph Burns. Sound: Jacob Coldsten. Art Director: Roger King. Sets: Marthe Pinfeau. Assistant Director: Donald P. H. Eaton. Production Designer: Penny Hadfield. Costumes: Del Adey-Jones. Premiered: 1989, N.B.C. Running Time: 104 minutes.

Leading Players: Mark Harmon (Chance Wayne), Elizabeth Taylor (Alexandra Del Lago), Rip Torn (Boss Tom Finley), Valerie Perrine (Miss Lucy), Cheryl Paris (Heavenly Finley), Kevin Greer (Tom Finley, Jr.), Seymour Cassell (Hatcher), Ronnie Claire Edwards (Aunt Nonnie), Ruta Lee (Sally Powers), Theodore Wilson (Fly), Charles Lucia (George Scudder), John W. Fleck (Heckler), Michael Wilding (Taylor's son), Megan Blake, Tom Nolan, Billy Ray Sharkey, Hal England, Avon Hill, Nurit Koppel, Angela Teek, Martha Miliken, Michael Shaner.

The Witches

Production: Lorimar Film Entertainment. Executive Producer: Jim Henson. Producer: Mark Shivas. Screenplay: Allan Scott, from a novel by Roald Dahl. Director of Photography: Harvey Harrison. Editor: Tony Lawson. Music: Stanley Myers. Sound: Rodney Glenn, Derek Holding, Peter Sutton. Art Director: Norman Dorme. Sets: Robin Tarsnane. Assistant Directors: Barry Wasserman, Callum McDougall, Mark Layton. Production Designer: Andrew Sanders. Animatronics: William Plant. Released: 1990. Running Time: 92 minutes.

Leading Players: Angelica Huston (Eva Ernst/Grand High Witch), Mai Zetterling (Helga), Bill Patterson (Mr. Jenkins), Brenda Blethyn (Mrs. Jenkins), Rowan Atkinson (Mr. Stringer), Jasen Fisher (Luke), Charlie Potter (Bruno Jenkins), Anne Lambton (woman in black), Jane Horrocks (Miss Irvine), Sukie Smith (Marlene), Rose English (Dora), Jenny Runacre (Elsie), Annabel Brooks (Nicola), Emma Relph (Millie), Nora Connolly (Beatrice), Rosamund Greenwood (Janice), Anjelique Rockas (Henrietta), Ann Tirad (first lady), Leila Hoffman (second lady), Roberta Taylor (witch chef), Brian Hawksley (elderly waiter), Debra Gillett (waitress), Jim Carter (head chef), Darcy Flynn (Luke's mother), Vincent Marzello (Luke's father), Serena Harragain (doctor), Greta Norda (Norwegian doctor), Elsie Eide (Erica), Kristen Steinsland (child Helga), Merete Armand (Erica's mother), Ola Otnes (Erica's father), Johan Sverre, Arvid Ones, Sverre Rossummoen (policemen).

Cold Heaven

Production: Hemdale Releasing Corporation. Executive Producer: Jack Schwartzmann. Producers: Allan Scott, Jonathan D. Krane. Screenplay: Allan Scott, from a novel by Brian Moore. Director of Photography: Francis Kenny. Editor: Tony Lawson. Songs: "Mariachi Walls," Jimme Haskell; "Mariachi Acapulco," P. Roy. Sets: Cliff Cunningham. Assistant Director: Donald P. H. Eaton. Production Designer: Steve Legler.

Leading Players: Theresa Russell (Marie Davenport), Mark Harmon (Dr. Alex Davenport), James Russo (Daniel Corvin), Talia Shire (Sister Martha), Will Patton (Father Niles), Richard Bradford (Monsignor Cassidy), Julie Carmen (Anna Corvin), Diana Douglas (Mother St. Agnes), Seymour Cassel (Tom Farrelly), Castulo Guerra (Dr. DeMenoos), Daniel Addes (Dr. Mendes), Jim Ishida (Dr. Tanaki), Jeanette Miller (Sister Katarina), Martha Milliken (Sister Anna), Margarita Cordova (registrar), Sal Lopez (young doctor), Gary Pagett (doorman), Helen Boll (maid), Dennis Kelly (first doctor), David Meyers (second doctor), Claudia Harrington (first nurse), Valerie Hastings (second nurse), Susan Sells (second nurse), Carmela Rioseco (Mexican nurse), Sam Vlahos (Alvarado), David Rodriguez (cab driver), Alex Alexander (waitress).

ADDITIONAL FILM WORK

The Miniver Story (H. C. Potter, 1950 Clapper boy)
Ivanhoe (Richard Thorpe, 1953 Focus Puller)
Gentlemen Marry Brunettes (Richard Sale, 1955 Camera)
Bhowani Junction (George Cukor, 1955 Camera operator)
Pacific Destiny (Wolf Rilla, 1956 Camera operator)
The Man Inside (John Gilling, 1957 Camera operator)
Island of the Sun (Robert Rossen, 1957 Camera operator)
The Great Van Operator (Max Varnell, 1958 Camera operator)
A Woman Possessed (Max Varnell, 1958 Camera operator)
Passport to Shame (Alvin Rakoff, 1958 Camera operator)
Moment of Indiscretion (Max Varnell, 1958 Camera operator)
The Child and the Killer (Max Varnell, 1958 Camera operator)
Jazzboat (Ken Hughes, 1959 Camera operator)
Tarzan's Greatest Adventure (John Guillerman, 1959 Camera)
The Trials of Oscar Wilde (Ken Hughes, 1960 Camera operator)
The Sundowners (Fred Zinneman, 1960 Camera operator)
Prize of Arms (Cliff Owen, 1961 Co-Screenwriter)
Sanders (Lawrence Huntington, 1961 Screenwriter)
Information Received (Robert Lynn, 1961 Lighting cameraman)
Lawrence of Arabia (David Lean, 1962 Second unit photography)
Dr. Crippen (Robert Lynn, 1962 Lighting cameraman)
Just for Fun (Gordon Fleming, 1962 Lighting cameraman)
The Caretaker/The Guest (Clive Donner, 1962 Second unit photography)
Nothing but the Best (Clive Donner, 1962 Lighting cameraman)

Every Day's a Holiday (James Hill 1964 Lighting cameraman)
Victim Five (Robert Lynn, 1964 Lighting cameraman)
The Masque of the Red Death (Roger Corman, 1964 Lighting cameraman)
The System / The Girl Getters (Michael Winner, 1964 Lighting cameraman)
A Funny Thing Happened on the Way to the Forum (Richard Lester, 1965
     Lighting cameraman)
Judith (Daniel Mann, 1965 Second unit direction, additional photography)
Fahrenheit 451 (François Truffaut, 1966 Lighting cameraman)
Casino Royale (John Huston, Kenneth Hughes, Val Guest, Robert Parrish, J.
     McGrath, 1967; additional photography [bubblebath sequence])
Far from the Madding Crowd (John Schlesinger, 1967 Lighting cameraman)
Petulia (Richard Lester, 1968 Second unit direction)
Glastonbury Fayre (Peter Neal, 1972 Co-producer, co-photographer)
Without You I'm Nothing (John Boskovitch, 1990 Executive producer)

ADDITIONAL TELEVISION WORK

Police Dog (1955 Photography)
Ghost Squad (1955 Photography)

INDEX

*Numbers in **boldface** refer to pages with photographs.*

219